外国人在穗指南（2021）

广州市人民政府外事办公室 / 编

中国·广州

图书在版编目（CIP）数据

外国人在穗指南：英汉对照 / 广州市人民政府外事办公室编 . -- 广州：南方日报出版社，2021.12
ISBN 978-7-5491-2455-8

Ⅰ . ①外… Ⅱ . ①广… Ⅲ . ①广州－概况－指南－汉、英 Ⅳ . ① K926.51-62

中国版本图书馆 CIP 数据核字（2021）第 233312 号

WAIGUOREN ZAI SUI ZHINAN

外国人在穗指南

编　　者：	广州市人民政府外事办公室
出版发行：	南方日报出版社
地　　址：	广州市广州大道中 289 号
出 版 人：	周山丹
责任编辑：	张　高　陈　焱
装帧设计：	邓晓童
责任技编：	王　兰
责任校对：	魏智宏
经　　销：	全国新华书店
印　　刷：	广州市岭美文化科技有限公司
开　　本：	880mm×1230mm　1/32
印　　张：	10.25
字　　数：	200 千字
版　　次：	2021 年 12 月第 1 版
印　　次：	2021 年 12 月第 1 次印刷
定　　价：	75.00 元

投稿热线：（020）87360640　　读者热线：（020）87363865
发现印装质量问题，影响阅读，请与承印厂联系调换。

《外国人在穗指南》编委会

主　编：詹德村

副主编：雷玮琚　　邓昌雄　　柳　柳　　金　澜
　　　　马满鹤　　涂宏哲　　黄穗雯　　旷昌平

编　委：广州市人民政府外事办公室领事与涉外安全处

翻　译：杜可君

目录

第一章　城市概况　001
一、基本情况　002
二、政区及人口　005
三、悠久历史　007
四、对外交往　009
五、政务办公　010

第二章　出入境及停留、居留　011
一、出入境检验检疫　012
二、旅客通关及海关申报　016
三、公自用物品出入境　021
四、签证证件办理　024
五、永久居留办理　032

第三章　生活百科　045
一、饮食娱乐　046
二、交通　049
三、通信、银行、邮电服务　055
四、就读　057
五、外国人来华工作许可　063

六、婚姻及收养	072
七、宗教及活动场所	080
八、医疗	084
九、殡葬	103
十、汉语学习	105

第四章　安全与法规　107

一、安全	108
二、纳税与免税	110
三、个人所得税	111
四、车船税	117
五、交通法规	120
六、法律纠纷	134

第五章　经商投资指引　137

一、投资环境及商务发展概况	138
二、产业扶持政策	139
三、重点经济开发区简介	145
四、知识产权保护	149

第一章
城市概况

一、基本情况

广州是广东省省会,全省政治、经济、科技、教育和文化中心。地处中国大陆南方,广东省东南部,珠江三角洲北缘,濒临南海,毗邻香港和澳门,是华南地区区域性中心城市、交通通信枢纽,是中国的"南大门"。

广州属亚热带季风气候,夏无酷暑,冬无严寒,雨量充沛,四季如春,繁花似锦。全年平均气温21—23摄氏度,平均相对湿度为75%,市区年降雨量为2100毫米以上。

广州是一座历史文化名城。据史籍记载,早在公元前214年,这里便修筑了城垣,建城至今已有2200多年的历史,留下了许多文化古迹,生动地反映了广州在各个历史阶段的发展。

广州,是中国古代"海上丝绸之路"的发祥地之一。自秦汉起2000多年间,广州一直作为对外贸易的重要港口,从发掘的造船遗址发现的秦汉时期带有舵、锚构件的大型木船；南越王二代墓穴出土的文物中，发现非洲的象牙和波斯银盒；唐宋时期，设有专门管理外贸的机构。这便是广州作为对外贸易重要口岸的最好证明。

广州还是近现代革命的策源地。1840年，当西方列强入侵中国的"南大门"时，三元里人民便发起了反抗侵略者的抗英斗争；洪秀全领导的农民起义；思想家康有为、梁启超等发起的维新变法；孙中山领导的反对封建统治的辛亥革命，以及著名的黄花岗起义，都与广州这片沃土息息相关。

今天，广州作为改革开放的前沿城市以及对外贸易的窗口，经济突飞猛进，各项事业得到全面的发展，成为中国经济最活跃的城市之一，经济综合实力位居全国主要城市的三甲之列。

经济的发展，促进了广州城市面貌和居住环境的不断改善。广州是京广、广深、广茂和广梅汕铁路的交汇点和华南民用航空交通中心，与全国各地的联系极为密切。已开通和运行15条线路的广州地铁、环城高速公路、丫髻沙大桥、广州国际会展中心、广州白云国际机场，以及广州大学城的落成，这些都证明了广州这座千年古城正日益显现出21世纪现代化国际大都市的无限魅力。

二、政区及人口

广州市总面积为7434.40平方千米,占全省陆地面积的4.21%。广州市辖越秀区、海珠区、荔湾区、天河区、白云区、黄埔区、花都区、番禺区、南沙区、从化区、增城区等11个区。

广州市2020年常住人口数量达18 676 605人,广州0—14岁人口占比13.87%;15—59岁人口占比达74.72%;60岁及以上人口占比为11.41%;65岁及以上人口占比达7.8%。

广州有少数民族人口82.7万,分属55个少数民族。其中,户籍少数民族人口约11.8万,人数较多的主要有壮族、回族、满族、土家族、瑶族;非户籍少数民族人口70.9万,人数较多的民族主要有壮族、回族、土家族、苗族、瑶族、侗族。广州市是全国少数民族人口增长最快、增幅最大的城市之一。全市有回民小学、满族小

学、畲族小学共3所民族小学，在校少数民族学生327人；1个少数民族聚居村（增城区正果镇畲族村，共88户，385人）；有10所招收新疆、西藏籍学生的学校（其中，广雅中学、市六中、市75中、玉岩中学、协和中学、禺山高中6所学校开办新疆内高班，市商贸职业学校、市政职业学校2所学校开设新疆内职班，广州市医药职业学校、广州卫生职业技术学院开设西藏内职班），在校学生1366人；有近2000家清真拉面店、餐馆；有市民族团结进步协会、市满族历史文化研究会、市回族历史文化研究会、市少数民族体育协会共4个市级民族团体。

三、悠久历史

广州是国务院颁布的全国第一批历史文化名城之一。早在六七千年前的新石器时期，先民们就在这块土地上生息繁衍，创造了灿烂的史前文明，揭开广州人文史的初页。广州又称为羊城、穗城。传说古代有5位仙人，骑五色羊，羊衔谷穗，降临广州，把谷穗赠与百姓，祝愿这里"永无饥荒"。如今，越秀公园的五羊雕像已成为广州的象征。

广州自秦汉至明清2000多年间，一直是中国对外贸易的重要港口城市。汉武帝时期，中国船队从广州出发，远航至东南亚和南亚诸国通商贸易，东汉时期航线更远达波斯湾。唐代，广州发展成为世界著名的东方大港，也是当时世界最长的海路航线"广州通海夷道"的起点，中央王朝首先委派专门管理对外贸易的官员市舶使到广州。宋代，在广州设立全国第一个管理外贸机构市舶司。明清时期，广州更是特殊开放的口岸，在较长一段时间内曾是全国唯一的对外贸易港口城市。

广州是具有光荣革命传统的英雄城市。在近代史上有三元里人民反抗外来侵略者的抗英斗争、孙中山领导的反对封建统治的"三·二九"起义（又称黄花岗起义）、中国共产党领导的广州起义。广州既是中国资产阶级民主革命的策源地，又是无产阶级政党领导人民群众进行革命斗争的英雄城市。

广州历代名人辈出，代代相传。秦朝任嚣，汉朝赵佗，晋朝葛洪，唐朝惠能，明朝湛若水，清朝学者屈大均、阮元，禁烟领袖林则徐，农民起义领袖洪秀全，洋务派代表人物张之洞，思想政治家康有为、梁启超，领导中国民主革命、推翻几千年封建统治的孙中山等，为广州名城的形成和发展作出卓越的贡献。

广州的文物古迹众多。南越王墓有2000多年历史，光孝寺、六榕寺、怀圣寺等有1000多年历史。始建于隋朝的南海神庙，明朝的五仙观、镇海楼、莲花塔，清朝的陈家祠、余荫山房等。近代革命历史纪念地有毛泽东同志主办的农民运动讲习所旧址、广州起义烈士陵园、黄花岗七十二烈士墓、黄埔军校旧址、中山纪念堂、洪秀全故居等。广州还有众多的风景名胜。宋、元、明、清历代都有评选"羊城八景"活动。中华人民共和国成立后，广州城市建设与发展日新月异。2011年5月18日，"羊城新八景"评选结果揭晓，新入选的"羊城新八景"为：塔耀新城、珠水流光、云山叠翠、越秀风华、古祠流芳、荔湾胜境、科城绵绣、湿地唱晚。

四、对外交往

广州是源远流长、闻名遐迩的国际都市。早在公元前就与国外有着密切友好往来，是著名的"海上丝绸之路"的发祥地之一，具有2000多年对外通商的历史。

截至2021年12月，广州市已与六大洲35个国家38个城市建立友好城市关系，其中欧洲10个国家12个城市、北美洲2个国家2个城市、拉丁美洲6个国家6个城市、亚洲11个国家12个城市、非洲4个国家4个城市、大洋洲2个国家2个城市。

截至2021年12月，广州市已与六大洲44个国家62个城市建立友好合作交流城市关系，其中欧洲13个国家23个城市、北美洲2个国家5个城市、拉丁美洲6个国家7个城市、亚洲13个国家15个城市、非洲7个国家7个城市、大洋洲2个国家3个城市。（详见广州市人民政府外事办公室官方网站。）

五、政务办公

广州的大部分涉外职能机构与部门均可以直接使用英语接待外国人的咨询、投诉以及业务办理。各政府机构都有相关中英文网站资源以帮助市民了解相关政策法规以及办事指南,其中工商、税务等业务可以在网上直接办理。政府部门的行政办公时间一般为周一至周五(国家规定的法定节假日除外),上午9:00至12:00,下午2:00至6:00。如有特殊需要在节假日办理业务者,可以提前与相关政府部门联系并预约。请浏览广州市政府门户网站(网址:www.gz.gov.cn),了解更多政府最新政策动态及生活信息。

广州市人民政府外事办公室建设的广州多语种公共服务平台960169热线为在穗外籍人士提供免费英、日、韩语公共事务翻译及相关政策咨询服务,并与12345、110、119、120、白云机场96158、广州交通96900等政府和公共服务热线通过三方通话方式建立联动,提供实时翻译服务。其中英语热线服务时间为24小时,日、韩语热线服务时间为9:00—21:00。

> **广州市人民政府外事办公室**
> 地址:广州市越秀北路311号
> 网址:http://www.gzfao.gov.cn

第二章
出入境及停留、居留

一、出入境检验检疫

（一）口岸健康申报

1. 国内外未发生重大传染病疫情时，出入境人员免于填报"出入境检疫健康申明卡"。但有发热、呕吐、咳嗽、呼吸困难、腹泻等症状，患有传染性疾病或精神病，携带微生物、人体组织、生物制品、血液及其制品、动植物及其产品等物品的出入境人员须主动口头向旅检通道检疫官员申报，并接受检验检疫。（摘自国家质检总局《关于简化全国口岸出入境旅客健康申报手续的公告》2008年第62号）

2. 国内外发生重大传染病疫情时，由国家质检总局发布对出入境交通工具和人员及其携带物采取临时性检验检疫强制措施的公

告，来自疫区的交通工具必须在指定的地点停靠；出入境人员必须逐人如实填报《出入境检疫健康申明卡》，并由检验检疫专用通道通行；出入境人员携带物必须逐件通过X光机透视检查。（摘自国家质检总局《关于简化全国口岸出入境旅客健康申报手续的公告》2008年第62号）

（二）入境人员检验检疫须知

1. 外国人来中国定居或者居留一年以上的，在申请入境签证时，还须交验所在国政府指定的卫生医疗部门签发的，或者卫生医疗部门签发的并经过公证机关公证的健康证明书。健康证明书自签发之日起六个月有效。（摘自《中华人民共和国外国人入境出境管理法实施细则》）

2. 来自黄热病疫区的人员，在入境时，必须向检验检疫机关出示有效的黄热病预防接种证书。（摘自《中华人民共和国国境卫生检疫法实施细则》）

3. 患有严重精神病、传染性肺结核病或者有可能对公共卫生

造成重大危害的其他传染病的外国人不准入境。(摘自《中华人民共和国外国人入境出境管理法实施细则》和《中华人民共和国国境卫生检疫法实施细则》)

(三)出境人员检验检疫须知

1. 前往黄热病疫区的人员出境时应出示黄热病预防接种证书。(摘自《入出境人员卫生检疫查验规程SN/T1344-2003》)

2. 根据前往国家的要求,出境人员应提供相应的预防接种证书。(摘自《入出境人员卫生检疫查验规程SN/T1344-2003》)

(四)出入境携带物品须知

1. 出入境人员携带下列物品,应当申报并接受检验检疫机构检疫:

(1)入境动植物、动植物产品和其他检疫物;

(2)出入境生物物种资源、濒危野生动植物及其产品;

(3)出境的国家重点保护的野生动植物及其产品;

(4)出入境的微生物、人体组织、生物制品、血液及血液制品等特殊物品;

(5)出入境的尸体、骸骨等;

(6)来自疫区、被传染病污染或者可能传播传染病的出入境的行李以及物品;

(7)国家质检总局规定的其他应当向检验检疫机构申报并接受检疫的携带物。(摘自国家质检总局第146号令《出入境人员携带物检疫管理办法》)

2. 出入境人员禁止携带下列物品进境:

(1)动植物病原体(包括菌种、毒种等)、害虫及其他有害生物;

(2)动植物疫情流行的国家或者地区的有关动植物、动植物产品和其他检疫物;

(3)动物尸体;

(4)土壤;

（5）《中华人民共和国禁止携带、邮寄进境的动植物及其产品名录》所列各物；

（6）国家规定禁止进境的废旧物品、放射性物质以及其他禁止进境物。（摘自国家质检总局第146号令《出入境人员携带物检疫管理办法》）

广州海关
地址：广州市珠江新城花城大道83号
邮编：510623
咨询电话：（8620）81102000
网址：http://guangzhou.customs.gov.cn/

二、旅客通关及海关申报

个人携带进出境的行李物品,以自用、合理数量为限,应当向海关如实申报,并接受海关查验。

非居民旅客携带拟留在中国境内的个人自用进境物品,总值在人民币2000元以内(含2000元)的,海关予以免税放行,单一品种限自用合理数量,但烟草制品、酒精制品等商品另按有关规定办理。

超出人民币2000元的,海关仅对超出部分的个人自用进境物品征税,对不可分割的单件物品,全部征税。

进出境物品的完税价格,由海关依法确定。

对来自和前往港澳地区的旅客每次进境可携带免税香烟200支,或雪茄50支,或烟丝250克;免税12度以上酒精饮料1瓶(0.75升以下)。其他旅客每次进境可携带免税香烟400支,或雪茄100支,或烟丝500克;免税12度以上酒精饮料2瓶(1.5升以下)。当天往返或短期内多次来往于港澳地区的旅客可携带免税香烟40支,或烟丝50克,雪茄5支;不准免税带进酒。

旅客入境时,携带途中必备的旅行自用物品超出照相机、便携式收音机、小型摄影机、手提式摄录机、手提式文字处理机每一种一件范围的,必须向海关申报并办理物品进境手续。

旅客携带人民币现钞超过20 000元或外币现钞折合超过5000美元进出境的(当天多次往返及短期内多次往返旅客携带外币另行规定),应当向海关书面申报。对15天内多次来往和经常出入境的外籍旅客,海关只免税放行其旅途必需物品。

持有中华人民共和国政府主管部门给予外交、礼遇签证以及其他享有免验礼遇的进出境旅客，可不填写申报单，但通关时应主动向海关出示本人有效证件，海关给予免验礼遇。

携带中药材、中成药出境，前往港澳地区的，总值限人民币150元；前往国外的，总值限人民币300元。

中国法规明文规定，珍贵文物和国家规定禁止出境的其他文物，不得出境。旅客携带、托运、邮寄文物出境，必须向海关申报。海关凭文物管理部门钤盖的鉴定标志及文物外销发货票，或文化部指定的文化行政管理部门开具的许可出口证明查验放行。

国家文物进出境审核广东管理处
地址：广州市水荫四横路32号
邮编：510075
电话：（8620）87047165

非居民长期旅客［经公安部门批准进境并在境内连续居留一年以上（含一年），期满后仍回到境外定居地的外国公民、港澳台地区人员、华侨］进出境自用物品，按照《中华人民共和国海关对非居民长期旅客进出境自用物品监管办法》办理手续。申请进境自用物品，可以由本人或者委托的报关企业向主管海关或口岸海关办理通关手续，并交验下列单证：

1. 身份证件；
2. 长期居留证件；
3. "中华人民共和国海关进出境自用物品申报单"；
4. 提（运）单、装箱单等相关单证。

对于非居民长期旅客进境应当征税的自用物品，海关按照《中华人民共和国进出口关税条例》的有关规定征收税款。根据政府间协定免税进境的非居民长期旅客自用物品，海关依法免征税款。

外国驻中国使、领馆人员，联合国及其专门机构，国际组织驻中国代表机构人员及其家属进出境的自用生活物品，按规定在直接需用数量范围内的,可以享受免税、免验待遇。由人社部、教育部或者其授权部门认定的高层次留学人才和海外科技专家进境的书籍和教学、科研物品,在自用合理数量范围内,可免征进口税。

> **有关规定及手续请咨询:**
> 电话:(8620)12360
> **广州海关**
> 地址:广州市珠江新城花城大道83号
> 网址:http://guangzhou.customs.gov.cn
> **黄埔海关**
> 地址:广州市黄埔区大沙地东333号
> 网址:http://huangpu.customs.gov.cn

为保护我国公民的健康安全,根据《中华人民共和国国境卫生检疫法》及其实施细则等法律法规的规定,提醒出入境人员关注国际旅行健康。

1. 出境前,可登录海关总署可登录海关总署和广州海关官方网站查询全球传染病疫情动态,也可向广州海关各隶属海关及其国际旅行卫生保健中心进行健康咨询。

2. 出境时如出现发热、头痛、咳嗽、呼吸困唯、恶心、呕吐、腹痛、腹泻、肌肉痛、关节痛、皮疹、黄疸等传染病症状(以下简称"传染病症状"),应主动向海关进行健康申报,可考虑取消或推迟出境行程,及时就医诊治。

3. 境外旅行途中应增强防病意识,尽量避免与有传染病症状人员授触;避免被鼠、蚁、蜱等病媒生物叮咬,保持良好的卫生习惯。如出现传染病症状应及时就医,必要时可向中国驻当地使领馆寻求帮助。

4. 归国途中如出现传染病症状,应及时、如实告知交通工具上的乘务人员,并配合乘务人员做好自己隔离和个人防护工作。

5. 入境时如出现传染病症状,应主动向海关卫生检疫人员进

行健康申报并如实告知旅行史和接触史,配合海关开展检疫排查工作。

6. 入境后密切关注身体状况,如出现传染病症状,应当立即就医并详细告知旅行史和接触史,同时将就医情况及时告知海关部门。

根据《中华人民共和国国境卫生检疫法》及其实施细则等法律法规规定:"携带微生物、人体组织、生物制品、血液及其制品等特殊物品出入境的,应当提前向目的地直属海关申请特殊物品审批,并在出入境时主动向海关申报。携带自用且仅限于预防或者治疗疾病用的血液制品或者生物制品出入境的,不需办理卫生检疫审批手续,出入境时应当向海关出示医院的有关证明;允许携带量以处方或者说明书确定的一个疗程为限。"

三、公自用物品出入境

（一）常驻机构公用物品及车辆

常驻机构申请进出境办公用品及机动车辆，以及常驻机构人员免税进境机动交通工具按相关规定办理。

上述免税进境的机动车辆自海关放行之日起超过4年，以及常驻人员任期届满的，可申请转让给其他常驻机构或常驻人员，或出售给特许经营单位，海关监管期限（6年）届满的，可申请转让、出售或移作他用。

（二）自用的机动车辆

取得境内长期居留证件的常驻人员可以进境征税机动车辆，每人限1辆，应当由本人或其委托的报关企业向主管海关提交书面申请。经主管海关审核批准后，凭审批单证和其他相关单证予以验放，并需照章征税。申请时应当向主管海关交验下列单证：

1. 身份证件；
2. 长期居留证件；
3. "中华人民共和国海关进出境自用物品申报单"；
4. 提（运）单、装箱单等相关单证；
5. 海关要求的其他证明材料。

主管海关核准后，开具《中华人民共和国海关监管车辆进/出境领/销牌照通知书》，常驻人员凭此向公安交通管理部门办理有关车辆转让过户手续。

有关规定及手续请咨询：
电话：（8620）12360

外国人在穗指南（2021）

> 广州海关
> 地址：广州市珠江新城花城大道83号
> 网址：http://guangzhou.customs.gov.cn
> 黄埔海关
> 地址：广州市黄埔区大沙地东333号
> 网址：http://huangpu.customs.gov.cn

（三）广州海关主要通关口岸主要职责及地铁交通情况

1. 广州海关隶属白云机场海关主要负责白云国际机场口岸进出境旅客行李物品监管通关工作。

地址：广州市白云区人和镇广州白云国际机场空港四路横一路。

公共交通：地铁3号线北延段"机场南"站。

2. 广州海关隶属车站海关主要负责天河铁路客运口岸进出境旅客行李物品监管通关工作。

地址：广州市天河区东站路1号。

公共交通：地铁1号线、3号线"广州东站"站G出口。

3. 广州海关隶属番禺海关主要负责番禺莲花山客运港进出境旅客行李物品监管通关工作。

地址：广州市番禺区石楼镇港前路1号莲花山客运港。

公交交通：番160路；地铁4号线石基站A出口转番92、93路。

4. 广州海关隶属南沙海关主要负责南沙客运港、南沙国际邮轮母港客运口岸进出境旅客行李物品监管通关工作。

地址：广州市南沙区海滨新城商贸大道南二路南沙客运港内、广州市南沙区兴沙路广州南沙国际邮轮母港港内。

公共交通：地铁4号线"南沙客运港"站G出口。

5. 广州海关隶属广州邮局海关主要负责广东省（除深圳、珠海、汕头、江门、东莞以外）以及河北省、甘肃省、青海省、宁夏回族自治区的进出境邮递物品、印刷品音像制品监管通关，全国其他省、市经本口岸进出境的国际邮袋的转关监管，以及邮政企业承运进出境货物、快件、跨境电子商务的监管通关工作。

地址：广州市越秀区站南路4号广州流花邮政大院内。公共交通：地铁2号线、5号线"广州火车站"站D2出口。

6. 广州海关隶属天河海关主要负责受理广州海关关区公自用物品出入境审核业务。

地址：广州市天河区华利路61号广州市政务服务中心四楼。

公共交通：地铁3号线"珠江新城"站B1出口。

四、签证证件办理

（一）签证种类

中国签证分为外交签证、礼遇签证、公务签证和普通签证，普通签证分为以下类别，并在签证上标明相应的汉语拼音字母：

1. C字签证，发给执行乘务、航空、航运任务的国际列车乘务员、国际航空器机组人员、国际航行船舶的船员及船员随行家属和从事国际道路运输的汽车驾驶员。

2. D字签证，发给入境永久居留的人员。

3. F字签证，发给入境从事交流、访问、考察等活动的人员。

4. G字签证，发给经中国过境的人员。

5. J1字签证，发给外国常驻中国新闻机构的外国常驻记者；J2字签证，发给入境进行短期采访报道的外国记者。

6. L字签证，发给入境旅游的人员；以团体形式入境旅游的，可以签发团体L字签证。

7. M字签证，发给入境进行商业贸易活动的人员。

8. Q1字签证，发给因家庭团聚申请入境居留的中国公民的家庭成员和具有中国永久居留资格的外国人的家庭成员，以及因寄养等原因申请入境居留的人员；Q2字签证，发给申请入境短期探亲的居住在中国境内的中国公民的亲属和具有中国永久居留资格的外国人的亲属。

9. R字签证，发给国家需要的外国高层次人才和急需紧缺专门人才。

10. S1字签证，发给申请入境长期探亲的因工作、学习等事由在中国境内居留的外国人的配偶、父母、未满18周岁的子女、配偶的父母，以及因其他私人事务需要在中国境内居留的人员；S2字签证，发给申请入境短期探亲的因工作、学习等事由在中国境内停留居留的外国人的家庭成员，以及因其他私人事务需要在中国境内停留的人员。

11. X1字签证，发给申请在中国境内长期学习的人员；X2字签证，发给申请在中国境内短期学习的人员。

12. Z字签证，发给申请在中国境内工作的人员。

（二）办理签证延期、换发所需材料

应当在签证停留期届满7日前申请签证延期或换发。

申请时需回答有关询问并提供以下材料：

1. 本人有效护照或其他国际旅行证件及签证的原件和复印件；

2. 填写"外国人签证证件申请表"；

3. 广东省出入境证件数码相片1张及该相片的"检测回执"；

4. 在穗有效"境外人员临时住宿登记表"；

5. 与签证事由有关的证明材料；

6. 公安机关认为需要提供的其他证明。

延长签证停留期限，累计不得超过签证原注明的停留期限。签证换发的停留期限自本次入境之日起连续累计不得超过1年。

（三）签证的补发

外国人入境后，由于所持普通签证遗失、被盗抢或损毁申请补发普通签证的，可为其补发与原签证种类、入境有效期、入境次数及停留有效期一致的普通签证。申请人应当按以下规定办理：

1. 签证遗失或被盗抢的，应当提交本人护照报失证明或者所属国驻华使领馆照会以及新护照或其他国际旅行证件。

2. 签证损毁的，出示损毁护照或者所属国驻华使领馆照会以及新护照或其他国际旅行证件。

3. 团体签证遗失、被盗抢或损毁的，当地接待旅行社证明函件、团体签证复印件。

4. 除提供以上资料外，还需提供申请人在穗有效"外国人住宿登记表"，广东省外国人签证相片1张及该相片的"检测回执"。

5. 公安机关认为需要提供的其他证明。

（四）居留证件种类

1. 工作类居留证件，发给来穗工作的外籍人员，持Z字签证入境，入境后30日内办理工作类居留许可。

2. 学习类居留证件，发给来穗长期学习的外国留学生，持X1签证入境，入境后30日内办理学习类居留许可。

3. 记者类居留证件，发给来华常驻外国记者，持J1签证入境，入境后30日内办理记者类居留许可。

4. 团聚类居留证件，发给因家庭团聚申请在穗居留的中国公民和在中国具有永久居留资格的外国人的外籍家庭成员，以及因寄养在穗外籍华人、华侨的未满18周岁外籍子女，持Q1签证入境，入境后30日内办理团聚类居留许可。

5. 私人事务类居留证件，发给因工作、学习等事由在穗居留外国人的配偶、父母、未满18周岁的子女、配偶的父母，以及因接受医疗救助、服务等其他私人事务需要在中国境内居留的外国人，持S1签证入境，入境后30日内办理私人事务类居留许可。

(五)办理相关签证证件所需材料

1. 首次办理工作类居留证件所需材料

来穗工作的外籍人员,持Z字签证入境,入境后30日内办理工作类居留许可。申请时需回答有关询问并提供以下材料:

(1)本人有效护照及签证的原件和复印件;

(2)填写"外国人签证证件申请表";

(3)广东省出入境证件数码相片1张及该相片的"检测回执";

(4)在穗有效"境外人员临时住宿登记表";

(5)广东出入境检验检疫局出具的"健康证明"(首次申请居留证件时提交);

(6)"外国人工作许可证"或"外国专家证"或"外国人就业证"或"外国人在中华人民共和国从事海上石油作业工作准证"或文化部及文化部授权部门批准演出的批件复印件(核对原件);

(7)工作单位证明函件;

(8)持其他种类签证入境,可凭人力资源社会保障、外专部门签发的工作许可证明申请有效期1年以内的工作类居留许可;

(9)公安机关认为需要提供的其他证明。

2. 办理工作类居留证件延期所需材料

(1)本人有效护照及签证的原件和复印件;

(2)填写"外国人签证证件申请表";

(3)广东省出入境证件数码相片1张及该相片的"检测回执";

(4)在穗有效"境外人员临时住宿登记表";

(5)"外国人工作许可证"或"外国专家证"或"外国人就业证"或"外国人在中华人民共和国从事海上石油作业工作准证"或文化部及文化部授权部门批准演出的批件复印件(核对原件);

(6)工作单位证明函件;

(7)公安机关认为需要提供的其他证明。

3. 就业者家属办理签证延期(S2签证)所需材料

因工作、学习等事由在中国境内停留居留的外国人的外籍家庭成员来华短期探亲(家庭成员包括配偶、父母、配偶的父母、子女、兄弟姐妹、祖父母、外祖父母、孙子女、外孙子女、子女的配

偶），需要在中国境内停留的外国人，持S2字签证入境，需在签证停留期限届满后继续停留的，应当在签证停留期届满7日前申请签证延期。

申请时需回答有关询问并提供以下材料：

（1）本人有效护照或其他国际旅行证件及签证的原件和复印件；

（2）填写"外国人签证证件申请表"；

（3）广东省出入境证件数码相片1张及该相片的"检测回执"；

（4）在穗有效"境外人员临时住宿登记表"；

（5）家庭成员关系证明、被探望人护照、签证或停留、居留证件复印件（核对原件）、被探望人出具的函件；

（6）公安机关认为需要提供的其他证明。

4. 就业者家属办理私人事务类居留证件所需材料

因工作、学习等事由在穗居留外国人的配偶、父母、未满18周岁的子女、配偶的父母需要在中国境内居留的外国人，持S1签证入境，入境后30日内办理私人事务类居留许可。

申请时需回答有关询问并提供以下材料：

（1）本人有效护照及签证的原件和复印件；

（2）填写"外国人签证证件申请表"；

（3）广东省出入境证件数码相片1张及该相片的"检测回执"；

（4）在穗有效"境外人员临时住宿登记表"；

（5）广东出入境检验检疫局出具的"健康证明"（首次申请居留证件时提交）；

（6）来华探望常住外国人的，还需提供被探望人有效护照和居留证件复印件（核对原件）以及工作、学习单位出具的证明函件、亲属关系证明；

（7）公安机关认为需要提供的其他证明。

5. 办理停留证件所需材料

就业者结束工作因人道原因需继续停留的，可以向停留地公安机关出入境管理部门申请办理停留证件。申请时须回答有关询问并提供以下材料：

（1）本人有效护照或其他国际旅行证件及签证的原件和复印件；

（2）填写"外国人签证证件申请表"；

（3）广东省出入境证件数码相片1张及该相片的"检测回执"；

（4）在穗有效"境外人员临时住宿登记表"；

（5）原单位的离职证明；

（6）公安机关认为需要提供的其他证明。

（六）办理签证证件补发所需材料

外国人入境后，由于所持有效的普通签证、停留证件或居留证件遗失、被盗抢或损毁申请补发的，可为其补发与原签证证件一致的普通签证、停留证件或居留证件。提供申请人需提交以下材料办理：

1. 基本材料

（1）申请人本人有效护照或其他国际旅行证件的原件和复印件；

（2）在穗有效"境外人员临时住宿登记表"；

（3）广东省出入境证件数码相片1张及该相片的"检测回执"；

（4）公安机关认为需要提供的其他证明。

2. 相关证明材料

（1）签证、停留证件遗失或被盗抢的：

本人"护照报失证明"或所属国驻华使领馆照会或《报警回执》。

（2）签证、停留证件损毁的：

①出示损毁护照；

②填写"案事件报告表"；

③如有所属国驻华使领馆照会的一并提交。

（3）团体签证遗失、被盗抢或损毁的：

①"派出所报案回执"；

②当地接待旅行社证明函件；

③团体签证复印件。

（4）居留证件遗失或被盗抢的：

①本人"护照报失证明"或所属国驻华使领馆照会或"报警回执"；

②外籍就业人员和学生需提交单位证明函件；

③境外遗失或被盗抢的还需提交入境时所持签证原件和复印件；

④境外遗失或被盗抢，且在境外时间停留超过30天的，需要重新体检。

（5）居留证件损毁的：

①出示损毁护照；

②填写"案事件报告表"；

③如有所属国驻华使领馆照会的一并提交；

④外籍就业人员和学生需提交单位证明函件；

⑤境外损毁的还需提交入境时所持签证原件和复印件；

⑥境外损毁，且在境外时间停留超过30天的，需要重新体检。

（七）办理签证证件的注意事项

1. 外国人进行签证、停留、居留证件申请，需先登录广州金盾网（www.gzjd.gov.cn）业务申请专区选择"外国人证件办理"进行网上预约申请，或亲临出入境大厦境外人员网上申请区进行现场预约。为外国人签证、停留、居留证件申请出具证明函件的单位还需登录广州金盾网业务申请专区选择"涉外单位备案"进行网上备案，备案审核通过后的单位在进行外国人签证、停留、居留证件申请时无需提交注册登记证明。

2. 外国人在中国境内工作必须同时持有工作许可和工作类居留证件。

3. 外国人居留证件登记事项发生变更的，持证件人应当自登记事项发生变更之日起10日内向居留证件签发机关申请变更。

4. 18至70周岁的申请人首次办理居留证件时应提交广东省出入境检验检疫局出具的"健康证明"。"健康证明"自开具之日起6个月内有效。

5. 境外机构出具的婚姻证明、出生证明、亲属关系证明、收养证明、姓名等资料变更证明，应经中国驻该国使领馆认证。有关外文证明材料应当经国内公证机关翻译成中文。

6. 在中国境内居留的外国人申请延长居留期限的，应当在居留证件有效期限届满30天前向居留地县级以上公安机关出入境管理部门提出申请。

7. 外国人申请签证证件符合受理规定的，公安机关出入境管理部门应当出具受理回执，并在受理回执有效期内作出是否签发的决定。办证时限为7个工作日（**有关事项需要公安机关调查核实的，调查时间不计入工作日**）。申请人所持护照或者其他国际旅行证件因办理证件被收存期间，可以凭受理回执在中国境内合法停留。如需乘坐飞机、火车等前往境内其他城市的可申请在受理回执上加盖出入境管理专用章。申请人应当在受理回执注明的取证日期当天前往公安机关出入境管理部门领取护照。

五、永久居留办理

(一) 符合在华永久居留申请条件的人员类别

1. 特殊人员

(1) 政府推荐类：符合认定标准，经广州市人民政府或广东省自贸办推荐的外籍高层次人才。

(2) 突出贡献类：对中国有重大、突出贡献以及国家特别需要的外国人。

2. 任职人员

(1) 积分评估类：根据广东自贸区或粤港澳大湾区9市外籍人才积分评估标准，达到70分以上的创新创业团队外籍成员和企业选

聘外籍技术人才。

（2）加注"人才"类：持工作类居留证件（加注"人才"）工作满三年的外籍高层次人才。

（3）市场认定类：在广东已连续工作满4年、每年在中国境内实际居住累计不少于6个月，申请时及申请之日前连续4年工资性年收入（税前）40万元人民币以上，每年缴纳个人所得税7万元人民币以上的外国人或者是工资性年收入不低于上一年度所在地区城镇在岗职工平均工资的6倍，每年缴纳个人所得税不低于工资性年收入的20%。

（4）一般任职类：在符合条件的单位担任副总经理、副厂长等职务以上或者具有副教授、副研究员等副高级职称以上以及享受同等待遇满4年，四年内在中国居留累计不少于3年，且纳税记录良好的外国人。

（5）华人博士类：具有博士研究生以上学历且持工作类居留许可在广州市工作的外籍华人。

（6）华人任职类：在广州市企业连续工作满4年、每年在中国境内实际居住累计不少于6个月的外籍华人。

3. 投资人员

（1）一般投资类：以自然人身份在中国投资合计200万美元或在国家颁布的《外商投资产业指导目录》鼓励类产业投资合计50万美元以上的，连续3年投资情况稳定，且纳税记录良好的外国人。

（2）大湾区投资类：以自然人身份或者通过本人以自然人身份作为控股股东的公司企业，在粤港澳大湾区9市内直接投资、连续3年投资情况稳定、投资数额合计100万美元（国家颁布的《外商投资产业指导目录》鼓励类产业投资合计50万美元）以上且纳税记录良好的外国人。

4. 随行家属

（1）配偶类：政府认定类、突出贡献类、一般任职类、一般投资类、华人博士类及任职类、市场认定类（工资性年收入不低于上一年度所在地区城镇在岗职工平均工资的6倍）人员的外籍配偶可随申请人同时申请在华永久居留。

（2）子女类：政府认定类、突出贡献类、一般任职类、一般投资类、华人博士类及任职类、市场认定类（工资性年收入不低于上一年度所在地区城镇在岗职工平均工资的6倍）人员的未满18周岁的外籍未婚子女可随申请人同时申请在华永久居留。

5. 团聚

（1）夫妻团聚类：配偶为广州市常住户籍的中国公民或者在中国获得永久居留资格的外国人，婚姻关系存续满5年且申请之日前已在中国连续居留满5年、每年在中国居留不少于9个月的外国人。

（2）亲子团聚类：父母双方或一方为广州市常住户籍的中国公民或者在中国获得永久居留资格的外国人，未满18周岁且未婚的外国人。

（3）亲属投靠类：在境外无直系亲属，且申请之日前已在中国连续居留满5年、每年在中国居留不少于9个月，投靠境内直系亲属的，年满60周岁的外国人。

（二）永久居留证件的换发与补发

1. 申请条件

外国人持有效永久居留证件，且未丧失在中国永久居留资格规定情形的，有下列条件之一，可以申请换发或者补发永久居留证件：

（1）外国人永久居留证件有效期满；

（2）外国人永久居留证件内容变更；

（3）外国人永久居留证件损坏或遗失。

2. 申请材料

（1）填写《外国人换发或补发永久居留证件申请表》（一式三份）。

（2）提交经检测合格的申请人近期正面免冠蓝底彩色照片（规格为：48mm×33mm）4张。

（3）有效护照。

（4）外国人永久居留证件。

（5）相关信息变更前后的证明材料（内容变更类提交）。

（6）报失地公安机关出具的报失证明或本人书写并签名的遗失说明（遗失证件类提交）。

（7）公安机关认为必须提交的其他证明。

3. 注意事项

（1）持有外国人永久居留证件的外国人应当在证件有效期满前一个月以内申请换发。

（2）证件内容变更的，应当在情况变更后一个月以内申请换发。

（3）证件损坏或遗失的，应当及时申请换发或者补发。

（三）国籍类业务办理

1. 恢复中国国籍

申请对象：曾经具有过中国国籍、并遵守中国宪法和法律的外国人。

2. 加入中国国籍

申请对象：外国人或无国籍人，愿意遵守中国宪法和法律，并具有下列条件之一的，可以申请加入中国国籍：

（1）中国人的近亲属；

（2）定居在中国的；

（3）有其他正当理由的。

3. 退出中国国籍

申请对象：中国公民具有下列条件之一的，可以经申请批准退出中国国籍：

（1）外国人的近亲属；

（2）定居在外国的；

（3）有其它正当理由。

（四）外国人住宿登记办理

外国人抵穗后，应按照《中华人民共和国出境入境管理法》第三十九条规定办理临时住宿登记手续。

住在酒店、宾馆等旅业部门的，由旅业部门为外国人办理住宿登记。

在旅馆以外的其他住所居住或者住宿的，应当在入住后24小时内由本人或者留宿人，向居住地的公安机关办理住宿登记。

住宿登记有效期满或签证证件发生变更的情况下，应及时更新临时住宿登记。

外国人租住的房屋必须符合安全要求并办理齐备我市相关房屋租赁登记备案手续。

申报住宿登记时应提交以下资料：

1. 住宿人的护照或有效证件（身份证件包括但不限于护照、国际旅行证件、临时证件、难民证、寻求庇护者证等）的身份资料页（有照片页）和有效签证页（须提供复印件一份并核验原件）。

2. 居住证明材料（须提供复印件一份并核验原件）。

（1）自购房的：不动产权证书或房地产权证。

（2）居住在出租屋的：出租人身份证件和与出租人签订的《房屋租赁合同》。出租屋主全权委托房屋中介出租管理的，应当视中介机构为留宿人，需提供中介机构法人身份证件。

（3）居住在留宿人家中的：留宿人身份证件。

（4）居住在有关机构的：留宿机构或接待单位出具的证明、所属机构法人代表身份证件。

（五）外国人临时住宿登记自助申报

1. 平台网址及链接

http://crjyw.gzjd.gov.cn/ELSCommunityinfoPutup

通过"广州金盾网—出入境业务—外国人住宿登记自助申报"链接登录。推荐使用谷歌浏览器，IE浏览器可能会显示不全。

2. 适用范围

（1）外国人临时住宿登记自助申报平台只适用在广州居住的外国籍人士。

（2）现持护照没有出入境记录的外国人、外国籍在华新出生婴儿、持用"中华人民共和国出入境通行证"出入境的境外人员及港澳台居民请到派出所现场办理。

3. 温馨提示

（1）请提供在华有效联系手机号码以便接收最新重要通知。

（2）按照要求填报后，请留意出入境部门发送的提示短信。如提示未能成功申报的，必须及时到居住地派出所现场办理。

（六）全市外国人签证证件办证网点

1. 广州市公安局出入境管理局

    地　　址：越秀区解放南路155号

    咨询电话：12345

    办公时间：周一至周五9:00—12:00 / 13:00—17:00

2. 海珠区公安分局出入境办证大厅

    地　　址：海珠区江南西紫龙大街18号

    咨询电话：12345

    办公时间：周一至周五9:00—12:00 / 13:00—17:00

3. 天河区公安分局出入境办证大厅

    地　　址：天河区软件路13号

    咨询电话：12345

    办公时间：周一至周五9:00—12:00 / 13:00—17:00

4. 白云区公安分局出入境办证大厅

    地　　址：白云区广云路11号

    咨询电话：12345

    办公时间：周一至周五9:00—12:00 / 13:00—17:00

5. 黄埔区公安分局出入境办证大厅

    地　　址：黄埔区香雪三路3号二楼

    咨询电话：12345

    办公时间：周一至周五9:00—12:00 / 13:00—17:00

6. 花都区公安局出入境办证大厅

    地　　址：花都区天贵路101号

    咨询电话：12345

    办公时间：周一至周五9:00—12:00 / 13:00—17:00

7. 番禺区公安分局出入境办证大厅

    地　　址：番禺区亚运大道550号

    咨询电话：12345

    办公时间：周一至周五9:00—12:00 / 13:00—17:00

8. 南沙区公安局出入境办证大厅

    地　　址：南沙区黄阁镇华梦街6号中国铁建环球中心5号楼2层

    咨询电话：12345

    办公时间：周一至周五9:00—12:00 / 13:00—17:00

9. 越秀区公安分局出入境办证大厅

    地　　址：越秀区海珠中路72号

    咨询电话：12345

    办公时间：周一至周五9:00—12:00 / 13:00—17:00

10. 荔湾区公安分局出入境办证大厅

    地　　址：荔湾区中山七路328号

    咨询电话：12345

    办公时间：周一至周五9:00—12:00 / 13:00—17:00

11. 增城区公安分局出入境办证大厅

    地　　址：增城区荔湖街景观大道北7号

    咨询电话：12345

    办公时间：周一至周五9:00—12:00 / 13:00—17:00

12. 从化区公安局出入境办证大厅

地　　址：从化区城郊街河滨北路128号

咨询电话：12345

办公时间：周一至周五9:00—12:00 / 13:00—17:00

（七）广州市各区外国人管理服务工作站一览表（2021年5月12日，共98个）

区	街镇	设置场所	地址	工作电话	联系人
越秀区 18个	登峰街	独立设置	童心路5号右侧二楼（广东省信托房产开发公司旁）	83492672	梁　烨 19966290490 池雨龙 13640728742
	华乐街	外国人综合服务中心	淘金坑68号一楼	83498020	杨致远 13533201059
	梅花村街	政务服务中心	梅花路21号首层14号窗	31651312	黄盈雅 37592527
	黄花岗街	来穗人员和出租屋服务管理中心	先烈中路84号	37619431	刘仲钦 18802032316
	建设街	独立设置	建设中马路2号	83523382	党从辉 83523382
	矿泉街	独立设置	瑶台西街85号（自编号）	86326382	吴雪婷 15099979894
	六榕街	六榕街道办事处大厅	六榕路109号之一	83185971	许穗卓 13632244019
	北京街	来穗人员和出租屋服务管理中心	惠福东路482号	31058899 31058897	陆文昭 13632292991
	大东街	党群服务中心	东仁新街8号首层	无	陈嘉恒 13710078144
	大塘街	政务服务中心	秉正街17号	83350595	曾绮卉 15914421516
	东山街	政务服务中心	寺右北二街26号之一二楼	87383516	邱鸿濂 13719037175
	洪桥街	北园社区居委会	小北路220号首层	无	游成柱 13925001352
	流花街	独立设置	环市中路209号之二	86661620	孙姝婧 83127280 18818854205
	人民街	街道出租屋服务管理中心	大新路257号	81092131	宋　麟 13826026221

039

外国人在穗指南（2021）

（续表）

区	街镇	设置场所	地址	工作电话	联系人
越秀区 18个	农林街	政务服务中心	执信南路64号	87660519	傅雪琳 13710907401
	珠光街	政务服务中心	珠光路54号	无	杨莹莹 13543432917
	白云街	政务服务中心	筑南大街8号	83884653	
	光塔街	综治信访维稳中心	解放中路云台里26号	83335087	梁　健 13724840290
海珠区 4个	赤岗街	政务服务中心	广州大道南448号财智大厦2楼	无	劳达城 18922187577
	新港街	政务服务中心	新港西路38号之二	无	林倩婷 13570480532
	滨江街	滨江派出所	海珠区滨江中逸民里15号地下	无	李金乐 18664877452
	琶洲街	东北社区居委会	宸悦路9号	89260554	苏敏莹 15818157347
荔湾区 22个	南源街	独立设置	南岸路荟文四街14号后座（警务室旁）	81022953	陈雪萍 13430258771 谢佩仪 13642779684
	逢源街	独立设置	荔湾区富力广场S栋一楼	81708945	李　穗 13326492523
	西村街	独立设置	西湾路151号	81670229 81670251	陈　实 18030592925
	站前街	独立设置	陈岗路51号大院门外（越秀车管所对面）	无	李英妹 13450203808
	白鹤洞街	独立设置	荔湾区鹤洞路42号之二首层东面	81557390	张敏莉 15914370900
	石围塘街	独立设置	兴东路7号之一	无	陈　茜 13828485969
	茶滘街	来穗人员和出租屋服务管理中心	茶滘路96号	81579169	关善明 13560089961
	冲口街	政务服务中心	芳村大道东88号三楼	81803162	陈思琼 13450472346
	多宝街	来穗人员和出租屋服务管理中心	多宝路121号首层	无	蔡晓婷 13826401131

(续表)

区	街镇	设置场所	地址	工作电话	联系人
荔湾区 22个	海龙街	政务服务中心	龙溪中路107号一楼	81415269	陈雪锋 19966230753 13570376393
	花地街	党群服务中心	芳村大道中187号	无	梁心怡 15017568391
	桥中街	政务服务中心	桥中南路169号	无	张恒烽 15622341831
	昌华街	政务服务中心	恩宁路逢庆首约33号之二首层	无	程嘉敏 18126844491
	东漖街	街道办事处	浣花路浣南街4号	81502025	黄桂红 13928840306
	东沙街	街道办事处	东沙大道玉兰路3号	无	魏志斌 15625093106
	金花街	政务服务中心	西华路金花直街79号	81089535	李晓聪 13535209329
	沙面街	政务服务中心	沙面一街1号地下	81218880	罗 侬 13611429608
	华林街	来穗人员和出租屋服务管理中心	兴贤坊34号1楼	无	蔡乐诗 13725324074 张洪梅 15014242905
	岭南街	政务服务中心	杉木栏路99号一楼	81859261	王丽婷 13610222016
	龙津街	政务服务中心	荔湾区欧家园52-54号	无	陈银铃 13570202420
	彩虹街	来穗人员和出租屋服务管理中心	冼家庄17号	81021610	陈满钰 13411160010 麦 圣 13826076482
	中南街	来穗人员和出租屋服务管理中心	增南路52号三楼	无	
天河区 18个	石牌街	独立设置	天河北路570号帝景苑商业中心六楼612室	87558146	官桂贤 13922110662 王 虹 13760758316
	林和街	政务服务中心	林和西路101号	83629417 38848305	郑宇东 13826087771 吴丽玲 13760777330
	五山街	来穗人员和出租屋服务管理中心	汇景南路201号（维伦特莱会所左侧）	38298306 85287435	刘 燕 13570550988 冯冠星 13751834628
	猎德街	独立设置	海明路20号	38211191	林 琳 13650713017

(续表)

区	街镇	设置场所	地址	工作电话	联系人
天河区 18个	天河南街	政务服务中心	体育西横街193号	37343867	李博浩 18565090409 沈思慧
	棠下街	棠下街政务中心	棠下棠德东横路1号一楼	无	潘锦霞 1351276620 满华云 13609007890
	天园街	政务服务中心	东方三路2号	88527736	洪军梅 13924001202
	龙洞街	政务服务中心	龙洞北路1号一楼大厅	32108252	谢振兴 13480265474
	车陂街	来穗人员和出租屋服务管理中心	东圃陂东路6号	32205635	杨惠媚 13824431416 林显杰 18198971207
	前进街	政务服务中心	桃园路3号	无	潘婷婷 13570350731 张晓雯 18126713681
	凤凰街	综治信访维稳中心	华美路88号	无	刘立峰 13560242029 吴俊安 13828407222
	黄村街	政务服务中心	荔苑路5号一楼	82307272	袁嘉琦 18602072823
	沙河街	政务服务中心	沙河大街89号首层	无	张志聪 15914390030
	新塘街	政务服务中心	合景路141-147号	82357233转812	吴侬霖 13143114510
	元岗街	政务服务中心	元岗路600号一楼	无	熊 蕾 18198971532
	长兴街	政务服务中心	长兴路289号一楼	无	李建中 13302211462
	珠吉街	来穗人员和出租屋服务管理中心	珠村东横五路2号二楼	32351603	廖月辰 13828467376
	冼村街	政务服务中心	平云路167号	38392756	林宛丽 13760715404
白云区 21个	松洲街	富力半岛（独立设置）	河畔东街39号	无	谭翩翩 13539479069
		富力桃园（独立设置）	富林街36号	无	沈嘉颖 18814106457
	棠景街	政务服务中心	三元里大道907号	无	暂无
	京溪街	政务服务中心	京溪中路18号	无	陈 颖 18825049495 吴志勇 13828413825

（续表）

区	街镇	设置场所	地址	工作电话	联系人
白云区 21个	金沙街	独立设置	汇才二街22号	37614323	沈春泉 13640692933 冯新文 18928872886
	同和街	政务服务中心	广州大道北2077号	无	龚 俊 13560451633
	黄石街	广外大社区警务室	丛云路19号	无	李 彬 13609012072
	白云湖街	政务服务中心	石夏路288号201	无	刘思佳 13631570625 罗永娴 13760726629 李惠娟 15914269467
	鹤龙街	来穗人员和出租屋服务管理中心	鹤龙一路629号	无	李显棹 18826101044
	嘉禾街	综治信访维稳中心	鹤龙二路1179号	81310021	刘绮妍 13609027965
	景泰街	政务服务中心	云苑三街31号	无	周嘉颖（景泰所辅警）15920131617
	均禾街	富力城社区警务室	均禾路富力城花语街26号首层	无	张 嫣 13826463520 杜燕仪 17322080816 张 浩 18316985517
	石门街	政务服务中心	石沙路石井工业区一横路12号政务中心10号窗	86166640	邱宇杰 13119590278
	同德街	政务服务中心	西槎路同德花园同雅街78号	无	梁颖昕 15017561882
	新市街	政务服务中心	新达路89号	无	周颖欣 18926211023
	永平街	政务服务中心	荟贤路1号	无	刘 正 18122717680
	云城街	来穗人员和出租屋服务管理中心	履泰西街1号	无	彭 茜 15218862190
	石井街	金碧新城居委会	金新三街40号	无	林海正 13922425228 黄永兆 15521065069
	人和镇	政务服务中心	鹤龙六路6号	36031153	周雪莹 15915812338
	钟落潭镇	社区警务室	长钟路2号	36774468	贺 毛 15602238851
	江高镇	来穗人员和出租屋服务管理中心	金沙南路1号	无	李 雁 18826466876

043

外国人在穗指南（2021）

（续表）

区	街镇	设置场所	地址	工作电话	联系人
黄埔区 3个	萝岗街	香雪社区居委会	山香路7号	89851230	聂　敏 15251516566
	云埔街	综治信访维稳中心	榕悦一街2号	82207380	金英虎 13073070066
	联和街	综治信访维稳中心	联和街道外管服务站	62208797	孙渝婷 13660064405
花都区 1个	花东镇	独立设置	花东镇富力金港城东区A1栋	36977400	江静仪 13710364240
番禺区 8个	洛浦街	独立设置	沿沙东路40号	84581515	陈舒慧 13570480270 黄紫贤 15902053988
	钟村街	缤纷汇社区党群服务中心	祈福新村学院路20号	84788095	温城锋 13824409885
	大石街	政务服务中心	岗东路149号	84785011	韩峻青 18688204768 李　婧 15920515616
	南村镇	政务服务中心	兴业大道1042号	84763275	梁敏珊 15814536732 郭钊华 13922739433
	小谷围街	政务服务中心	中心南大街28号	34729905	黄司雅 13535477741 陈紫君 13711254950
	石楼镇	亚运城媒体村物业服务中心	广州亚运城兴亚二路1号	84658890	陈杰汶 13560430003 梁炳培 13560320403
	新造镇	来穗中心	兴华路9号	无	黎杰开 15914398101 陈耀锋 18820000796
	石壁街	广州南站维稳中心	汇骏路广州南站维稳综治中心	39267235	黄耀东 15322062854 李涛宇 13678973738
南沙区 1个	南沙街	独立设置	南沙碧桂园天玺湾2号门口左侧第二间铺（暂未编号）	34684563	罗菲菲 13535438848
从化区 1个	温泉镇	独立设置（小区临街门面）	温泉镇冲口路167号	87990806	梁嘉雯 18826262295
增城区 1个	永宁街	永新派出所凤凰城社区警务室	永宁街碧桂园凤凰城凤妍苑五街8号	32169393	列肇强 13580510980 詹嘉琳 13430365849

第三章
生活百科

一、饮食娱乐

(一) 食在广州

"食在广州"历史悠久、闻名遐迩,据考证,该美誉已经有2000年的历史。粤菜是中国八大菜系之一,其食材多样丰博、制作精细,讲求色、香、味、形、鲜。粤菜的口味较为清淡,配合季节性变化,突出其新鲜与营养科学的特点。广州的北京路、上下九步行街、西关美食街一带,随处可见广州著名的小吃、点心和风味食品。煲汤、饮茶、吃夜宵也是广州饮食文化的一部分。

广州有一大批百年老字号的粤菜酒楼、潮菜酒楼,以及经营其他中国菜系的酒楼,例如湘菜馆、川菜馆、鲁菜馆、淮扬菜馆等等。广州也有许多西方美食的好去处,例如西餐厅、咖啡馆、麦当劳、必胜客等,同时还有不少平民化的小餐馆、大排档、传统小吃店等经营特色小菜、火锅、烧烤和小吃。

（二）岭南佳果

广州地处亚热带，一年四季都有新鲜水果上市，被誉为"水果之乡"。广州的水果有数百种之多，其中以荔枝、香蕉、木瓜、菠萝著名，并称"岭南四大名果"。此外，芒果、杨桃、石榴、龙眼、白榄、乌榄、黄皮、杨梅、菠萝蜜、三华李、西瓜等水果也颇受欢迎。

（三）购物

广州是"购物天堂"，大到世界各地的知名品牌和奢侈品，小到超市里的各国生活用品、食品、衣服鞋帽，应有尽有。还有各类出口全球的专业批发市场，完全可以满足来穗经商、居住或旅游的外国人不同层次的需求。

外国游客如果需要购买广州的特产馈赠亲朋好友，可以去北京路的新大新百货超市，也可以选择莲香楼的各式糕点饼食，广州酒家利口福连锁店的腊味食品，还可以去天河城、正佳广场以及各旅游景点购买旅游纪念品等。

（四）文化娱乐活动

身处广州，可以享受丰富多彩的娱乐活动，感受各种层次的文化盛宴。广州大剧院、星海音乐厅、友谊剧院、中山纪念堂经常有经典的中外演出；广州美术馆、广州艺术博物馆、广州图书馆、广东美术馆等场馆有各类异彩纷呈的展览；长隆欢乐世界、天河城、正佳广场等都有机动游乐设施，可以放松身心；香江野生动物园、鳄鱼公园、广州动物园、白云山风景区等是休闲观光、亲近自然的好去处；从化温泉、碧水湾度假村、金叶子度假酒店、锦绣香江温泉城可以泡温泉，也可以承办大型的团体会议；珠江夜游、华纳金逸影城、KTV、酒吧等是享受浪漫夜生活的最佳选择。广州有多个酒吧聚集区域，著名的有：珠江两岸的芳村酒吧街、滨江路酒吧街、外国人云集的市中心环市路的酒吧街和珠江琶醍酒吧街等。

广州也不乏大型运动场所，如麓湖高尔夫球场、沙面、二沙岛的网球场和羽毛球场，瑜伽馆、力美健健身俱乐部等，可以锻炼身体、放松身心。

二、交通

（一）广州白云国际机场

广州白云国际机场位于广州市区以北的花都区，是中国三大枢纽机场之一。白云机场交通便利，除了机场高速公路直达，大型综合交通枢纽集合了多种便捷的交通方式，旅客可以选择自驾、乘坐出租车、地铁3号线、空港快线大巴以及城际轨道抵离白云机场。

目前，白云机场共设有8个停车场面向社会公众开放，分别为P1、P2、P3、P4、P5、P6、P7、P8，其中P1—P5在一号航站楼（T1）周边，P6-P8在二号航站楼（T2）周边，共有8400多个停车位。小型机动车停车收费标准为：前15分钟（含15分钟）免费，前2个小时每小时10元，不足1小时按1小时计，第3个小时起每小时加收5元，一天24小时封顶60元。

乘坐空港快线大巴，广州市区可往返白云机场至广州白马大厦、广州天河区华师大厦酒店、海珠区珀丽酒店、开发区万科尚城御府；珠三角地区可往返白云机场至从化、增城、珠海（经停官塘、唐家、香洲）、深圳（经停宝安）、中山、中山古镇（经停横栏）、中山小榄（经停东升）、惠州（经停博罗）、佛山、佛山顺德（经停陈村）、顺德龙山、佛山桂城（经停大沥）、佛山高明（经停三水）、佛山西樵（经停狮山）、肇庆（经停四会）、东莞市区（经停南城）、东莞松山湖（经停东城）、东莞万江、江门、江门台山、清远（经停好来登酒店）、阳江（经停址山、恩平）、河源、云浮、韶关等地。旅客可通过当地的乘车点、城市候机楼或是白云机场的自助售票机及人工售票柜台购票乘车。

广清城际（花都站至清城站）、广州东环城际（花都站至白云机场北站）让清远和花都的旅客往返白云机场更加快捷便利。广清城际、广州东环城际采用"清城—花都—白云机场北"贯通运营。

从清城站至花都站，大站停最快行程时间约16分钟，若搭乘站站停的班次，行程时间约33分钟；从花都站至白云机场北站，大站停单程时间约14分钟，若搭乘站站停班次列车，行程时间约21分钟。

白云机场客服热线

电话：(8620) 96158

白云机场官网：http://www.gbiac.net

（二）铁路

中国铁路广州局集团有限公司管内有动车组列车和普速旅客列车。高铁动车组设有商务座（仅限少数车次）、特等座、一等座、二等座和无座等票种，普速旅客列车设有高级软卧、软席卧铺、硬席卧铺、软座、硬座和无座（高级软卧、软席卧铺仅限部分车次）等票种，另外还有空调列车和非空调列车之分。动车组列车和长途列车设有餐车车厢供旅客点餐用餐。

近年来，中国铁路经历了快速发展，为旅客提供了快捷方便、安全舒适、经济实惠的出行方式。目前广州已开通当日可到达北京、石家庄、郑州、武汉、长沙、上海、南京、杭州、福州、合肥、南昌、济南、西安、南宁、贵阳、成都、重庆、兰州、银川、昆明等省会城市以及香港的高速铁路，除台湾、澳门外，其他省会城市均有普速旅客列车可以到达。

广州市现有四个火车站：广州站位于越秀区，广州东站位于天河区，广州南站位于番禺区，广州北站位于花都区。

广州站的旅客列车主要开往北京、上海、武汉、成都、重庆、贵阳、拉萨、乌鲁木齐、南宁、海口、西安、银川、宁波等城市；广州东站的旅客列车主要开往香港红磡、深圳、汕头、梅州、厦门、哈尔滨、长春等城市，还有部分开往华东地区（京九线）、北京、上海等大城市；广州南站主要开行当日可到达的高速动车组列车和珠海城际动车组列车。

旅客可登录中国铁路客户服务中心网站（www.12306.cn）或使用"铁路12306"手机客户端办理电子客票购票、改签、退票等业务，可通过火车站售票厅人工窗口办理购票、改签、退票等线下服务，也可使用车站自动购票机自助购买电子客票，或拨打95105105进行电话订票。广州市内各代售点均可办理电子客票售票业务。

（三）地铁

广州地铁集团成立于1992年，是广州市政府全资大型国有企业。目前广州地铁已开通15条线路，分别为1号线、2号线、3号线（含3号线北延段）、4号线、5号线、6号线、7号线、8号线、9号线、13号线、14号线（含知识城线）、18号线、21号线、APM线（珠江新城旅客自动输送系统）和广佛地铁，共设290座车站（含换乘站34座），运营里程589.4公里，线路横跨广佛两地，遍布全市11个行政区，无缝衔接白云机场、高铁站、火车站及各大客运站等主要交通枢纽，实现"广佛同城""区区通地铁"。广州有轨电车运营线路共有2条，即广州有轨电车海珠环岛线（THZ1）和黄埔有轨电车1号线（THP1），运营里程约为22.1公里，共设30座车站。

广州地铁线网票价按里程分段计价：起步4公里内2元；4—12公里内每递增4公里加1元；12—24公里内每递增6公里加1元；24公里以后，每递增8公里加1元。APM线、有轨电车均为票价2元/人次。乘客可使用乘车码、羊城通、岭南通、全国一卡通、地铁日

票、银联信用卡或单程票等搭乘广州地铁。目前,可搭乘广州地铁的乘车码入口分别有广州地铁APP、微信小程序、支付宝小程序、羊城通APP等;其中,广州地铁官方APP乘车码已实现了与北京、上海、重庆3座城市地铁乘车码的互联互通,方便市民异地搭乘城市轨道交通。

作为市民乘客首选的公共交通出行方式,广州地铁始终不忘肩负的社会责任,坚持"全程为你"品牌理念,以乘客满意为导向,提供"爱心候车区""爱心专座""爱心直通车"预约等系列爱心服务,推行"便民雨伞""便民药箱""准妈咪徽章""绿色通道"等人性化举措,致力满足各类乘客群体出行需求。

广州地铁服务热线:96891
广州地铁官网:www.gzmtr.com
广州地铁官方APP二维码:

(四)公共交通

广州市巡游出租汽车运价为起步12元/3公里,超出3公里部分,续租价2.6元/公里,返空费实行阶梯附加,15至25公里按照续租价加收20%,25公里以上按续租价加收50%,夜间(23:00—次日5:00)按续租价加收30%。通过需另行收费的道路、桥梁时费用由乘客另外支付。司机和乘客必须系好安全带。付完车费后,乘客可索取车票,下车时记得拿好自己的行李物品。

如需了解长途汽车客运班次、公交车线路、水上巴士线路等相关情况,可以使用行讯通APP或小程序查询客车班次客票情况、购票、生成检票码等,查询公交车实时到站情况;在乘坐公共交通工具或进入客运站场时,需按要求做好相关疫情防控措施;如对广州

外国人在穗指南（2021）

正规客运站场发班或进入的长途汽车客运、公共交通的营运、服务有不满，请拨打"12345"热线进行咨询、意见反馈或实名投诉；如遗漏行李物品在公交车、出租车上，根据《广州市人民政府办公厅关于印发广州市拾遗物品管理规定的通知》（穗府办规〔2021〕1号）的相关规定，请向公共交通工具所属单位查询。

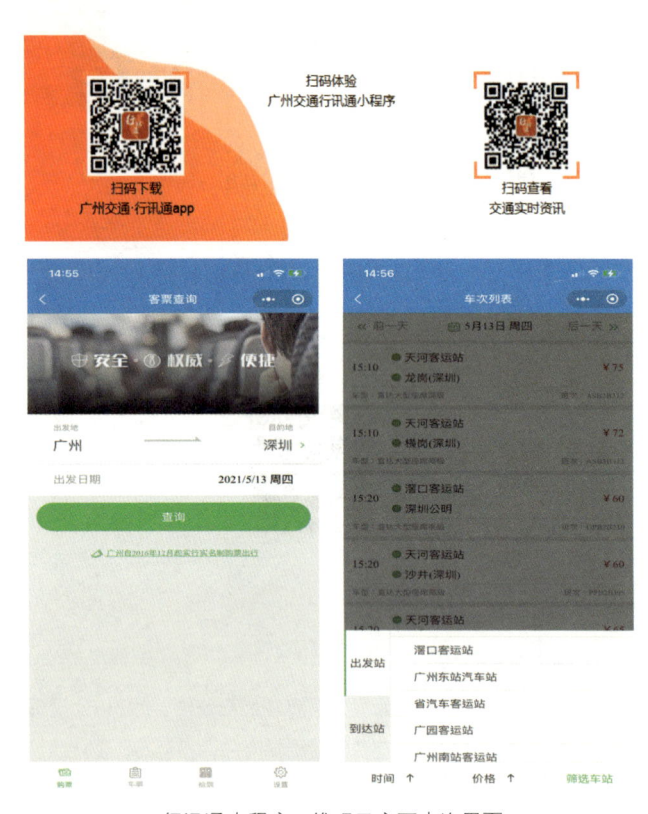

行讯通小程序二维码及客票查询界面

三、通信、银行、邮电服务

（一）电信及移动通信

广州的酒店内的客房电话一般都可以直接拨打国际长途（IDD），酒店除代收电信通话费用外，一般要加收10%—15%不等的服务费用。在商店购买IP电话卡或电话充值卡并使用公共电话可以直接拨打国际、国内长途电话。拨打10000（中国电信）、10050（铁路通信）或到电信的营业厅可以申请安装电话和宽带互联网服务。酒店的客房、商务中心、对外营业的网吧等也提供上网服务。广州有GSM、CDMA两种移动通信网络，并可以提供无线互联网服务。

详情请到运营商的营业厅了解或致电：10086（中国移动）10010（中国联通）。

（二）银行服务

广州各大银行的网点可以进行外币兑换以及退汇手续，三星级以上酒店可以提供外币兑换人民币服务。广州的星级酒店、部分餐馆、大型百货商场以及超市都可使用境外信用卡结账。中国银行的大部分网点可以办理旅行支票兑现或托收业务。

（三）邮政及快递服务

邮电局的服务网络遍布广州。邮电局全周营业，可办理收寄国际/国内信函、包裹、特快邮件及国际商业信函、电报、电话、电传等业务，另外一些邮政储蓄所可办邮政储蓄、汇款、电报汇款等业务。主要街道的路边都设有绿色标志的邮筒，以便人们投寄国内、国际信件。

四、就读

中国的现行学制规定：义务教育为9年，高中教育为3年，专科教育为2—3年，本科教育为4—5年，硕士研究生教育为2—3年，博士研究生教育为3—4年。

（一）义务教育和高中教育阶段

广州市已将"海外华侨华人子女""持'外国人永久居留身份证'的外籍人员随迁子女（含未成年的持证人本人）""驻穗领事馆等外交人员的适龄子女"等纳入义务教育阶段政策性照顾学生范围，他们享受与户籍适龄儿童同等入学待遇，由各区教育局按免试就近入学原则安排义务教育学位；其他外籍适龄儿童少年还可按属地区指引自行报读符合条件的义务教育民办学校。

广州市已将"驻穗领事馆等外交人员的适龄子女"纳入高中阶段政策性照顾学生范围，他们在我市参加高中阶段学校招生考试，可报考公办普通高中、民办普通高中和中等职业学校，与户籍生享受同等待遇。具有我市初中学籍的外籍人员子女，或经批准的国外来穗升学生，可报考我市民办普通高中、中等职业学校。

需要转学入读广州市普通中小学的外籍学生，可根据《广东省教育厅关于中小学生学籍管理的实施细则（试行）》的规定，自行联系学校，经学校核实同意后，由学校按要求办理转学、入学事宜。

此外，外籍人士适龄子女，可自行向在穗外籍人员子女学校申请入读。

（二）高等教育阶段

具有相当于中国高中毕业或以上学历，身体健康，持普通护照的外国公民，可申请到有招收国际学生资质的高等学校中学习或进修。

在广州市高等院校就读，可根据教育部、外交部、公安部关于《学校招收和培养国际学生管理办法》执行。国际学生应当在入境前根据其学习期限向中国驻其国籍国或居住地国使领馆或外交部委托的其他驻外机构申请办理X1字或X2字签证，按照规定提交经教育主管部门备案的证明和学校出具的录取通知书等相关材料。国际学生所持学习类签证注明入境后需要办理居留证件的，应当自入境之日起三十日内，向广州市公安局出入境管理支队申请办理学习类外国人居留证件。（详见广州金盾网：www.gzjd.gov.cn）

（三）在穗外籍人员子女学校名单

广州英国学校
The British School of Guangzhou
地址：广州市白云区同和路983-3
邮编：510515
电话：020-87094788
网址：www.bsg.org.cn

广州美国人国际学校
Ameircan International School of Guangzhou
地址：广州市越秀区二沙岛烟雨南街3号（K-5年级）
　　　广东省广州市黄埔区科翔路19号（6-12年级）
邮编：510105（K-5年级）
　　　510663（6-12年级）
电话：020-3213555
网址：www.aisgz.org

广州日本人学校
広州日本人学校/Japanese School of Guangzhou
地址：广州市科学城风信路10号
邮编：510663
电话：020-61397023
网址：jsgcn.com

广州奥伊斯嘉日本语幼儿园
オイスカ広州日本語幼稚園/OISCA Guangzhou Japanese Kindergarten
地址：广州市科学城风信路10号
邮编：510663
电话：020-61397023

广州恩慧学校
Guangzhou Grace Academy
地址：广州市番禺区大石镇桔树村"万兴围"厂房A、B
邮编：511431
电话：020-84500180
传真：020-34506248

广州暨大港澳子弟学校

Affiliated School of JNU for Hong Kong and Macao Students

地址：广州市天河区龙洞街道荟龙路18号

邮编：510520

电话：020-87085090

传真：020-87085090

网址：暂无

广州誉德莱国际学校

Utahloy International School Guangzhou

地址：广州市白云区沙太北路800号

邮编：510515

电话：020-87202019

网址：www.utahloy.com/gz/

增城誉德莱国际学校

Utahloy International School Zengcheng

地址：广州市增城区增江街大埔围

邮编：511325

电话：020-82913201

网址：www.utahloy.com/zc/

广州韩国学校
광저우한국학교/Guangzhou Korean School
地址：广州市番禺区石楼镇兴海路6号
邮编：511447
电话：020-39298661
传真：020-39298663
网址：www.gks.or.kr

广州爱莎外籍人员子女学校
ISA International School of Guangzhou
地址：广州市天河区员村四横路128号红专厂创意园C2-2
邮编：510655
电话：020-88900909
网址：www.isagzth.com

广州市加拿大外籍人员子女学校
Canadian International School of Guangzhou
地址：广州市番禺区东艺路122号
邮编：511400
电话：020-39939920
网址：www.cisgz.com

广州贝赛思外籍人员子女学校
BASIS International School Guangzhou
地址：广州市黄埔区科学城尖塔山路8号
邮编：510663
电话：020-37781086
网址：bigz.basischina.com

广州市英伦外籍人员子女学校
Britannia International School Guangzhou
地址：广州市白云区金沙洲创佳路4号
邮编：510168
电话：020-66606886
网址：www.bisgz.com

广州科学城爱莎外籍人员子女学校
ISA Science City International School
地址：广州市黄埔区玉树南路66号
邮编：510700
电话：020-37362580
网址：www.isagzsc.com

五、外国人来华工作许可

（一）适用范围

外国人在中国境内工作，应当按规定取得工作许可和工作类居留许可证件。任何单位和个人不得聘用未取得工作许可和居留许可证件的外国人。

（二）主要内容

境外外国人来华工作许可、境内许可、短期许可；许可证的延期、变更、补办；许可证、许可通知的注销等业务。

（三）申请渠道

在"外国人来华工作管理服务系统"（https://fuwu.most.gov.cn/lhgzweb/）在线办理，常年受理，无需缴纳任何费用。

（四）外国人才分类标准

1. 外国高端人才（A类）

外国高端人才是指符合"高精尖缺"和市场需求导向，中国经济社会发展需要的科学家、科技领军人才、国际企业家、专门特殊人才等，以及符合计点积分（85分及以上）外国高端人才标准的人才。外国高端人才无数量限制，可不受年龄、学历和工作资历限制。具体见外国人来华工作分类标准（试行）。

2. 外国专业人才（B类）

外国专业人才是指符合外国人来华工作指导目录和岗位需求，属于经济社会发展急需的人才，具有学士及以上学位和2年及以上相关工作经历或者符合计点积分60分及以上，年龄不超过60周岁。对确有需要，符合创新创业人才、专业技能类人才、优秀外国

外国人在穗指南（2021）

毕业生、符合计点积分外国专业人才标准的以及执行政府间协议或协定的，可适当放宽年龄、学历或工作经历等限制。具体见外国人来华工作分类标准（试行）。国家对专门人员和政府项目人员有规定的，从其规定。

3. 其他外国人员（C类）

其他外国人员是指满足国内劳动力市场需求，符合国家政策规定的其他外国人员。具体见外国人来华工作分类标准（试行）。

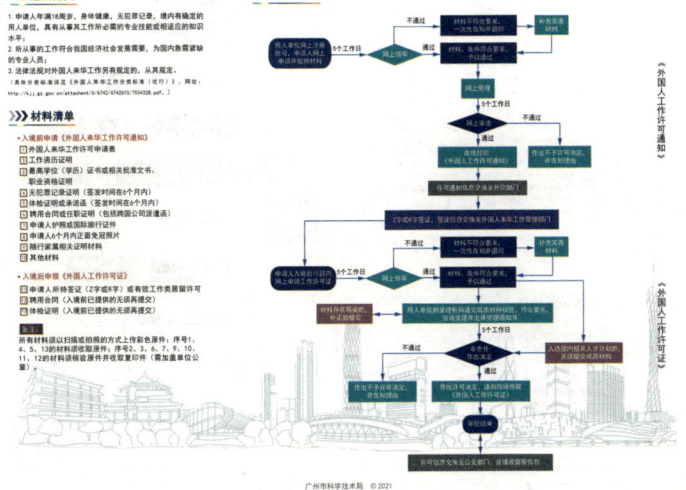

第三章 生活百科

▶▶▶ 领证须知及注意事项

1. 申请人本人或经办人（如非系统登记的经办人，需出具用人单位的授权委托书）凭本人有效身份证明文件，携带《外国人来华工作许可受理通知》至受理机构领取证件。或用人单位在网上提起申请时已勾选通邮寄，决定通过后，受理机构将所申请的《外国人工作许可证》邮寄给用人单位（邮费到付）。

2. 领证后可到公安出入境部门申请办理居留证件。

扫描以下二维码
获取完整版《申办指引》

服务窗口

广州市外国人工作许可服务窗口
（受理除黄埔区、南沙区以外其他区单位业务）
地址：广州市天河区珠江新城华利路
61号5楼517、518号窗口

广州南沙政务服务中心涉外综合服务平台
（受理南沙辖区内单位业务）
地址：广州市南沙区凤凰大道1号一楼
广州南沙政务服务中心
涉外综合服务平台外办、5室口

黄埔区科学技术局服务窗口
（受理黄埔辖区内单位业务）
地址：广州市黄埔区香雪三路3号
政务服务中心四楼区401、402窗口

办公时间：星期一至星期五
9:00-12:00, 13:00-17:00
（国家法定节假日除外）

咨询电话：020-12345

境外申办（90日以上）
外国人来华工作许可申办指引

业务办理请登录"外国人来华工作管理服务系统"
（网址：https://fuwu.most.gov.cn/lhgzweb/）
业务办事指引请登广州市科学技术局官网
"外籍和港澳台人才业务"栏目
（网址：http://kjj.gz.gov.cn/attachment/6/6742/6742652/7034328.pdf）

▶▶▶ 适用范围

1. 申请人年满18周岁，身体健康，无犯罪记录，境内有确定的用人单位，具有从事其工作所必需的专业技能或相应的知识水平；
2. 所从事的工作符合我国经济社会发展需要，为国内急需紧缺的专业人员；
3. 法律或对外国人来华工作另有规定的，从其规定。

（具体分类标准请查看《外国人来华工作分类标准（试行）》，网址：http://kjj.gz.gov.cn/attachment/6/6742/6742045/7034328.pdf）

▶▶▶ 材料清单

- **入境前申请《外国人来华工作许可通知》**
  1. 外国人来华工作许可申请表
  2. 工作资质证明
  3. 最高学位（学历）证书或其批准文书、职业资格证明
  4. 无犯罪记录证明（签发时间在6个月内）
  5. 体检证明或承诺函（签发时间在6个月内）
  6. 聘用合同或任职证明（包括跨国公司派遣函）
  7. 申请人的护照或国际旅行证件
  8. 申请人6个月内正面免冠照片
  9. 随行家属相应证明材料
  10. 其他材料

- **入境后申请《外国人工作许可证》**
  1. 申请人所持签证（Z字或R字）或有效工作类居留许可
  2. 聘用合同（入境前已提供的无须再提交）
  3. 体检证明（入境前已提供的无须再提交）

注3：
所有材料请以扫描或拍照的方式上传彩色原件；序号1、4、5、13的材料请收取原件；序号2、3、6、7、9、10、11、12的材料需核验原件并收取复印件（需加盖单位公章）

▶▶▶ 办理流程

广州市科学技术局 ©2021

外国人在穗指南（2021）

扫描以下二维码
获取完整版《申办指引》

服务窗口

广州市外国人工作许可服务窗口
（受理越秀区、南沙区以外其他区单位业务）
地址：广州市天河区珠江新城华利路
61号5楼517、518号窗口

广州南沙政务服务中心涉外综合服务平台
（受理南沙区内单位业务）
地址：广州市南沙区凤凰大道1号一楼
广州南沙政务服务中心
涉外综合服务平台外4、5窗口

黄埔区科学技术局服务窗口
（受理黄埔区内单位业务）
地址：广州市黄埔区香雪三路3号
政务服务中心四楼A区401、402窗口

办公时间：星期一至星期五
9：00-12：00，13：00-17：00
（国家法定节假日除外）

咨询电话：020-12345

境内申办（90日以上）
外国人来华工作许可申办指引

业务办理请登录"外国人来华工作管理服务系统"
（网址：https://fuwu.most.gov.cn/lhgzweb/）
业务办事指引请见广东省科学技术厅官网
"外籍和港澳台人才业务"栏目
（网址：http://kjj.gz.gov.cn/attachment/
6/6742/6742652/7034328.pdf）

>>> 适用范围

1. 申请人年满18周岁，身体健康，无犯罪记录，境内有确定的用人单位，具有从事其工作所必需的专业技能或相适应的知识水平；
2. 所从事的工作符合我国经济社会发展需要，为国内急需紧缺的专业人员；
3. 法律法规对外国人来华工作另有规定的，从其规定。
（具体积分赋分标准见《外国人来华工作分类标准（试行）》，网址：http://kjj.gz.gov.cn/attachment/6/6742/6742610/7034328.pdf ）
4. 须符合以下情形之一：

(1) 在华工作的外国人变换用人单位，但工作岗位（职业）未变动，且工作地属留许可在有效期内的；
(2) 中国公民的外籍配偶或子女、华侨本人及留居工作的外国人的配偶或子女，持有有效签证或有效居留许可的；
(3) 符合自由贸易区、全面创新改革试验区相关优惠政策的；
(4) 用人单位为外事有国跨国公司在华地区总部组长代表处的；
(5) 企业集团的核心人员流动的；
(6) 执行政府间合作项目的；
(7) 已持工作居留证促进入境的经华机构代表人员，已获得来华工作90日以下的外国人工作许可的，在其聘雇有效期内，被境内用人单位聘用的；
(8) 其他审批机构认定符合条件的。

>>> 办理流程

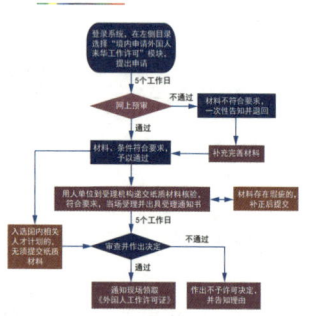

登录系统，在左侧目录
选择"境内申请外国人
来华工作许可"模块，
提出申请
↓
5个工作日
↓
网上预审 —不通过→ 材料不符合要求，一次性告知并退回
↓通过
材料、条件符合要求，不予通过 —→ 补充完善材料
↓
用人单位到受理机构送交纸质材料核验，
符合要求，当场受理并出具受理通知书
↓ 5个工作日
↓
入选国内相关 ← 审查并作出决定 —不通过→ 材料存在瑕疵的，种正后提交
人才计划的，
无须提交纸质材料
↓通过
通知现场领取
《外国人工作许可证》
↓
作出不予许可决定，
并告知理由

>>> 材料清单

① 外国人来华工作许可申请表
② 工作资历证明
③ 最高学位（学历）证书或相关批准文书、职业资格证明
④ 无犯罪记录证明（签发时间在6个月内）
⑤ 体检证明或声语言（签发时间在6个月内）
⑥ 聘用合同或任职证明（包括跨国公司派遣函）
⑦ 申请人护照或国际旅行证件
⑧ 申请人在中国免签居留
⑨ 申请人所持签证（Z字或R字）或有效居留许可
⑩ 随行家属相关证明材料
⑪ 其他材料

强注：
在境内变换用人单位，但工作岗位（职业）未变动的，可免交2、3、4材料，但须提交原工作许可注销证明或原工作许可证。

>>> 领证须知及注意事项

1. 申请人本人或经办人（如非系统登记的经办人，需出具用人单位的授权委托书）凭本人有效身份证明文件，携带《外国人来华工作许可受理通知书》至受理机构领取证件，或用人单位在网上提起办理时提出邮政速递服务，决定通过后，受理机构将所申请的《外国人工作许可证》邮寄给用人单位（邮费到付）。
2. 领证后可到公安出入境部门申请办理居留许可。

广州市科学技术局 © 2021

066

第三章 生活百科

短期来穗工作（90日及以下）外国人来华工作许可申办指引

扫描以下二维码获取完整版《申办指引》

服务窗口

广州市外国人工作许可服务窗口
（受理除黄埔区、南沙区以外其他区单位业务）
地址：广州市天河区珠江新城华利路61号5楼517、518号窗口

广州南沙政务服务中心涉外综合服务平台
（受理南沙辖区内单位业务）
地址：广州市南沙区凤凰大道1号一楼广州南沙政务服务中心涉外综合服务平台内4、5号口

黄埔区科学技术局服务窗口
（受理黄埔辖区内单位业务）
地址：广州市黄埔区香雪三路3号政务服务中心四楼A区401、402窗口

办公时间：星期一至星期五
9:00—12:00，13:00—17:00
（国家法定节假日除外）

咨询电话：020-12345

业务办理请登录"外国人来华工作管理服务系统"
（网址：https://fuwu.most.gov.cn/lhgzweb/）
业务办事指引详见广州市科学技术局官网"外籍和港澳台人才业务"栏目
（网址：http://kjj.gz.gov.cn/attachement/6/6742/6742570/7034328.pdf）

》》适用范围

申请短期（90日及以下）来穗工作的外国人，需申请外国人来华工作许可通知（90日及以下）
申请人符合以下情形之一：
- 到境内合作方完成某项技术、科研、管理、指导等工作
- 到境内体育机构进行试训（包括教练员、运动员）
- 拍摄影片（包括广告片、纪录片）
- 时装表演（包括车模、拍摄平面广告等）

》》材料清单

1. 外国人来华工作许可申请表
2. 工作合同（项目合同、合作协议）、邀请单位邀请说明
3. 申请人护照或国际旅行证件
4. 其他材料

》》办理流程

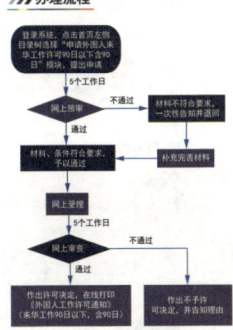

登录系统，点击首页左侧目录树中选择"申请外国人来华工作许可90日以下"模块，提出申请

↓ 5个工作日

网上预审 —不通过→ 材料不符合要求，一次报告知并退回
↓ 通过
材料、条件符合要求，予以通过 → 补充完善材料
↓
网上受理
↓ 5个工作日
网上审查 —不通过→ 作出不予许可决定，并告知理由
↓ 通过
作出许可决定，在线打印《外国人工作许可通知》（来华务工90日以下，含90日）

》》领证须知及注意事项

1. 办理《外国人许可通知》的，系统自动生成许可通知，用人单位自行打印并发送申请人；申请人凭打印的《外国人工作许可通知》及其所需材料向我驻外使领馆申办理Z字或F签证。
2. 持Z字签证入境后，停留期不超过30日的，不办理工作类居留证件；停留期超过30日的（含30日），须办理工作类居留证件。

广州市科学技术局 © 2021

067

外国人在穗指南（2021）

扫描以下二维码
获取完整版《申办指引》

服务窗口

广州市外国人工作许可服务窗口
（受理除黄埔区、南沙区以外其他区单位业务）
地址：广州市天河区珠江新城华利路
61号5楼517、518号窗口

广州南沙政务服务中心涉外综合服务平台
（受理南沙辖区内单位业务）
地址：广州市南沙区凤凰大道1号一楼
广州南沙政务服务中心
涉外综合服务平台台外4、5窗口

黄埔区科学技术局服务窗口
（受理黄埔辖区内单位业务）
地址：广州市黄埔区香雪三路3号
政务服务中心四楼401、402窗口

办公时间：星期一至星期五
9:00—12:00、13:00—17:00
（国家法定节假日除外）

咨询电话：020-12345

外国高端人才确认函申办指引

业务办理请登录"外国人来华工作管理服务系统"
（网址：https://fuwu.most.gov.cn/lhgzweb/）
业务办事指引详见广州市科学技术局官网
"外籍和港澳台人才业务"栏目
（网址：http://kjj.gz.gov.cn/attachment/
6/6742/6742571/7034328.pdf）

>>> 适用范围

符合《外国人来华工作分类标准（试行）》中外国高端人才（A类）标准条件，为我国经济社会发展需要的外国高层次人才和急需紧缺人才，以及符合"高精尖缺"和市场需求导向的科学家、科技领军人才、国际企业家、专门人才和高技能人才等，可申请《外国高端人才确认函》，持《外国高端人才确认函》可申请人才签证（R签证）。

>>> 材料清单

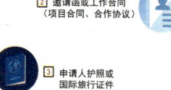

1. 外国高端人才确认函申请表
2. 邀请函或工作合同（项目合同、合作协议）
3. 申请人护照或国际旅行证件
4. 符合《外国人来华工作分类标准（试行）》A类条件的相关认定材料
5. 其他材料

>>> 办理流程

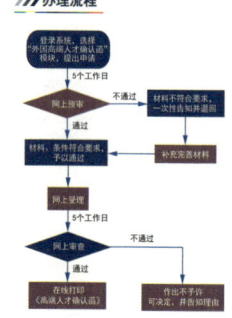

登录系统，选择"外国高端人才确认函"模块，提出申请
↓ 5个工作日
网上接审 —— 不通过 → 材料不符合要求，一次性告知并退回
↓ 通过
材料、条件符合要求，予以通过 ← 补充完善材料
↓
网上受理
↓ 5个工作日
网上审查 —— 不通过 → 作出不予作可决定，并告知理由
↓ 通过
在线打印《高端人才确认函》

>>> 领证须知及注意事项

《外国高端人才确认函》在线自行下载打印，无需再到受理机构领取。

第三章 生活百科

领证须知及注意事项

1. 不涉及《外国人工作许可证》卡面信息变更的，系统将自动更新芯片信息，申请人或单位可自行扫描二维码确认信息变更情况；涉及卡面信息变更的（包括姓名、类别等），在领取新的《外国人工作许可证》及《准予行政许可决定书》时，需将旧的《外国人工作许可证》交受理机构剪退回。

2. 申请人本人或经办人（如非系统登记的经办人，需出具用人单位的授权委托书）凭本人身份证件及相关原件材料到受理机构领取《准予行政许可决定书》或《外国人工作许可证》。

3. 以上也可通过在申请时提出速递需求，申请邮政速递送达，邮费到付。

扫描以下二维码
获取完整版《申办指引》

服务窗口

广州市外国人工作许可服务窗口
（受理除黄埔区、南沙区以外其他区单位业务）
地址：广州市天河区珠江新城华利路
61号5楼517、518号窗口

广州南沙政务服务中心涉外综合服务平台
（受理南沙区内单位业务）
地址：广州市南沙区凤凰大道一号一楼
广州南沙政务服务中心
涉外综合服务平台01、4、5窗口

黄埔区科学技术局服务窗口
（受理黄埔区内单位业务）
地址：广州市黄埔区香雪三路3号
政务服务中心四楼A区401、402窗口

办公时间：星期一至星期五
9:00-12:00, 13:00-17:00
（国家法定节假日除外）

咨询电话：020-12345

许可证延期、变更、补办
外国人来华工作许可申办指引

业务办理请登录"外国人来华工作管理服务系统"
（网址：https://fuwu.most.gov.cn/lhgzwwb/）
业务办事指引请见广州市科学技术局官网
"外国和港澳台人才业务"栏目
（网址：http://kjj.gz.gov.cn/attachment/6/6742/6742779/7034328.pdf）

（一）外国人工作许可证延期

适用范围

用人单位在原岗位（职业）继续聘用本人入境工作（90日以上，不含90日），且此前已领取《外国人工作许可证》的申请人，应当在申请本人的《外国人工作许可证》有效期届满前30日-90日按本指引提出延期业务申请。

材料清单

- 外国人工作许可证延期申请表
- 聘用合同证明
- 雷试或有效期内护照
- 其他材料

备注：所有材料须以扫描或拍照的方式上传彩色原件；序号1的材料须收取原件；序号2、3、4的材料须核验原件并收取复印件（需加盖单位公章）。

办理流程

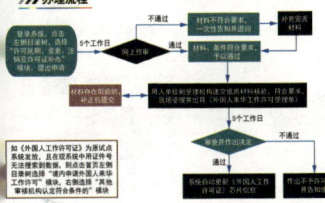

（流程图）

领证须知及注意事项

1. 申请人本人或经办人（如非系统登记的经办人，需出具用人单位的授权委托书）凭本人有效身份证件及《外国人来华工作许可受理通知》到受理机构领取《准予行政许可决定书》；涉及个人信息变更需要的，需到受理机构领取新的许可证书；以上也可通过在申请时提出速递需求，申请邮政速递送达，邮费到付。

2. 领取前可到公安认入境《外国人来华工作居留证件》手续。

3. 用人单位在收到《外国人工作许可证》有效期届满前30日-90日内加上系统提出延期申请，若有效期不足30日的，系统自动生成撤回通知单，申请通过确认工作许可证延期。

重新办理工作许可证。（A类按流程重新申请工作许可证，B、C类按境外程序重新申请工作许可通知。）

4. 变任新岗位（职业），或国籍变更的，须重新申请办理外国人来华工作许可证。（A类按内程序重新申请工作许可证，B、C类按境外程序重新申请工作许可通知。）

（二）外国人工作许可证变更、补办

适用范围

变更：已取得《外国人工作许可证》的外国人个人信息（姓名、护照号、职务、类别）等事项发生变更的，应当自变更事项发生之日起10个工作日内申办。

补办：《外国人工作许可证》遗失或损毁的，申请人应当自证件遗失（损毁）之日起发现遗失（损毁）之日起申办。

材料清单

变更
- 外国人来华工作许可变更申请表
- 申请变更事项的证明文件
- 其他材料

备注：
1. 全流程网办，无须收取纸质材料；所有材料须以扫描或拍照的方式上传彩色原件。

补办
- 外国人来华工作许可补办申请表
- 关于《外国人工作许可证》遗失或损毁情况说明
- 其他材料

备注：
1. 全流程网办，无须收取纸质材料；所有材料须以扫描或拍照的方式上传彩色原件。

办理流程

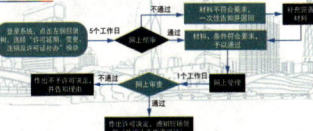

（流程图）

广州市科学技术局 © 2021

069

外国人在穗指南（2021）

>>> 领证须知及注意事项

决定通过后，许可通知自动失效，可在系统的境外速递提出新的申请，无须再到受理机构递交材料。

扫描以下二维码
获取完整版《申办指引》

服务窗口

广州市外国人工作许可服务窗口
（受理除黄埔区、南沙区以外其他地区单位业务）
地址：广州市天河区珠江新城华利路
61号6楼517、518号窗口

广州南沙政务服务中心涉外综合服务平台
（受理南沙辖区内单位业务）
地址：广州市南沙区凤凰大道1号一楼
广州南沙政务服务中心
涉外综合服务平台外4、5窗口

黄埔区科学技术局服务窗口
（受理黄埔辖区内单位业务）
地址：广州市黄埔区香雪三路3号
政务服务中心D栋A区401、402窗口

办公时间：星期一至星期五
9:00-12:00, 13:00-17:00
（国家法定节假日除外）

咨询电话：020-12345

许可证、许可通知注销
外国人来华工作许可申办指引

业务办理请登录"外国人来华工作管理服务系统"
（网址：https://fuwu.most.gov.cn/lhgzxxb/）
业务办事指引详见广州市科学技术局官网
"外籍和港澳台人才业务"栏目
（网址：http://kj.gz.gov.cn/attachment/6/6742/6742779/7034328.pdf）

（一）外国人工作许可证注销

>>> 适用范围

1. 《外国人来华工作许可证》有效期届满未延续的，自动注销；依法被撤销、撤回的，以及许可证作依法被吊销的，由决定机构注销。
2. 申请人死亡或者失行为能力或履约终止合同，解除聘用关系的，用人单位于事项发生之日起10个工作日内向决定机构申请注销。
3. 用人单位歇业的，申请人可以向决定机构申请注销工作许可。

>>> 材料清单

- 外国人来华工作许可注销申请表
- 聘用关系解除、合同终止或其他关系解除相关证明材料
- 其他材料

备注： 所有附件须以扫描或拍照的方式上传彩色原件；序号1的材料收取原件；序号2和3的材料均须核查原件并收取复印件。

>>> 办理流程

登录系统，点击左侧"业务申请栏"选择"申请撤销、变更、注销许可证业务"模块，提交申请 → 5个工作日内 → 网上预审 → [不通过：材料不符合要求，一次性告知并退回 → 补齐完善材料] → [通过：材料、条件符合要求，不以过通] → 用人单位按照申请机构提交纸质材料后，再符合要求，由决定机构作出同意注销决定。 → 1个工作日 → 审批作件出具决定 → [不通过：作出不予许可决定，并告知理由] → [通过：作出同意注销决定，按照程序出具注销证明]

（二）外国人工作许可通知注销

自《外国人工作许可通知》签发之日起，超过3个月仍未在中国境外便，领馆办理相关字词字签证入境，如需继续申请中的，须先注销该许可通知后重新申请《外国人工作许可通知》；因聘用单位或申请人原因，无法入境履行劳动合同任务，应及时注销通知；短期（90日及以下）《外国人来华工作许可通知》的注销，应在工作合同生效前提起注销申请，如合同已生效，则不予注销。

>>> 材料清单

- 外国人来华工作许可通知注销申请表
- 其他材料

备注： 1. 全流程网办，无须收取纸质材料。2. 所有材料须以扫描或拍照的方式上传彩色原件。

>>> 办理流程

登录系统，点击左侧"业务申请"业务申请栏选择"申请撤销、变更、注销许可证业务"模块，提交申请 → 5个工作日内 → 网上预审 → [不通过：材料不符合要求，一次性告知并退回 → 补齐完善材料] → [通过：材料、条件符合要求] → 网上受理 → 1个工作日 → 网上审查 → [不通过：作出不予许可决定] → [通过：作出同意注销决定]

广州市科学技术局 © 2021

070

第三章 生活百科

领证须知及注意事项

1. 申请人本人或经办人（如非系统登记的经办人，需出具用人单位的授权委托书）凭本人有效身份证明，携带《外国人来华工作许可受理单》受理通知机构领取证件。或用人单位在网上提起申请时提出邮政速递要求，决定通过后，受理机构将所申请的《外国人工作许可证》邮寄给用人单位（邮费到付）。

2. 外籍应届高校毕业生领取证件后向公安机关申请办理工作类居留许可。

扫描以下二维码
获取完整版《申办指引》

服务窗口

广州市外国人工作许可服务窗口
（受理除黄埔区、南沙区以外其他区单位业务）
地址：广州市天河区珠江新城华利路
61号5楼517、518号窗口

广州南沙政务服务中心涉外综合服务平台
（受理南沙辖区内单位业务）
地址：广州市南沙区凤凰大道1号一楼
广州南沙政务服务中心
涉外综合服务平台台4、5窗口

黄埔区科学技术局服务窗口
（受理黄埔辖区内单位业务）
地址：广州市黄埔区香雪三路3号
政务服务大厅（四楼A区401、402窗口

办公时间：星期一至星期五
9:00-12:00, 13:00-17:00
（国家法定节假日除外）

咨询电话：020-12345

外籍高校毕业生
外国人来华工作许可申办指引

业务办理请登录"外国人来华工作管理服务系统"
（网址：https://fuwu.most.gov.cn/lhgzweb/）
业务办事指引请登广州市科学技术局官网
"外籍和港澳台人才业务"栏目
（网址：http://kj.gz.gov.cn/attachment/6/6742/6742782/7034328.pdf）

适用范围

在境内知名高校取得硕士及以上学位且毕业一年以内的外籍毕业生，或在中国境内高校取得硕士及以上学位且毕业一年以内的外国留学生。

审批条件：
1. 年满18周岁，身体健康；
2. 无犯罪记录；
3. 学习成绩优秀，平均成绩不低于80分（百分制，其他制换算成百分制处理）或B+/B（四级制）以上，在校期间无不良行为记录；
4. 取得相应的学历与学位；

5. 确定的聘用单位，从事工作岗位与所学专业对口，薪酬原则上不低于当地城镇在岗职工平均工资，具体标准由各省级人力资源社会保障部门根据就业市场实际和引进人才工作的需要合理确定；
6. 持有有效护照或能代替护照的其他国际旅游证件。

办理流程

材料清单

● 入境前
☐ 外国人来华工作许可申请表
☐ 履历证明（简历）
☐ 最高学位（学历）证书
☐ 无犯罪记录证明（签发时间在6个月内）
☐ 体检证明或体格表（签发时间在6个月内）
☐ 聘用意向书
☐ 申请人护照或国际旅行证件
☐ 申请人6个月内正面免冠照片
☐ 聘用（包括在校应届毕业生可以做为记录、成绩单、用人单位在当地公共就业和人才服务机构查询到的劳动者公开发布招聘信息满30日的证明）

● 入境后
☐ 申请人所持签证（工作或X学）或有效居留许可
☐ 聘用合同（入境前已提供的无需再提交）
☐ 体检证明（入境前已提供的无需再提交）

备注：
1. 在境外高校取得硕士的外籍毕业生须凭境外途径申请，入境时交与入境的材料申办《外国人工作许可通知》，得入境后，按入境的材料申领《外国人工作许可证》；在境内高校取得学位的外籍毕业生及凭国口上入境的及入境的材料清单整理提交，接境内的途径申请。
2. 所有材料须以A4（297×210mm）的方式上传彩色原件。
3. 序号1、2、4、5、12的材料须签章。
4. 序号6、7、8、9、10、11须核验原件并收取复印件（需加盖单位公章）。

广州市科学技术局 © 2021

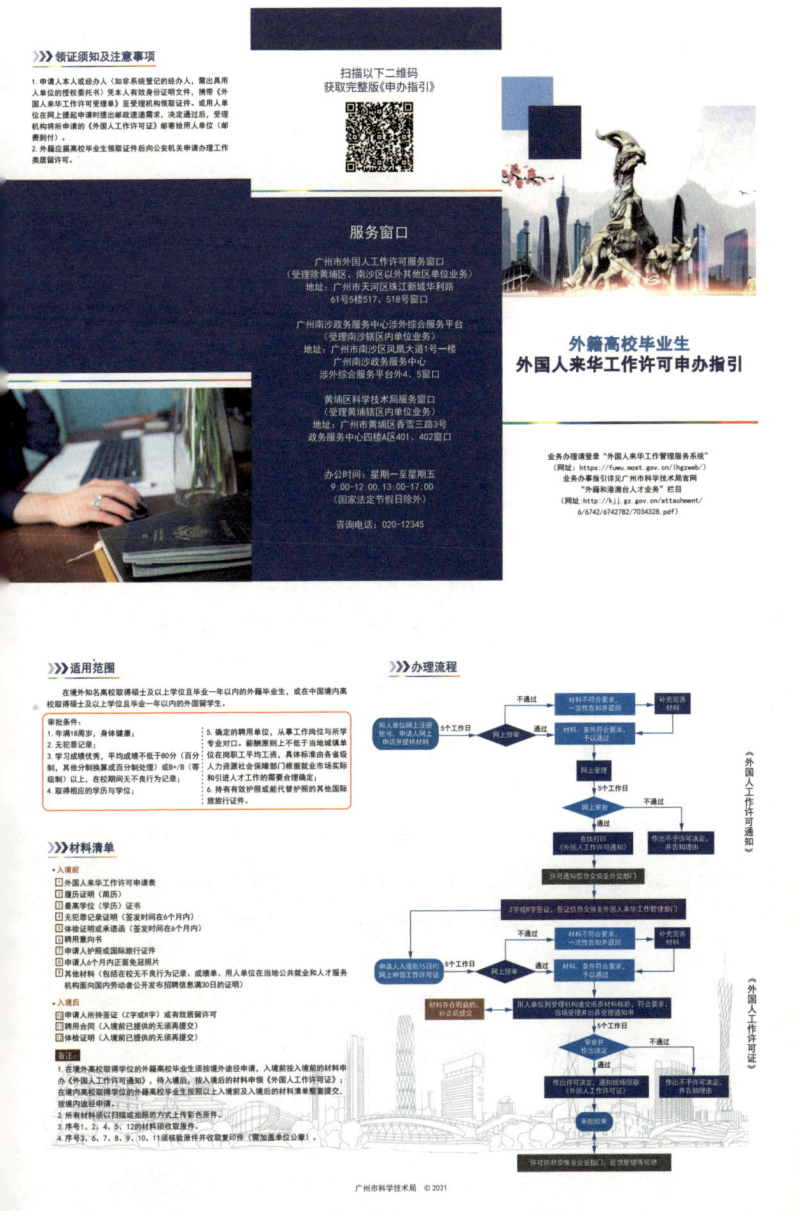

071

六、婚姻及收养

（一）结婚登记

要求结婚的男女双方应当亲自到婚姻登记机关申请结婚登记。符合规定的，予以登记，发给结婚证。完成结婚登记，即确立婚姻关系。

1. 结婚登记受理条件

（1）婚姻登记机关具有管辖权；

（2）男女双方完全自愿结婚；

（3）男年满22周岁，女年满20周岁；

（4）要求结婚的男女双方应当亲自到婚姻登记机关申请结婚登记；

（5）男女双方均无配偶（未婚、离婚、丧偶）；

（6）男女双方没有直系血亲或者三代以内旁系血亲关系；

（7）男女双方持有规定的有效身份证件、证明材料。

2. 办理结婚登记应提供的材料

（1）当事人双方3张2寸近6个月内半身免冠合影红底彩色照片。

（2）有效身份证件、证明材料。

内地居民：本人有效的户口簿和居民身份证（当事人为集体户口无法提供户口簿首页原件的，可以提供加盖户口簿保管单位公章的首页复印件和本人页原件）。居民身份证过期或遗失的，可凭有效临时身份证办理。

外国人：本人的有效护照或者其他有效的国际旅行证件；所在国公证机构或者有权机关出具的、经中华人民共和国驻该国使（领）馆认证或者该国驻华使（领）馆认证的本人无配偶的证明，或者所在国驻华使（领）馆出具的本人无配偶的证明。

与中国无外交关系的国家出具的有关证明，应当经与该国及中国均有外交关系的第三国驻该国使（领）馆和中国驻第三国使（领）馆认证，或者经第三国驻华使（领）馆认证。

(二)离婚登记

夫妻双方自愿离婚的,应当书面签订离婚协议,并亲自到婚姻登记机关申请离婚登记。自婚姻登记机关收到离婚登记申请之日起三十日内,任何一方不愿离婚的,可以向婚姻登记机关撤回离婚登记申请。前款规定届满后三十日内,双方应当亲自到婚姻登记机关申请发给离婚证。未申请的,视为撤回离婚登记申请。

1. 离婚登记受理条件

(1)婚姻登记机关具有管辖权;

(2)男女双方自愿离婚;

(3)男女双方应当亲自到婚姻登记机关申请办理离婚登记;

(4)男女双方均具有完全民事行为能力;

(5)男女双方对子女抚养、财产以及债务处理等事项协商一致;

(6)男女双方持有内地婚姻登记机关或者中国驻外使(领)馆颁发的结婚证;

(7)男女双方均无重婚情形;

(8)男女双方持有规定的有效身份证件、证明材料。

2. 离婚登记办理流程

(1)申请。夫妻双方自愿离婚的,应当提供离婚协议,持证件和证明材料共同到具有管辖权的婚姻登记机关提出申请,在婚姻登记机关现场填写"离婚登记申请书"。

(2)受理。婚姻登记机关对当事人提交的证件和证明材料进行初审,初审无误后,发给"离婚登记申请受理回执单"。不符合离婚登记申请条件的,不予受理。当事人要求出具"不予受理离婚登记申请告知书"的,应当出具。

(3)冷静期。离婚登记当事人收到"离婚登记申请受理回执单"之日起三十日内(自婚姻登记机关收到离婚登记申请之日的次日开始计算期间,期间的最后一日是法定休假日的,以法定休假日结束的次日为期间的最后一日),任何一方不愿离婚的,可以持本人有效身份证件等材料向受理离婚申请的婚姻登记机关撤回离婚登记申请,并亲自填写"撤回离婚登记申请书"。经婚姻登记机关核实无误后,发给"撤回离婚登记申请确认单"。自离婚冷静期届满后三十日内,双方未共同到婚姻登记机关申请发给离婚证的,视为撤回离婚登记申请。

(4)审查。自离婚冷静期届满后三十日内(自冷静期届满日的次日开始计算期间,期间的最后一日是法定休假日的,以法定休假日结束的次日为期间的最后一日),双方当事人应持规定有效的证件和证明材料,共同到婚姻登记机关申请发给离婚证。婚姻登记机关依据相关规定对当事人的真实意愿、证件和证明材料、离婚协议书等进行审查。对不符合离婚登记条件的不予办理。当事人要求出具"不予办理离婚登记告知书"的,应当出具。

(5)登记(发证)。婚姻登记机关按照相关法律法规的规定予以登记,发给离婚证。

3. 离婚登记申请应提供的材料

(1)内地婚姻登记机关或者中国驻外使(领)馆颁发的结婚证。

(2)有效身份证件、证明材料。

内地居民:本人有效的户口簿和居民身份证(当事人为集体户口无法提供户口簿首页原件的,可以提供加盖户口簿保管单位公章的首页复印件和本人页原件)。居民身份证过期或遗失的,可凭有效临时身份证办理。

外国人:本人的有效护照或者其他有效的国际旅行证件。

(3)在婚姻登记机关现场填写的"离婚登记申请书"。

4. 申请发给离婚证应提供的材料

(1)内地婚姻登记机关或者中国驻外使(领)馆颁发的结婚证。

(2)有效身份证件、证明材料。

内地居民:本人有效的户口簿和居民身份证(当事人为集体户口无法提供户口簿首页原件的,可以提供加盖户口簿保管单位公章的首页复印件和本人页原件)。居民身份证过期或遗失的,可凭有效临时身份证办理。

外国人:本人的有效护照或者其他有效的国际旅行证件。华侨、外国人办理离婚登记时换领新护照的,应当同时提交办理结婚登记时使用的旧护照;无法提交的,应当提交有权机关出具的护照号码变更证明。新护照上已载明旧护照号码的,可不提交上述证件或者材料。

(3)双方当事人共同在婚姻登记员面前签署的离婚协议书(一式三份)。

(4)双方当事人2张2寸单人近6个月内半身免冠红底彩色照片。

(5)如当事人身份及信息变更的,需提供有权机关或部门出具的相关变更证明。

(6)"离婚登记申请受理回执单"或者该回执单遗失的证明材料。

5. 离婚登记程序

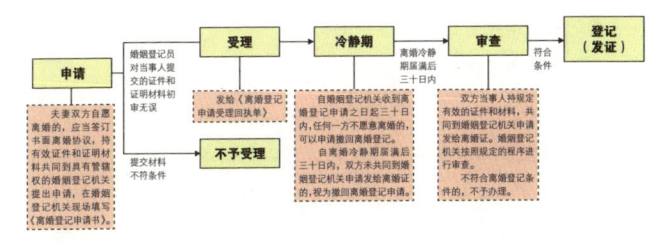

（三）补领婚姻登记证

当事人遗失、损毁婚姻登记证，或婚姻登记证上的个人信息与现持有的有效身份证件上的个人信息不一致的，可以申请补领婚姻登记证。

1. 补领婚姻登记证受理条件

（1）婚姻登记机关具有管辖权。

（2）当事人在内地婚姻登记机关或者中国驻外使（领）馆依法登记结婚或者离婚，现今仍然维持该状况。

（3）当事人遗失、损毁婚姻登记证的。

（4）当事人持有规定的有效身份证件、证明材料。

（5）当事人持有婚姻登记档案保管部门或经办婚姻登记机关出具的婚姻登记记录证明或加盖印章的婚姻登记档案复印件。

2. 补领婚姻登记证应提供的材料

（1）有效身份证件

内地居民：本人有效的常住户口簿、居民身份证（当事人为集体户口无法提供户口簿首页原件的，可以提供加盖户口簿保管单位公章的首页复印件和本人页原件）。居民身份证过期或遗失的，可凭有效临时身份证办理。

外国人：本人的有效护照或者其他有效的国际旅行证件。华侨、外国人办理补领婚姻登记证时换领新护照的，应当同时提交办理婚姻登记时使用的旧护照；无法提交的，应当提交有权机关出具的护照号码变更证明。新护照上已载明旧护照号码的，可不提交上述证件或者材料。

（2）证明材料

a. 加盖原婚姻登记机关或档案保管部门公章的婚姻登记档案复印件或"档案遗失证明"等其他证明材料；

b. 如有证件信息或人员身份变更，导致现持有的身份证件上的信息与结（离）登记档案信息不一致的，需提供有权机构出具的相关变更证明。

c. 婚姻登记档案遗失或身份证件信息与婚姻登记档案信息不一致的，具体办事材料请咨询户口所在地或原办理婚姻登记的婚姻登记机关。

（3）照片

申请补领结婚证的，双方当事人提供3张2寸近6个月内半身免冠合影红底彩色照片；申请补领离婚证的，双方当事人提供2张2寸单人近6个月内半身免冠红底彩色照片。

（四）其他说明

（1）当事人提交的证件证明材料是外国语言文字的，应当全文同等格式翻译成中文。当事人未同时提交证件证明材料中文译文的，视为未提交该文件。

婚姻登记机关可以接受由当事人所在国驻华使（领）馆或者当地有资格的翻译机构出具的翻译文本。

（2）结婚登记或者补领结婚证的双方当事人均不通晓汉语的，应当自带翻译人员；离婚登记或者补领离婚证的一方当事人不通晓汉语的，应当自带翻译人员。

翻译人员应当提交本人有效身份证件，如实翻译，并确认当事人已知晓无误，在需要署名的文件、材料上亲笔签名、书写日期。

（五）广州市各区民政局婚姻登记处服务信息一览表

办事机构	地址	服务时间	联系电话
越秀区民政局婚姻登记处	广州市水荫路110号（东风公园西门）	星期一至星期五 上午：9:00—12:00 下午：13:00—17:00 星期六 上午：9:00—12:00	83814282
海珠区民政局婚姻登记处	广州市海珠区南田路302号（海珠区婚育服务中心）		34073601
荔湾区民政局婚姻登记处	广州市荔湾区逢源路逢源北街26号1楼		81379313
天河区民政局婚姻登记处	广州市天河区黄埔大道中256号恒安大厦1楼		37127127
白云区民政局婚姻登记处	广州市白云区白云大道北880号"安华汇"A馆六楼		36637461

(续表)

办事机构	地址	服务时间	联系电话
黄埔区民政局婚姻登记处	广州市黄埔区开达路77号乐飞家园A5栋首层	星期一至星期五 上午：9:00—12:00 下午：13:00—17:00 星期六 上午：9:00—12:00	82112103
花都区民政局婚姻登记处	广州市花都区新华街公益路35号一楼	星期一至星期五 上午：9:00—12:00 下午：13:00—17:00 星期六 上午：9:00—12:00	36897638
番禺区民政局婚姻登记处	广州市番禺区市桥街兴泰路274号基盛大厦C3栋3层		84834583
南沙区民政局婚姻登记处	广州市南沙区环市大道中19号		34689076 84941999 婚姻家庭辅导和法律咨询：84998789
从化区民政局婚姻登记处	广州市从化区温泉镇明月山溪大道2号2—3栋首层		87839333
增城区民政局婚姻登记处	广州市增城区荔湖街景观大道北7号区政务服务中心B区婚姻登记服务厅		82655833 82655838

（六）收养登记

1. 登记机关

广东省收养登记中心受广东省民政厅委托，具体承办涉外收养登记工作。

办公地址：广州市越秀区大德路233号富华商贸大厦8楼

2. 外国收养人来粤申请办理收养登记程序

（1）预约登记时间。外国收养人接到由中国儿童福利和收养中心签发的"来华收养子女通知书"后，应在来粤办理收养登记前十天与广东省收养登记中心预约办理收养登记日期。

收养登记预约电话：020-83318577、83368441

电子邮箱：gd_adoption@163.com

（2）交接孩子仪式。收养人与被收养人见面，并在省收养登记中心举行交接仪式，禁止到酒店交接孩子。

（3）签订融合协议。外国收养人与送养人签订《融和期间委托监护协议》，融合期为48小时以内，融合期间发生的异常情况应及时向广东省收养登记中心报告。

（4）办理收养登记。融合期满，收养双方当事人无异议的，收养人、送养人和被收养人必须亲自到广东省收养登记中心办理收养登记，收养人交验的证件和材料如下（全部材料应为国内A4规格纸张，复印清晰整齐，文字内容应用签字笔书写）：

a. "来华收养子女通知书"原件1份；

b. 收养人的护照正本及复印件1份；

c. 收养人填写的"收养登记申请书"（上贴收养人夫妻双方大一寸照片各1张）；

d. 收养人、送养人签订的"收养协议""融合期间委托监护协议"原件各1份；

e. 夫妻共同收养子女，有一方不到场的，应出具经所在国公证机关公证并经中国驻该国使领馆认证的收养授权委托书原件1份。

以上证件及材料齐全有效，对符合《中华人民共和国民法典》和《外国人在中华人民共和国收养子女登记办法》规定的，登记员为收养人办理收养登记，呈省民政厅审批，7日内发给"收养登记证"，收养关系自登记之日起成立。

七、宗教及活动场所

（一）在中国境内进行宗教活动的规定

外国人进入中国国境，可以携带本人自用的宗教印刷品、宗教音像制品和其他宗教用品；携带超出本人自用的宗教印刷品、宗教音像制品和其他宗教用品入境，按照中国海关的有关规定办理相关手续。禁止携带有危害中国社会公共利益内容的宗教印刷品和宗教音像制品入境。

外国人可以在中国境内的寺院、宫观、清真寺、教堂等宗教活动场所参加宗教活动。经省、自治区、直辖市以上宗教团体邀请的外国人，可以在中国宗教活动场所讲经、讲道。

以宗教教职人员身份来访的外国人，经省、自治区、直辖市以上宗教社会团体邀请，可以在依法登记的宗教活动场所讲经、讲道。

以其他身份入境的外国宗教教职人员，经省、自治区、直辖市以上宗教社会团体邀请，并经省级以上人民政府宗教事务部门同意，可以在依法登记的宗教活动场所讲经、讲道。

应邀在依法登记的宗教活动场所讲经、讲道的外国宗教教职人员，应该遵守该场所的管理规章，尊重该场所人员的信仰习惯

经中国的宗教社会团体同意，境内外国人可以邀请中国宗教教职人员按各教习惯为其进行洗礼、婚礼、葬礼和道场、法会等宗教仪式。其中，举行婚礼的外国人必须是已经依法缔结婚姻关系的男女双方。

在中国境内的外国人集体进行宗教活动，要在由县级以上人民政府宗教事务部门认可的，经依法登记的寺院、宫观、清真寺、教堂，或者在由省、自治区、直辖市人民政府宗教事务部门指定的临时地点进行。

外国组织或个人向中国提供的以培养宗教教职人员为目的的出

国留学人员名额或资金,由中国全国性宗教团体根据需要接受并统筹选派出国留学人员。

外国组织或个人不得在中国境内擅自招收以培养宗教教职人员为目的的出国留学人员。

外国人到中国宗教院校留学,须符合《高等学校接受外国留学生管理规定》的有关规定,并经全国性宗教社会团体批准、向国家宗教事务局备案。

外国人到中国宗教院校讲学,须根据《宗教院校聘用外籍专业人员办法》的规定办理。

外国人在中国境内进行宗教活动,应当遵守中国的法律、法规。外国人不得干涉中国宗教社会团体、宗教活动场所的设立和变更,不得干涉中国宗教社会团体对宗教教职人员的选任和变更,不得干涉和支配中国宗教社会团体的其他内部事务。

外国人在中国境内不得以任何名义或形式成立宗教组织、设立宗教办事机构、设立宗教活动场所或者开办宗教院校、举办宗教培训班;不得在中国公民中委任宗教教职人员、发展宗教教徒、擅自在宗教活动场所讲经、讲道;不得未经批准在依法登记的宗教活动场所以外的处所讲经、讲道,进行宗教聚会活动;不得在宗教活动临时地点举行有中国公民参加的宗教活动(**被邀请主持宗教活动的中国宗教教职人员除外**);不得制作或销售宗教书刊、宗教音像制品、宗教电子出版物等宗教用品,散发宗教宣传品。

(二)对外开放的宗教活动场所

广州宗教源远流长,佛教、道教、伊斯兰教、天主教、基督教五大宗教齐全。其中,佛教、道教、伊斯兰教传入广州已有上千年,天主教、基督教也有两三百年历史,文化底蕴深厚。在广州旧城区中轴线上,矗立着五大宗教共十间寺观教堂,形成了独具特色的文化奇观。目前全市登记开放的84处宗教活动场所中,属国家级重点文物保护单位的有6个,省级重点文物保护单位2个,市级重点文物保护单位10个。这些寺观教堂积淀了广州宗教深厚的文化底蕴,共同见证着广州这座历史文化名城的沧桑变化。

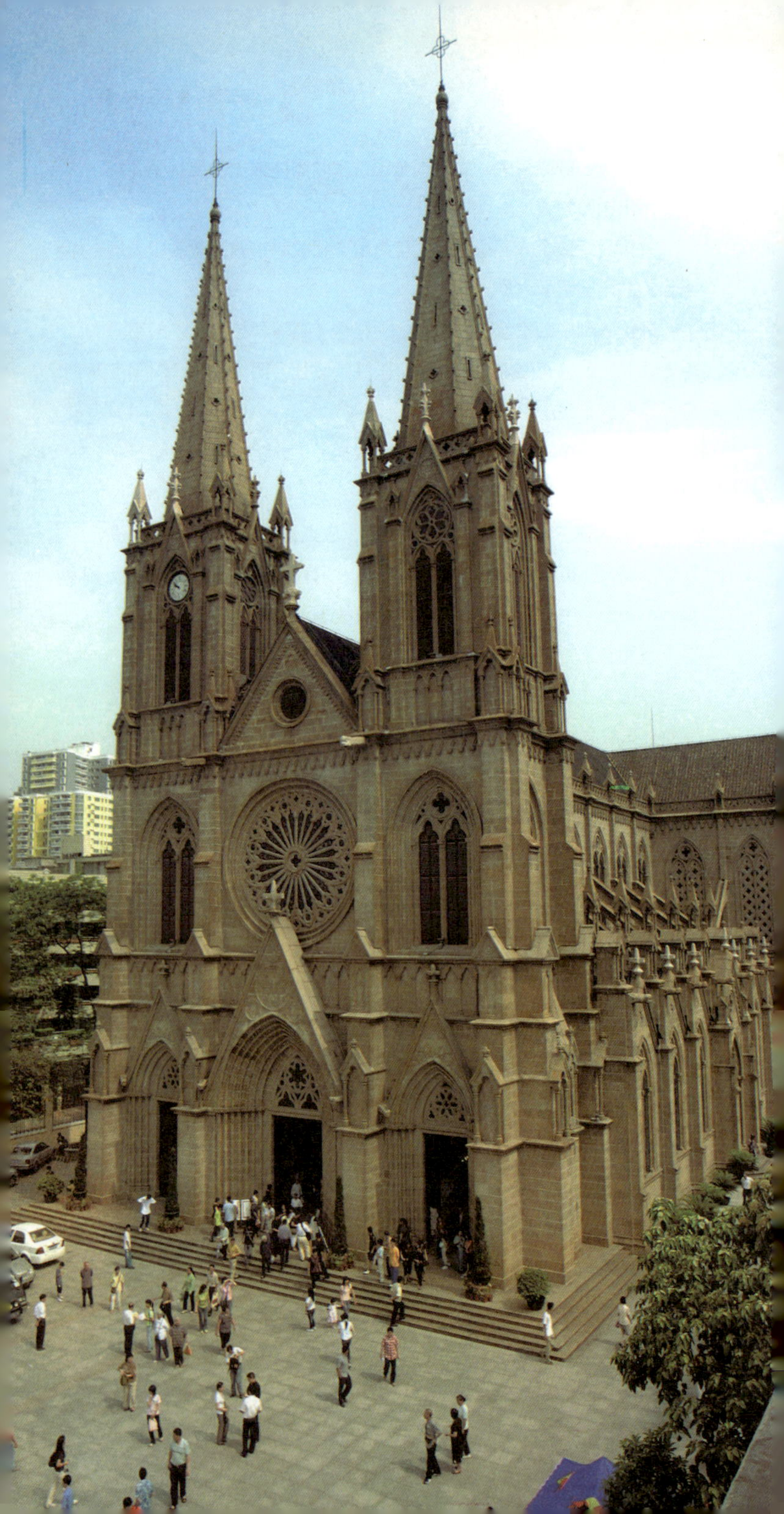

第三章 生活百科

宗教场所	地址	联系电话
佛教		
六榕寺	越秀区六榕路87号	83392843/83357754
光孝寺	越秀区光孝路109号	81088867
大佛寺	越秀区惠福东路惠新中街21号	83393455
华林禅寺	荔湾区下九路华林寺前31号	81387849
海幢寺	海珠区南华中路188号	84399172
道教		
三元宫	越秀区应元路11号	83551548
纯阳观	海珠区瑞康路268号	84189071
黄大仙祠	荔湾区百花路黄大仙道1号	81561855
仁威祖庙	荔湾区泮塘路仁威祖庙前街22号	81705462
都城隍庙	越秀区中山四路忠佑大街48号	83378036
基督教		
东山堂	越秀区寺贝通津9号	87776305/87305377
锡安堂	越秀区人民中路392号	81889054
救主堂	越秀区万福路184号	83335778
光孝堂	越秀区光孝路29号	81087837
河南堂	海珠区洪德路洪德五巷23号	84422935
天主教		
石室圣心堂	越秀区一德路旧部前56号	83334180
露德圣母堂	荔湾区沙面大街14号	81217858
伊斯兰教		
怀圣光塔寺	越秀区光塔路56号	83333593
濠畔寺	海珠区濠畔街378号	81091123
先贤古墓清真寺	越秀区解放北路901号	86692743

注：伊斯兰教活动场所一般不对游客开放。

八、医疗

（一）就诊

广州有很完善的医疗保健网络，综合性医院和专科医院遍布广州的每一个行政区。外国人可自行前往医院就医。如果不能自行前往医院的，可拨打急救电话120或指定医院的电话，呼叫救护车上门接收病人到就近的相关医院接受治疗。此项服务为收费服务，视运送距离及医疗用药情况收取一百至数百元人民币不等的费用。

医院现提供多种形式的预约挂号服务（如广州健康通、医院官网、微信公众号、12320热线等），病人亦可自行前往门诊挂号，就诊流程为：挂号分诊→排队候诊→医生问诊→交费检查检验（视情况所需，某些检查需另外预约时间）→直接开处方或根据检查检验结果开处方→交费→取药。

疫情防控期间进入医院，应按照属地统一防控要求，提供以下健康证明之一：穗康码（蓝码、绿码）、粤康码（绿码）、医学观察期满通知书、核酸检测报告、身份证明等。

广州市三级医院名单（截至2021年3月）

广东省人民医院
地址：广州市中山二路106号
电话：020-83827812-2507

广东省第二人民医院
地址：广州市海珠区新港中466号
电话：020-84219338-20007

广东省中医院
地址：广州市大德路111号
电话：020-81887233

广东省中医院大学城医院
地址：广州市番禺区大学城内环西路
电话：020-81887233-31228

广东省中医院二沙岛医院
地址：广州市大通路261号
电话：020-87351238

广州市慈善医院（广东省中医院芳村分院）
地址：广州市芳村区花地涌岸街36号
电话：020-81499866

广东省第二中医院
地址：广州市恒福路60号
电话：020-83585617

中山大学附属第一医院
地址：广州市中山二路58号
电话：020-87755766-8504

中山大学孙逸仙纪念医院
地址：广州市沿江西路107号
电话：020-81332199

中山大学附属第三医院
地址：广州市天河路600号
电话：020-85253210

中山大学第三附属医院岭南医院
地址：广州市黄埔区开创大道2693号
电话：020-82111376

中山大学附属第六医院
地址：广州市天河区员村二横路26号
　　　广州市天河区瘦狗岭路17号
电话：020-38254000

中山大学附属口腔医院
地址：广州市陵园西56号
电话：020-83862558

中山大学中山眼科中心
地址：广州市先烈南路54号
电话：020-87333209

中山大学肿瘤防治中心
地址：广州市东风东路651号
电话：020-87343088

南方医科大学南方医院
地址：广州市广州大道北1838号
电话：020-61641888

南方医科大学南方医院白云分院
地址：广州市白云区黄石街元下底路23号、广州市广州大道中
　　　1305号、越秀区水荫路水荫直街西二巷8—12号
电话：020-87240021

南方医院太和分院
地址：广州市白云区太和镇太和中路53号
电话：020-87429013

南方医科大学珠江医院
地址：广州市海珠区工业大道中253号
电话：020-84339888-43022

南方医科大学第三附属医院
地址：广州市中山大道西183号
电话：020-62784240

南方医科大学第五附属医院
地址：广州市从化区城郊街从城大道566号
电话：020-61780008

南方医科大学中西医结合医院
地址：广州市海珠区石榴岗路13号
电话：020-61650057

南方医科大学皮肤病医院、广东省皮肤病医院
地址：广州市越秀区麓景路2号
电话：020-83027506

南方医科大学口腔医院
地址：广州市海珠区江南大道南366号
电话：020-84427034

广州中医药大学第一附属医院
地址：广州市机场路14号、16号
电话：020-36591730

广州中医药大学第一附属医院白云医院
地址：广州市白云区人和镇鹤龙七路2号
电话：020-86452816

广州中医药大学第三附属医院（广州中医药大学第三临床医学院、广州中医药大学附属骨伤科医院）
地址：广州市荔湾区龙溪大道261、263号
电话：020-22292888

广州中医药大学金沙洲医院
地址：广州市白云区礼传东街1号
电话：020-81330999

暨南大学附属第一医院
地址：广州市天河区黄埔大道西613号
电话：020-38688036

广东药科大学附属第一医院
地址：广州市农林下路19号
电话：020-61325637

广东省妇幼保健院
地址：广州市广园西路13号
电话：020-61118777

广东省职业病防治院
地址：广州市海珠区新港西路海康街165号
电话：020-89022988

广东省计划生育专科医院
地址：广州市越秀区梅东路17号
电话：020-87776784

第三章 生活百科

广东省工伤康复医院
地址：广州市白云区启德路68号、广州市从化区温泉镇温泉东路117号
电话：020-87830238

广州市第一人民医院
地址：广州市盘福路1号
电话：020-81048808

广州市第十二人民医院
地址：广州市黄埔大道西天强路1号、广园中路景泰直街35号、白云山黄婆洞、广州市黄埔大道西43号瑞达大厦首层
电话：020-85591881-3332

广州医科大学附属第一医院
地址：广州市沿江路151号
电话：020-83337616

广州医科大学附属第二医院
地址：广州市海珠区昌岗东路250号
电话：020-34152464

广州医科大学附属第三医院
地址：广州市多宝路63号
电话：020-81292135

广州医科大学附属第五医院
地址：广州市黄埔区港湾路621号
电话：020-82279975-2462

广州医科大学附属肿瘤医院
地址：广州市麓湖路横枝岗78号
电话：020-83595032

广州医科大学附属口腔医院
地址：广州市黄沙大道31号
电话：020-61359477

广州医科大学附属中医医院
地址：广州市荔湾区珠玑路16号
电话：020-81886504

广州医科大学附属脑科医院
地址：广州市荔湾区明心路36号
电话：020-81891425

广州医科大学附属市八医院
地址：广州市东风东路627号、广州市白云区华英路8号
电话：020-83816453

广州市妇女儿童医疗中心
地址：广州市天河区珠江新城金穗路9号
电话：020-87036039

广州市红十字会医院
地址：同福中路396号
电话：020-34403815

广州市胸科医院
地址：广州市横枝岗路62号
电话：020-83595977

广州市荔湾中心医院
地址：广州市荔湾区荔湾路35号
电话：020-81346935

广州爱尔眼科医院
地址：广州市越秀区环市中路191号
电话：020-87313480

广州复大医疗有限公司复大肿瘤医院
地址：广州市天河区棠德西路2号及2号之二，广州市海珠区赤
　　　岗聚德中路91号、93号
电话：020-3899396

广州市民政局精神病院
地址：广州市白云区石井街东秀路143号
电话：020-86441601

广州市白云区妇幼保健院
地址：广州市白云区机场路1128号；广州市广园西路344号、
　　　黄石路黄园一街4号、三元里大道1148号
电话：020-86329682

广州市白云区第二人民医院
地址：广州市白云区江高镇北胜街16号之一、白云区胜利路
　　　80号
电话：020-86601231

广东三九脑科医院
地址：广州市沙太路南路578号
电话：020-87736999

白云精神病康复医院

地址：广州市白云区同和街握山新村17号

电话：020-36314381

广州新市医院

地址：广州市白云区新市街新市新街79号之一、之二

电话：020-86307051

白云精康医院

地址：广州市白云区龙归街北村鹤龙五巷2号

电话：020-37379393、37386065

广州开发区医院

地址：广州经济技术开发区友谊路196号

电话：020-82215578

广州市番禺区中医院

地址：番禺区市桥街桥东路65号、93号

电话：020-84822332

第三章 生活百科

广州市番禺区中心医院
地址：广州市番禺区桥南街福愉东路8号
电话：020-84826647

广州市番禺区妇幼保健院（广州市番禺区何贤纪念医院、广州市番禺区何贤纪念医院互联网医院）
地址：广州市番禺区清河东路2号；广州市番禺区沙湾镇茂源大街12号；广州市番禺区市桥街环城东路99、101、103、105、107号；广州市番禺区市桥街石桥新村一座101、102
电话：020-84629993

广东祈福医院
地址：广州市番禺区鸿福路3号
电话：020-84518222

广州市花都区人民医院
地址：花都区新华街新华路48号、广州市花都区新华街公园前路60号、广州市花都区新华街曙光路10号
电话：020-86838973

广州市中西医结合医院、广州市中西医结合医院互联网医院
地址：花都区新华街迎宾大道87号，花都区新华街福宁路8号；花都区花城街玫瑰路7号都会雅苑5、6、7、8、10-1、17、18、19、26、34号商铺及首层自编1号中间商场
电话：020-86888997

广州市花都区妇幼保健院（胡忠医院）
地址：花都区新华街建设路51号、花都区新华街松园路7号、花都区新华街工业大道17号、花都区新华街公益路35号
电话：020-86825072

广州市增城区人民医院

地址：广州市增城区增江街光明东路1号、广州市增城区增江街纺织路26号、广州市增城区增江街增正路120号

电话：020-82735052

广州市增城区中医医院

地址：广州市增城区荔城街民生路50号、广州市增城区荔城街和平路31号、广州市增城区荔城街和平路22号北楼301室

电话：020-82758895

前海人寿广州总医院

地址：广州市增城区新城大道703号

电话：020-32632102

广州市增城区中心医院

地址：广州市增城区宁西街创新大道28号

电话：020-62707024

（二）传染病或重大疫情处理

1. 被动物（犬、猫、鼠等）咬伤、抓伤的，应立即到就近的医疗机构就医，对伤口进行清洗等处理后，再到广州市第八人民医院（东风院区和嘉禾院区，24小时提供服务）接种狂犬疫苗，或到就近的指定的狂犬病疫苗接种点（登录"广州游疾病预防控制中心网站"→"服务指南"→"免疫接种"→"广州市狂犬疫苗接种门诊分布"查询）接种狂犬疫苗。

2. 如果在医疗机构被诊断为法定传染病或疑似传染病的，应配合医疗卫生机构做好检查、隔离、流行病学调查等各项措施，并按有关规定转至指定的医疗机构进行治疗。

广州市疾病预防控制中心

地址：广州市白云区启德路1号

电话：(8620) 36052333, 83822400

网址：http://www.gzcdc.org.cn

广州市胸科医院

地址：广州市越秀区横枝岗路62号

电话：(8620) 83595977

广州市第八人民医院

地址：（东风院区）广州市越秀区东风东路627号

（嘉禾院区）广州市白云区嘉禾华英路8号

电话：(8620) 83838688, 83800419（东风院区）

(8620) 36549012（嘉禾院区）

3. 在穗外籍人士适龄人群新冠病毒疫苗接种指引

广州市已启动在穗外籍人士适龄人群接种国产新冠病毒疫苗工作。根据"知情、自愿、自费、风险自担"原则，广州市在11个区各指定了1家新冠疫苗接种单位为外籍人士接种疫苗。根据现阶段国家政策规定，在广东省内年龄18周岁至59周岁，以及部分60周岁以上因特殊原因需接种、且身体基础状况较好的自愿接种的外籍人士，可通过粤健通微信服务平台在线预约登记疫苗接种。广州市目前使用的是国产新冠病毒灭活疫苗，全程需接种两剂。已参加广东省社会保障医疗保险的外籍人士，现场出示有效医保参保凭证，享受与其他参保中国公民同等待遇。未参加广东省社会保障医疗保险的外籍人士，自费接种疫苗，费用为100元/剂次。

预约方式如下：扫描二维码（附后），进入粤健通微信服务平台的外籍人士新冠疫苗接种服务页面进行信息填报、预约。预约成功后在指定时间、地点，携带中华人民共和国外国人永久居留身份证或护照及有效停居留证件、医保参保凭证前往。在指定接种点接种前，按程序签署知情同意书、免责承诺书等，做好个人防护并主动告知健康状况，由专业人员判定是否符合接种条件。接种14天内请密切关注自身身体情况，如有不适，请及时就医。

预约app二维码

在穗外籍人士新冠病毒疫苗定点接种点名单

序号	接种点名称	接种点地址	咨询电话
1	越秀区中医医院	越秀区正南路6号	83330808-8124 83331597
2	广东省第二人民医院	海珠区新港中路466号	89168015
3	广州市荔湾中心医院	荔湾路35号	81349306
4	广州市第十二人民医院	天河区天强路1号	38981247
5	南方医科大学南方医院白云分院	白云区黄石街元下底路23号	4000201120
6	中山大学附属第三医院岭南医院	黄埔区开创大道2693号	82179413
7	花都区人民医院（花都体育馆接种点）	花都区秀全大道41号	020-62935411
8	广东祈福医院	番禺区钟村街鸿福路3号	020-84518222转70700
9	广州市第一人民医院南沙医院	南沙区丰泽东路105号	020-28698677
10	南方医科大学第五附属医院	从化区从城大道566号	020-61780566
11	省水电医院（凤凰院区）	增城区永宁街汽车城东路4—6号	66266953

在穗外籍人士新冠病毒疫苗接种工作流程

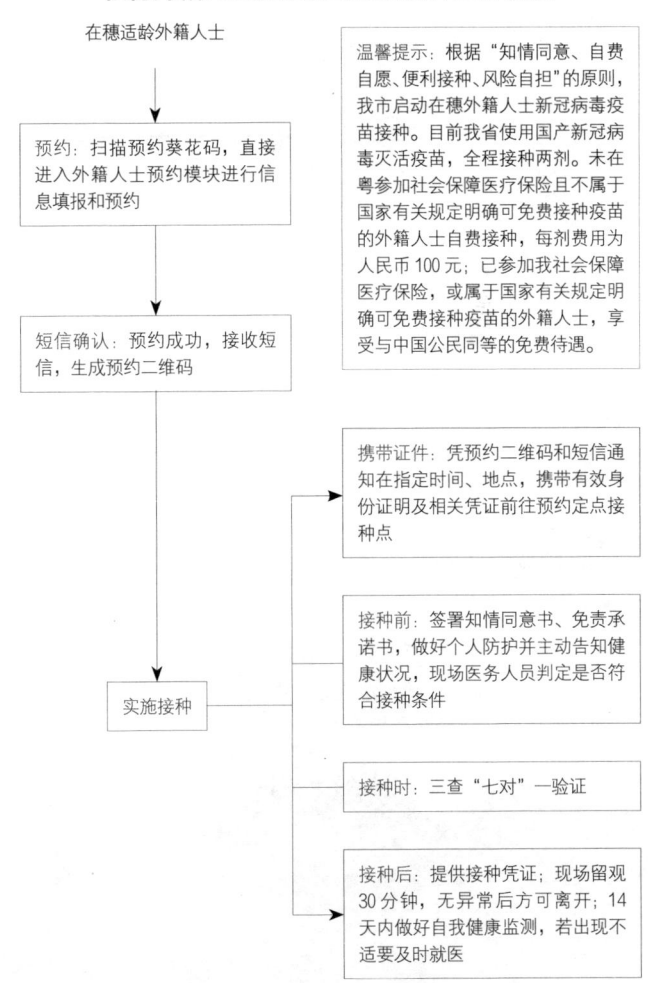

在穗适龄外籍人士
↓
预约：扫描预约葵花码，直接进入外籍人士预约模块进行信息填报和预约
↓
短信确认：预约成功，接收短信，生成预约二维码
↓
实施接种

温馨提示：根据"知情同意、自费自愿、便利接种、风险自担"的原则，我市启动在穗外籍人士新冠病毒疫苗接种。目前我省使用国产新冠病毒灭活疫苗，全程接种两剂。未在粤参加社会保障医疗保险且不属于国家有关规定明确可免费接种疫苗的外籍人士自费接种，每剂费用为人民币100元；已参加我社会保障医疗保险，或属于国家有关规定明确可免费接种疫苗的外籍人士，享受与中国公民同等的免费待遇。

携带证件：凭预约二维码和短信通知在指定时间、地点，携带有效身份证明及相关凭证前往预约定点接种点

接种前：签署知情同意书、免责承诺书，做好个人防护并主动告知健康状况，现场医务人员判定是否符合接种条件

接种时：三查"七对"一验证

接种后：提供接种凭证；现场留观30分钟，无异常后方可离开；14天内做好自我健康监测，若出现不适要及时就医

外国人在穗指南（2021）

4. 在穗外籍人士HIV自愿咨询检测预约指引

广州市为所有在穗外籍人士提供免费的HIV自愿咨询检测服务，预约方式如下：

微信扫二维码或搜索"查呗"，进入查呗小程序。

点击"预约HIV检测"按钮。

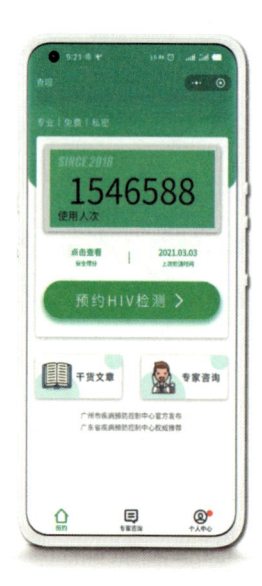

第三章　生活百科

在列表模式或地图模式中选择合适的咨询检测门诊。

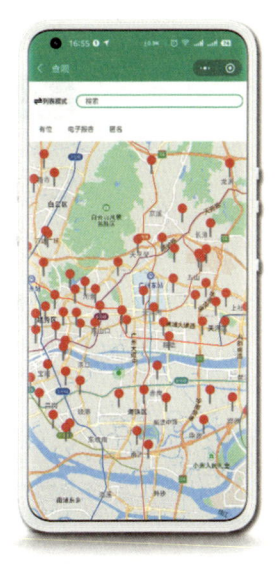

进入"查看可预约时间",选择合适的时间预约。

外国人在穗指南（2021）

　　填写称呼、手机号码，获取验证码，填写验证码，点击"确认预约"。

　　预约成功页面中可查看已预约时间，以及门诊的地址、地图和咨询电话。

如果有事无法赴约，请点击"取消预约"。

5. 在穗外国友人健康防护指引

为做好新型冠状病毒感染肺炎疫情常态化防控，在穗外国友人健康防护指引如下：

（1）关注权威信息。请关注广州市卫生健康委员会"广州卫健委"等官方媒体微信公众号，获取新型冠状病毒感染肺炎疫情官方通报及防治指引措施等信息，或致电广州市卫生热线12320咨询。如果您需要英语、日语或韩语服务，请您致电广州多语种公共服务平台960169。广州多语种公共服务平台译员会为您连接12320进行三方通话，解答您的问题。

（2）加强自我防护。保持良好的卫生习惯，勤洗手。咳嗽、打喷嚏时务必使用纸巾或肘部捂住口鼻，不随地吐痰，废弃口罩按规定规范投放。适当开窗通风，注意保持室内环境卫生。避免接触任何野生动物或禽类动物，肉类和蛋类请彻底煮熟后食用。

（3）尽量减少不必要的外出。不前往中、高风险地区和其他出现疫情的城市。尽量避免前往人员密集的场所，尽量减少聚会、聚餐等集体活动，保持社交距离。若必须前往，请正确佩戴口罩，首选医用外科口罩，在手机上及时刷新准备好健康码。

（4）配合卫生防疫医务人员工作。如果您14天内到访过中、高风险地区，应当及时向当地疾病预防控制机构或指定部门报告，并密切关注自身的身体状况，居家休息，减少外出。如果有政府、社区工作人员、医务人员询问您的情况，请您积极配合他们的工作。若出现发热、咳嗽、胸闷、乏力等症状，须佩戴口罩到就近医院的发热门诊就诊，如实告知医生自己14天内的出行史。遵守政府防疫规定，自觉接受当地核酸检测安排。

（5）接种疫苗。中国国产的多款新冠疫苗已有亿计的安全接种，在全球多个国家和地区接种证实是安全和有效的，并被世界卫生组织（WHO）认可推荐，接种疫苗对您大有裨益。广东省卫生当局在2021年4月已将在华外籍人士纳入疫苗接种人群范围，只要是适龄（目前是18岁以上）和适合接种的对象都可以付费接种。如果您加入省、市社会保障医疗保险计划，还可以享受与我市其他参保中国公民的同等待遇。如有接种意愿，请预约接种，广州各区都有指定外籍人士接种服务医疗机构。

目前广州市共有114家医疗机构设有发热门诊，遍及11个区，请扫下方葵花码了解详情。

（三）儿童预防接种

在广州出生或居住的儿童，其家长或监护人应当带儿童到居住地的预防接种单位［本街（镇）的卫生服务中心］接种疫苗并领取预防接种证，按规定的免疫程序和时间完成疫苗接种。

儿童因迁移、长期外出或居住外地等原因未完成规定的免疫接种的，可凭接种证在迁移后的新居住地预防接种单位继续完成规定的疫苗接种。儿童监护人应保管好接种证，以备孩子入托、入学查验。

九、殡葬

1. 殡葬惠民减免政策

2016年9月28日后在广州市辖区内死亡,并在辖区内殡葬服务单位实行遗体火化的非广州市户籍人员。其家属或委办人可申请减免以下6项基本服务费用,最高可申请减免1330元。

(1)遗体接运,每具费用不超过180元。

(2)遗体消毒,每具费用不超过100元。

(3)冷藏防腐(不超过3天),每具费用不超过300元。

(4)遗体告别厅租用费,每具费用不超过400元。

(5)遗体火化,每具费用不超过250元。

(6)普通骨灰盅,每个费用不超过100元。

2. 办理程序及所需材料:

丧事委办人可直接在经办殡葬服务单位办理减免手续,办理时需提供下列材料:

(1)殡葬基本服务费用减免申请表(经办殡仪馆提供);

(2)出示公安部门或医疗机构出具的"居民死亡医学证明(推断)书";

(3)出示丧事委办人居民身份证。

殡葬服务单位负责对丧事委办人提供的上述材料进行核实(除减免申请表外,其余复印留存),按规定的项目及标准直接减免。

3. 办事指引

广州市范围内5个殡仪馆均可办理外国人遗体接运、火化等业务,办理人可通过拨打"12349"或各殡仪馆报丧电话以及登陆穗好办APP等方式,上报遗体接运需求。遗体接运至殡仪馆之后,办理人到经办殡仪馆办理具体业务。外国人遗体、骨灰需要外运出境的，统一由中国殡葬协会国际运尸网络服务中心和其委托机构承办。广州市国际运尸承运单位服务站设在广州市殡仪馆，服务电话：87087506。

4. 广州市殡葬管理服务单位联系方式

（1）政策咨询

广州市殡葬管理处：天河区燕岭路394号，87053456

（2）业务服务（报丧电话）

广州市殡仪馆：天河区燕岭路418号，87744444

花都区殡仪馆：花都区新华街农新路164号，86863490

番禺区殡仪馆：番禺区石壁街屏山二村，84774444

从化区殡仪馆：从化区江埔街下罗村，87980145

增城区殡仪馆：增城区增江街工业路19号，82742322

十、汉语学习

五行教育自主研发《国际职场通用汉语》6+N系列教材涵盖国际职场中60+主题下100+工作场景1000+实用句子,听说为主兼顾读写快速提升汉语表达能力,助您职场沟通无障碍,搭配CHIease APP,随时随地想学就学。

线上自学+线下强化,即学即用、省时省钱。

每天10分钟,学有用的汉语!

Contact Us
Tel: (8620) 80502829
Wechat: 18144892155
E-mail: info@5dieachinese.com
Twitter: 5dieachinese
Facebook: 5ideaAPP
Add: 1F, Building 6, No. 48 Chenjiaci Road, Liwan District, Guangzhou

微信联系课程顾问，免费领体验券：

下载CHIease APP，随时随地轻松学：

第四章
安全与法规

一、安全

（一）治安管理

1. 在宾馆、酒店住宿的外国人，需向服务员提供身份证件原件并按规定办理临时住宿的登记手续。
2. 到宾馆、酒店探访的外国人，需按规定办理来访登记手续。
3. 吸食毒品、卖淫、嫖娼、打架、斗殴等行为均触犯中国法律。

（二）突发事件处理

外国人如遇到交通事故或突发事件，应立即拨打以下电话求助，警方和急救中心可处理英语来电。

匪警电话：110
火警电话：119
急救电话：120
交通事故：122

广州的各个街道及繁华路段均有派出所及其执勤点。派出所24小时值班并执行任务，同时有警车24小时巡逻当值，处理市民的求助以及执行110报警台的出警任务。

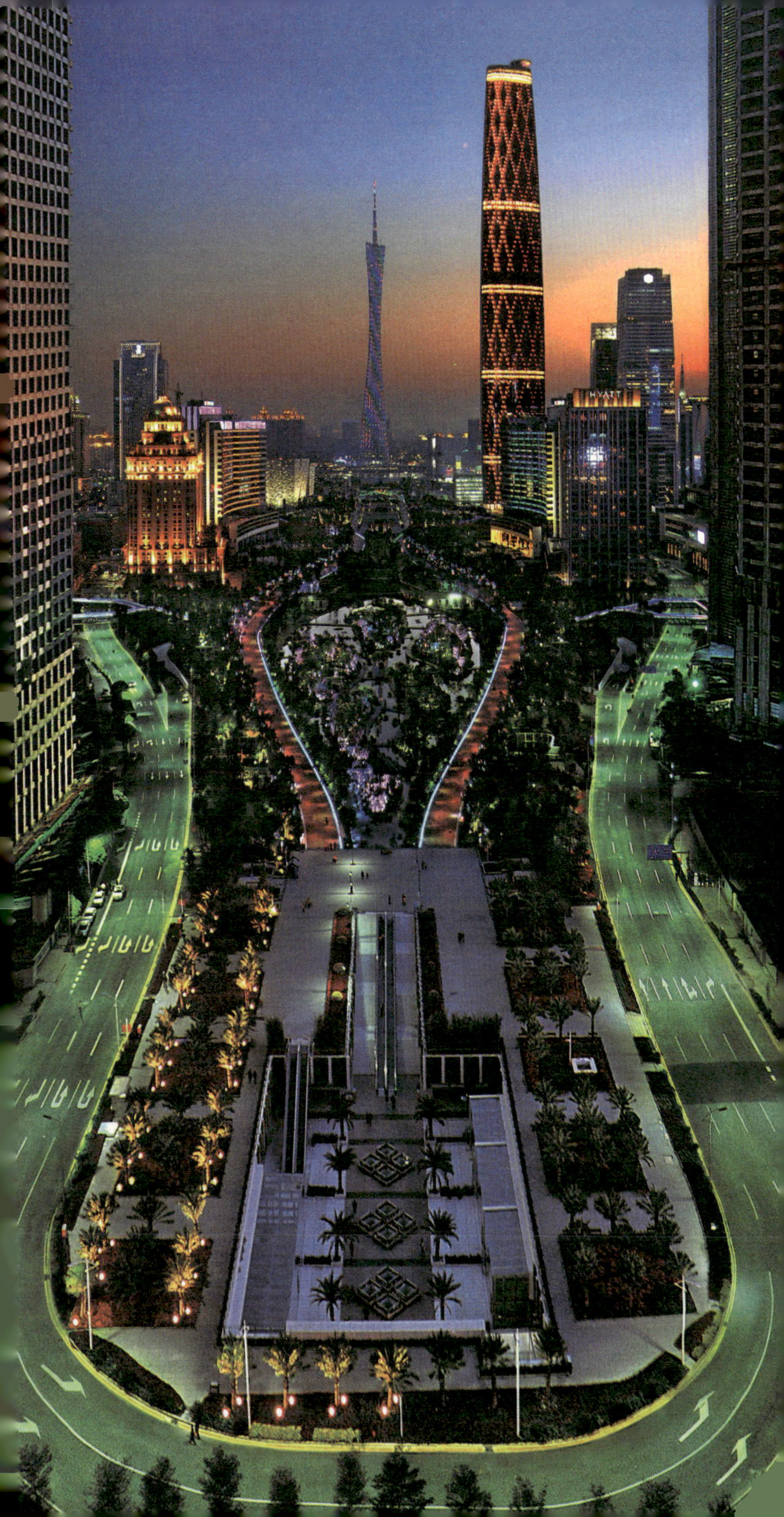
HYATT

二、纳税与免税

国家税务总局广州市税务局贯彻执行税收、社会保险费和有关非税收入法律、法规、规章和规范性文件，组织落实国家规定的税收优惠政策，负责所辖区域内各项税收、社会保险费和有关非税收入征收管理。

外国人在广州设立企业，应在开展生产经营或发生涉税事项时到税务机关办理纳税人身份信息确认或者纳税人（扣缴义务人）身份信息报告。已领取加载统一社会信用代码营业执照的企业，凭加载统一社会信用代码的营业执照可替代税务登记证使用，无需办理税务登记，不需领取税务登记证。

> **国家税务总局广州市税务局**
> 电话：020-12366
> 网址：http://guangdong.chinatax.gov.cn/gdsw/gzsw/gzsw_index.shtml

三、个人所得税

个人所得税以所得人为纳税人,是依照税法规定负有直接纳税义务的个人。

纳税人分为居民个人和非居民个人,承担不同的纳税义务。居民个人指在中国境内有住所,或者无住所而一个纳税年度内在中国境内居住累计满183天的个人。居民个人从中国境内和境外取得的所得,均应缴纳个人所得税。但是,在中国境内无住所的个人,在中国境内居住累计满183天的年度连续不满6年的,经向主管税务机关备案,其来源于中国境外且由境外单位或者个人支付的所得,免予缴纳个人所得税。

在中国境内无住所又不居住,或者无住所而一个纳税年度内在中国境内居住累计不满183天的个人,为非居民个人。非居民个人从中国境内取得的所得,缴纳个人所得税。但是,在中国境内无住所的个人,在一个纳税年度内在中国境内居住累计不超过90天的,其来源于中国境内的所得,由境外雇主支付并且不由该雇主在中国境内的机构、场所负担的部分,免予缴纳个人所得税。

(一)应缴纳个人所得税的所得

在《中华人民共和国个人所得税法》和《中华人民共和国个人所得税法实施条例》中列举了个人所得税的九项所得项目及相应的范围,个人取得这些收入时,都应该按相应的要求计算缴纳个人所得税。

表1 所得项目范围

所得项目	范围
1. 工资、薪金所得	个人因任职或者受雇取得的工资、薪金、奖金、年终加薪、劳动分红、津贴、补贴以及与任职或者受雇有关的其他所得

（续表）

所得项目	范围
2. 劳务报酬所得	个人从事劳务取得的所得，包括从事设计、装潢、安装、制图、化验、测试、医疗、法律、会计、咨询、讲学、翻译、审稿、书画、雕刻、影视、录音、录像、演出、表演、广告、展览、技术服务、介绍服务、经纪服务、代办服务以及其他劳务取得的所得
3. 稿酬所得	个人因其作品以图书、报刊等形式出版、发表而取得的所得
4. 特许权使用费所得	个人提供专利权、商标权、著作权、非专利技术以及其他特许权的使用权取得的所得；提供著作权的使用权取得的所得，不包括稿酬所得
5. 经营所得	①个体工商户从事生产、经营活动取得的所得，个人独资企业投资人、合伙企业的个人合伙人来源于境内注册的个人独资企业、合伙企业生产、经营的所得 ②个人依法从事办学、医疗、咨询以及其他有偿服务活动取得的所得 ③个人对企业、事业单位承包经营、承租经营以及转包、转租取得的所得 ④个人从事其他生产、经营活动取得的所得
6. 利息、股息、红利所得	个人拥有债权、股权等而取得的利息、股息、红利所得
7. 财产租赁所得	个人出租不动产、机器设备、车船以及其他财产取得的所得
8. 财产转让所得	个人转让有价证券、股权、合伙企业中的财产份额、不动产、机器设备、车船以及其他财产取得的所得
9. 偶然所得	个人得奖、中奖、中彩以及其他偶然性质的所得

居民个人取得上述第1项至第4项所得（以下称综合所得），按纳税年度合并计算个人所得税；非居民个人取得上述第1项至第4项所得，按月或者按次分项计算个人所得税。纳税人取得上述第5项至第9项所得，依照个人所得税法规定分别计算个人所得税。

（二）个人所得税的税率

在中国，不同的应税所得项目适用不同的个人所得税税率。

1. 综合所得适用3%至45%的七级超额累进税率。

表2 综合所得年度税率表（适用于居民个人）

级数	全年应纳税所得额	税率（%）	速算扣除数
1	不超过 36 000 元的部分	3	0
2	超过 36 000 元至 144 000 元的部分	10	2520
3	超过 144 000 元至 300 000 元的部分	20	16 920
4	超过 300 000 元至 420 000 元的部分	25	31 920
5	超过 420 000 元至 660 000 元的部分	30	52 920
6	超过 660 000 元至 960 000 元的部分	35	85 920
7	超过 960 000 元的部分	45	181 920

表3 按月换算后的综合所得税率表（适用于非居民个人）

级数	全月应纳税所得额	税率（%）	速算扣除数
1	不超过 3000 元的部分	3	0
2	超过 3000 元至 12 000 元的部分	10	210
3	超过 12 000 元至 25 000 元的部分	20	1410
4	超过 25 000 元至 35 000 元的部分	25	2660
5	超过 35 000 元至 55 000 元的部分	30	4410
6	超过 55 000 元至 80 000 元的部分	35	7160
7	超过 80 000 元的部分	45	15 160

2. 经营所得适用5%至35%的五级超额累进税率。

表4 经营所得税率表

级数	全年应纳税所得额	税率（%）	速算扣除数
1	不超过 30 000 元的部分	5	0
2	超过 30 000 元至 90 000 元的部分	10	1500
3	超过 90 000 元至 300 000 元的部分	20	10 500
4	超过 300 000 元至 500 000 元的部分	30	40 500
5	超过 500 000 元的部分	35	65 500

3. 利息、股息、红利所得，财产租赁所得，财产转让所得和偶然所得，适用20%的比例税率。

(三)外国人享有的税收优惠

1. 外籍个人补贴、津贴免税

外籍个人(包括港、澳、台同胞)取得的以下津补贴、暂免征收个人所得税:

(1)以非现金形式或实报实销形式取得的住房补贴、伙食补贴、搬迁费、洗衣费;

(2)因到中国任职或离职,以实报实销形式取得的搬迁费,不包括雇主以搬迁费名义每月或定期向外籍雇员支付的费用;

(3)按合理标准取得的境内、外出差补贴;

(4)取得的探亲费,且在合理数额内的部分,合理数额只指个人在我国的受雇地与其家庭所在地(包括配偶或父母居住地)之间搭乘交通工具且每年不超过两次的费用;

(5)在中国境内接受语言培训以及子女在中国境内接受教育取得的语言培训费和子女教育费补贴,且在合理数额内的部分;

(6)因家庭原因居住在香港、澳门的外籍人员享受六项补贴的特殊情形。

自2004年1月1日起,受雇于我国境内企业的外籍个人(不包括香港、澳门居民个人),因家庭等原因居住在香港、澳门,每个工作日往返于内地与香港、澳门等地区,由此境内企业(包括其关联企业)给予在香港或澳门住房、伙食、洗衣、搬迁等非现金形式或实报实销形式的补贴,凡能提供有效凭证的,经主管税务机关审核确认后,可以免予征收个人所得税。前述外籍个人就其在香港或澳门进行语言培训、子女教育而取得的费用补贴,凡能提供有效支出凭证等材料的,经主管税务机关审核确认为合理的部分,可以免予征收个人所得税。

2019年1月1日至2021年12月31日期间,外籍个人符合居民个人条件的,可以选择享受个人所得税专项附加扣除,也可以选择享受住房补贴、语言培训费、子女教育费等津补贴免税优惠政策,但不得同时享受。外籍个人一经选择,在一个纳税年度内不得变更。自2022年1月1日起,外籍个人不再享受住房补贴、语言培训费、子女教育费津补贴免税优惠政策,应按规定享受专项附加扣除。

2. 外国派出单位发给包干款项

外国来华工作人员,由外国派出单位发给包干款项,其中包括个人工资、公用经费(邮电费、办公费、广告费、业务上往来必要的交际费)、生活津贴费(住房费、差旅费),凡对上述所得能够划分清楚的,可只就工资薪金所得部分按照规定征收个人所得税。

3. 股息税收优惠

外籍个人(包括港、澳、台同胞)从外商投资企业取得的股息、红利所得暂免征收个人所得税。

4. 外籍专家工资薪金所得免税

凡符合下列条件之一的,外籍专家(包括港、澳、台同胞)取得的工资薪金所得可免征个人所得税:

(1)根据世界银行专项贷款协议由世界银行直接派往我国工作的外国专家;

(2)联合国组织直接派往我国工作的专家;

(3)为联合国援助项目来华工作的专家;

(4)援助国派往我国专为该国无偿援助项目工作的专家;

(5)根据两国政府签订文化交流项目来华工作两年以内的文教专家,其工资薪金所得由该国负担的;

(6)根据我国大专院校国际交流项目来华工作两年以内的文教专家,其工资薪金所得由该国负担的;

(7)通过民间科研协定来华工作的专家,其工资薪金所得由该国政府机构负担的。

5. 股票转让所得免税

自2014年11月17日，对香港市场个人投资者投资上海证券交易所上市A股取得的转让差价所得，暂免征收个人所得税；自2016年12月5日起，对香港市场个人投资者投资深交所上市A股取得的转让差价所得，暂免征收个人所得税。

自2015年12月18日起，对香港市场个人投资者通过基金互认买卖内地基金份额取得的转让差价所得，暂免征收个人所得税。

（四）个人所得税申报方式

表5　申报方式

所得项目	居民个人		非居民个人
工资、薪金所得、劳务报酬所得、特许权使用费所得和稿酬所得	综合所得	按年计算个人所得税，有扣缴义务人的，先由扣缴义务人按月或按次预扣预缴税款，符合汇算清缴情形的，纳税人需要在年度终了后办理汇算清缴	按月或按次分项计算个人所得税，由扣缴义务人代扣代缴，无需办理汇算清缴；在中国境内从两处以上取得工资、薪金所得的，需办理自行申报
利息、股息、红利所得，财产租赁所得，财产转让所得或者偶然所得		按月或者按次，由扣缴义务人依法办理全员全额扣缴申报；扣缴义务人未扣缴税款的，次年6月30日前办理纳税申报，税务机关通知限期缴纳的，应当按照期限缴纳税款	
经营所得		按年计算个人所得税，按月（季）度预缴申报，年度终了后办理汇算清缴	

有下列情形之一的，纳税人应当依法办理纳税申报：

1. 取得综合所得需要办理汇算清缴；

2. 取得应税所得没有扣缴义务人；

3. 取得应税所得，扣缴义务人未扣缴税款；

4. 取得境外所得；

5. 因移居境外注销中国户籍；

6. 非居民个人在中国境内从两处以上取得工资、薪金所得。

纳税人可以使用手机个人所得税APP或自然人电子税务局web端实现网络申报，或者采用邮寄方式申报，也可以直接到办税服务厅申报。

四、车船税

1. 在中华人民共和国境内属于"车船税税目税额表"规定的车辆、船舶(以下简称"车船")的所有人或者管理人,为车船税的纳税人,应当依法缴纳车船税。

广东省车船税税目税额表(从2018年度开始执行)

税 目		计税单位	适用税额(元/年)	备 注
乘用车[按发动机汽缸容量(排气量)分档]	10升(含)以下的	每辆	60	核定载客人数9人(含)以下
	10升以上至16升(含)的		300	
	16升以上至20升(含)的		360	
	20升以上至25升(含)的		660	
	25升以上至30升(含)的		1200	
	30升以上至40升(含)的		2400	
	40升以上的		3600	
商用车	中型客车(核定载客10—19人)	每辆	480	核定载客人数9人以上,包括电车
	大型客车(核定载客≥20人)		510	
	货车	整备质量每吨	16	包括半挂牵引车、三轮汽车和低速载货汽车等
挂车		整备质量每吨	8	
其他车辆	专用作业车	整备质量每吨	16	不包括拖拉机
	轮式专用机械车	每吨	16	

(续表)

税 目		计税单位	适用税额（元/年）	备 注
摩托车		每辆	36	
船舶	机动船舶	净吨位≤200吨 每吨	3	
		净吨位201—2000吨 每吨	4	
		净吨位2001—10 000吨 每吨	5	
		净吨位≥10 001吨 每吨	6	拖船、非机动驳船分别按照机动船舶税额的50%计算
	游艇	长度≤10米 每米	600	长度指游艇总长度
		长度11—18米 每米	900	
		长度19—30米 每米	1300	
		长度≥31米 每米	2000	
	辅助动力帆船	每米	600	

2. 依照法律规定应当予以免税的外国驻华使领馆、国际组织驻华代表机构及其有关人员的车船免征车船税。

3. 车船税的纳税地点为车船的登记地或者车船税扣缴义务人所在地。依法不需要办理登记的车船，车船税的纳税地点为车船所有人或者管理人所在地。

4. 车船税纳税义务发生时间为取得车船所有权或者管理权的当月。

5. 车船税按年申报，分月计算，一次性缴纳。纳税年度为公历1月1日至12月31日。

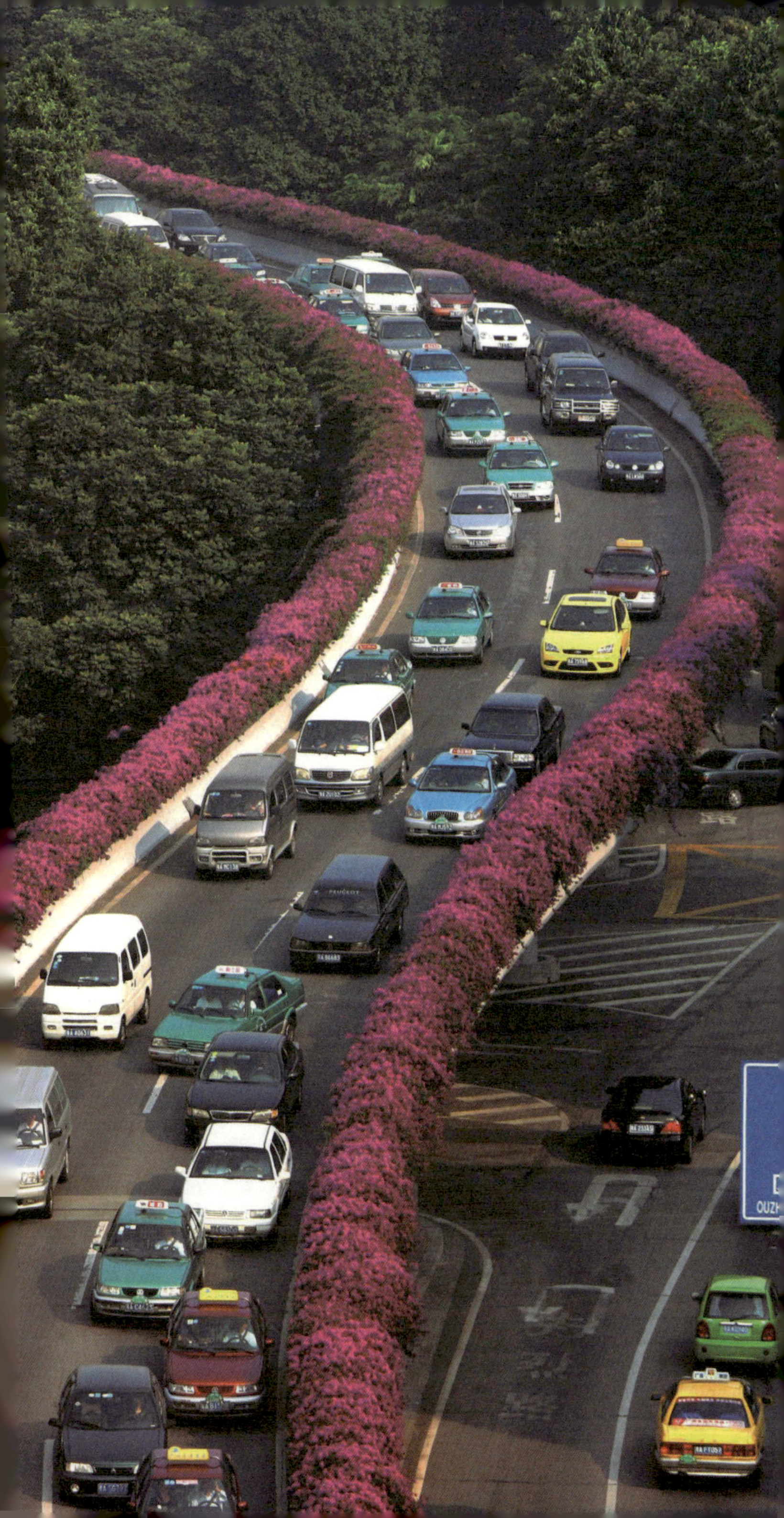

五、交通法规

（一）驾驶机动车须遵守的交通安全法规

1. 驾驶机动车须持有公安机关交通管理部门核发有效机动车驾驶证。
2. 不准使用涂改、伪造、挪用或骗取的机动车牌证、驾驶证、通行证或其他交通管理证。
3. 不准驾驶号牌不齐全或因遮挡、污损等造成号牌字迹辨认不清的机动车。
4. 驾驶机动车时不准接打移动电话或查询移动电话信息，不准向车外抛掷物品影响交通安全。
5. 不准使用与交通管理有关的各种失效证件。
6. 不得在设有禁停标志的路段临时停车；在非禁停路段临时停车的，驾驶人不得离开驾驶室，不准影响道路畅通，妨碍交通安全。有民警在场的，听从现场民警指挥。
7. 不得在道路上进行机动车驾驶训练。
8. 避让出入站台的公共电/汽车。
9. 驾驶汽车时配有效的灭火器具。
10. 遵守中华人民共和国各级政府的其他交通安全法规。

广州已经在市区范围内禁止摩托车在道路上行驶，但其他机动车辆仍日益增多，在早上7:00—9:00、下午5:00—8:00出现交通拥挤的情况难以避免。因此，外国朋友最好在熟悉路况之后再自行驾驶，并尽量在交通高峰时段使用出租车或者地铁等公共交通工具。

（二）非机动车安全出行常识

1. 非机动车应走非机动车道，停车时不要超越停车线；在未设有非机动车的道路上，应尽量靠路的右侧通行，不得进入机动车道。

2. 在设有禁止非机动车通行标志的道路上，应在人行道上下车推行。

3. 在横过路口时，应严格遵循"红灯停、绿灯行"原则，按人行道交通信号灯指示通行，在人行横道上要下车推行过路口。

4. 在设有人行横道的路口，应根据机动车车道信号指示通行，尽量靠近机动车道右侧通过。

5. 在路口转弯前减速慢行、向后瞭望、伸手示意，不要争道抢行、急转猛拐。

6. 道路设有中心护栏实施封闭的，骑车人应按照交通标志指示，由行人隧道或过街天桥推行。

7. 骑非机动车时，不得超过规定的尺寸、重量搭载货物，在城市市区道路上不得搭载乘客。须知：行人、非机动车驾驶人违反道路交通安全法规的，最高可罚款50元；拒绝接受罚款处罚的，可被扣留其非机动车；妨碍民警执行公务的，可依法处以15日以下的行政拘留。情节严重的，追究其刑事责任。

（三）步行、乘车安全出行常识

1. 遇有人行横道和红绿灯的路口，行人应严格遵循"红灯停、绿灯行"原则，按交通信号灯指示通行，横过马路应走人行横道线，不翻越隔离护栏，严禁闯红灯、乱过马路。

2. 在绿灯信号指示下，行人应快速通过人行横道线，遇到绿灯闪烁还没有进入人行横道线的，应在人行横道或安全岛上停留等待。

3. 在没有人行横道线的路口横过马路时，应注意观察双向来往的车辆，在确保安全的情况下迅速通过。

4. 道路设有中心护栏实施封闭时，行人应按照交通标志指示，由行人隧道或过街天桥通过。

5. 搭乘公共汽车时，乘客应在公交车站内等候，不能站在车道上；待车停稳后，依次上车。搭乘出租车时，不可在禁止出租车停车的地方或车道上招呼出租车，待出租车停稳后，从右边上车。

6. 下车时要往车后瞭望，确认没有车辆驶近再下车。下车后不要在机动车道上逗留，要立即走上人行道。

7. 搭乘汽车时，在设有安全带的座位上要系好安全带，不可将头、手伸出车外，不可向窗外丢杂物。下车开门时要留意其他车辆，不可在路口50米范围内或者禁停路段停车、下车。

（四）机动车注册登记

1. 有关规定。

（1）国家对机动车实行登记制度。机动车经公安机关交通管理部门登记后，方可上路行驶。

（2）初次申领机动车号牌、行驶证的，机动车所有人应当向住所地的车辆管理所申请注册登记。

（3）申请注册登记的机动车必须符合国家、广州市关于机动车辆污染物排放标准的规定。

（4）确定机动车号牌号码有五种形式：一是继续使用原机动车号牌号码；二是计算机自动选取号码；三是按照机动车号牌标准规定自编自选号码（仅限小型汽车号牌）；四是小型汽车号竞价发放；五是互联网预选号牌号码。

（5）进口机动车、危险化学品运输车、校车及中型（含中型）以上客载汽车只能在广州市区的车管分所申请注册登记业务；小型、微型载客汽车只能在广州市区的车管分所或增城、花都番禺车管所申请注册登记业务。

（6）代理人申请机动车登记业务时，应当提交代理人的身份证和机动车所有人的书面委托。

（7）申请中小客车注册登记的还需符合《广州中小客车总量调控管理办法》的有关规定。

（8）属于中小客车申请注册登记的，应先通过网上车管所（www.gzjd.gov.cn/cgs）、手机APP（*移动用户——广州警民通、联*

通用户——沃警民通、电信用户——天翼警民通)和客服电话(联通客服电话116114、移动客服电话12580、电信客服电话114)预约。

2. 办理业务所需资料。

(1)"机动车注册、转移、注销登记/转入申请表"。

(2)机动车所有人的身份证明原件及复印件。

(3)机动车来历证明原件。

(4)机动车交通事故责任强制保险凭证的第三联原件。

原件丢失的。提交其他任一联的复印件并加盖保险公司印章或保险公司提供的补办证。

(5)国产机动车整车出口合格证明原件或进口机动车进口凭证原件,有底盘合格证的须提供原件。

(6)车辆的置税完整证明或者免税凭证。

(7)查验民警确认机动车后出具的"机动车查验记录表"原件。

(8)机关、企业、事业单位购买19座(含19座)以下载客汽车的,须提供"定编小汽车指标使用许可证";外商独资企业、中外合资(合作)企业、集体企业、私营企业购买19座(含19座)以下载客汽车的,须提供验资报告的原件及复印件。

(9)车船税纳税或免税证明。

(10)属于中小客车的,还应当提交广州市中小客车指标证明文件。

(11)救护车、消防车、工程救险车须提交相关主管部门出具的车辆使用性质证明。其他机动车使用性质由机动车所有人按规定自主申报。

(12)法律、行政法规规定应当在机动车登记时提交的其他证明、凭证的原件及复印件。

3. 身份证明是指:

(1)外国驻华使馆、领馆和外国驻华办事机构、国际组织驻华代表机构的身份证明,是该使馆、领馆或者该办事机构、代表机构出具的证明及相关人员身份证件。

(2)外国人的身份证明,是其入境时所持有的护照或者其他旅行证件（属外文登记的需提供中文公证翻译件）、居（停）留期为六个月以上的有效签证或者居留许可，以及公安机关出具的住宿登记证明。

（3）外国驻华使馆、领馆人员和国际组织驻华代表机构人员的身份证明，是外交部核发的有效身份证件。

机动车来历凭证是指在国内购买的机动车，其来历证明是全国统一的机动车销售发票或者二手车交易发票。在国外购买的机动车，其来历证明是该车销售单位开具的销售发票及其翻译文本，但海关监管的机动车不需提供来历证明。

广州市车辆管理所名单

岑村总所
地址：广州市天河区岑村华观路1732号

天河分所
地址：广州市天河区岑村华观路1732号

越秀分所
地址：广州市荔湾区陈岗路34号

荔湾分所
地址：广州市荔湾区芳村大道西563号

化龙分所
地址：广州市番禺区化龙镇创展大道18号

白云分所
地址：广州市白云区太和镇鹤龙四路97号

东漖机动车登记服务点
地址：广州市荔湾区龙溪大道414号

番禺分所
地址1：广州市番禺区亚运大道550号（车管综合业务）
地址2：广州市番禺区沙湾镇福涌村福北路359号（机动车业务和教考场）

花都分所
地址1：广州市花都区天贵路101号
地址2：广州市花都区炭步镇四角围民主村（教考场）
地址3：广州市花都区芙蓉大道东边村（机动车业务）

南沙分所
地址：广州市南沙区横沥镇广珠路513号

增城分所
地址：广州市增城区朱村街朱村大道东1号（车管综合业务、机动车业务、科目一考场）

从化分所
地址1：广州市从化区环市东路106号
地址2：广州市从化区青云路353号（车管综合业务）
地址3：广州市从化区鳌头镇横坑村（教考场）

咨询投诉电话
广州市公安局：110
广州市公安局交警支队：020-83118400
广州市公安局交警支队车辆管理所：020-12345

（五）办理机动车驾驶证

申请中华人民共和国机动车驾驶证的外国人，应当符合国务院公安部门规定的驾驶许可条件；经考试合格后，由公安机关交通管理部门发给相应类别的机动车驾驶证。持有境外机动车驾驶证的外国人，符合国务院公安部门规定的驾驶许可条件，经公安机关交通管理部门考核合格的，可以发给中国的机动车驾驶证。

1. 未持有境外驾驶证的外国人初次申请中国驾驶证所需资料：

（1）填写"机动车驾驶证申请表"（由报考的驾驶人培训班提供）。

（2）申请人身份证明的原件及复印件。外国人的身份证明，是其入境时所持有的护照或者其他旅行证件、居（停）留期为三个月以上的有效签证或者居留许可或者"中华人民共和国外国人永久居留证"，以及公安机关出具的住宿登记证明。或外国驻华使馆、领馆人员及国际组织驻华代表机构人员的身份证明是外交部核发的有效身份证件。

（3）需提供有资质的县级或者部队团级以上医疗机构的"机动车驾驶人身体条件证明"。

（4）申请人近期免冠、白底背景、人头像约占相片长度三分之二的彩色正面光学小一寸相片四张。

【备注】申请人需到驾驶人培训班报考，由各驾驶人培训班到广州市公安局交通警察支队车辆管理所（广州市天河区华观路1732号）办理。

2. 已持有境外驾驶证的外国人申请换领中国驾驶证所需资料：

（1）"机动车驾驶证申请表"（车管所提供，免填写）。

（2）申请人身份证明的原件及复印件。外国人的身份证明，是其入境时所持有的护照或者其他旅行证件、居（停）留期为三个月以上的有效签证或者居留许可或者"中华人民共和国外国人永久居留证"，以及公安机关出具的住宿登记证明。或外国驻华使馆、领馆人员及国际组织驻华代表机构人员的身份证明是外交部核发的有效身份证件。

（3）需提供有资质的县级或者部队团级以上医疗机构的"机

动车驾驶人身体条件证明"（申请人为外国驻华使馆、领馆人员及国际组织驻华代表机构人员的，不审核"机动车驾驶人身体条件证明"）。

（4）有效期内的境外机动车驾驶证原件及复印件（属外文记载的需提供中文翻译文本）。

（5）申请人近期免冠、白底背景、人头像约占相片长度三分之二的彩色正面光学小一寸相片四张。

（6）属外国驻穗领事、领馆人员、行政人员的除按上述要求外，还需要领事官证或公务人员证的原件及复印件，并且护照的复印件或中文翻译文本上需要具备领事官负责人的签字和领事馆公章，同时提供广东省人民政府外事办出具的"办理领事车辆各相关证件业务通知单"。办理地址：广州市公安局交通警察支队车辆管理所综合业务B厅（广州市天河区华观路1732号）。

3. 临时驾驶许可：

适用于临时进入中华人民共和国境的机动车驾驶人。

（1）申请临时驾驶许可所需资料：

①入出境身份证件。

②境外机动车驾驶证，属于非中文表述的，还应当出具中文翻译文本。

③申请人近期免冠、白底背景、人头像约占相片长度三分之二的彩色正面光学小一寸相片两张。

（2）临时驾驶许可有效期。临时入境人员在中国境内短期停留的，临时驾驶许可有效期为三个月；停居留时间超过三个月的，临时驾驶许可有效期与准许入境期限一致，但有效期最长不超过一年；临时驾驶许可有效期内可多次入境使用，无需重新申请。

（3）时限要求。收到申请材料之日起，当日进行审查，符合规定的，在组织学习三小时的道路交通安全法律、法规后，当日核发临时机动车驾驶许可。

（4）其他说明：

①港澳台居民的入出境身份证件，是"港澳居民来往内地通行证""台湾居民来往大陆通行证"或者外交部核发的"中华人民

共和国旅行证"。

②华侨的入出境身份证件,是"中华人民共和国护照"。

③外国人的入出境身份证件,是其入境时所持有的护照或者其他有效入出境证件、有效签证或者停留、居留证件;属于免签的,入出境身份证件是其入境时所持有的护照或者其他有效入出境证件。

④"境外机动车驾驶证"是指外国,香港、澳门特别行政区,台湾地区核发的具有单独驾驶资格的机动车驾驶证。

⑤"准许入境期限"是指临时入境人员入出境身份证件上签注的准许入境期限。

⑥港澳台居民持"港澳台居民居住证"申请临时驾驶许可的,不需要再提交入出境身份证件。

⑦临时入境人员申请临时驾驶许可、临时入境机动车牌证时,所持境外机动车驾驶证、境外主管部门核发的机动车登记证明属于非中文表述的,还应当出具中文翻译文本。

⑧临时机动驾驶许可应当与所持境外机动车驾驶证及其中文翻译本同时使用。

4. 有关规定:

(1)持境外机动车驾驶证申请机动车驾驶证的,应当考试科目一。申请准驾车型为大型客车、牵引车、城市公交车、中型客车、大型货车机动车驾驶证的,还应当考试科目三。

属于外国驻华使馆、领馆人员及国际组织驻华代表机构人员申请的,应当按照外交对等原则执行。

(2)有下列情形之一的,不得申请机动车驾驶证:

①有器质性心脏病、癫痫病、美尼尔氏症、眩晕症、癔病、震颤麻痹、精神病、痴呆以及影响肢体活动的神经系统疾病等妨碍安全驾驶疾病的;

②三年内有吸食、注射毒品行为或者解除强制隔离戒毒措施未满三年,或者长期服用依赖性精神药品成瘾尚未戒除的;

③造成交通事故后逃逸构成犯罪的;

④饮酒后或者醉酒驾驶机动车发生重大交通事故构成犯罪的;

⑤醉酒驾驶机动车或者饮酒后驾驶营运机动车依法被吊销机动车驾驶证未满五年的;

⑥醉酒驾驶营运机动车依法被吊销机动车驾驶证未满十年的;

⑦因其他情形依法被吊销机动车驾驶证未满二年的;

⑧驾驶许可依法被撤销未满三年的;

⑨法律、行政法规规定的其他情形。

未取得机动车驾驶证驾驶机动车,有上述第5项至第7项行为之一的,在规定期限内不得申请机动车驾驶证。

(3)年龄条件:

①申请小型汽车、小型自动挡汽车、残疾人专用小型自动挡载客汽车、轻便摩托车准驾车型的,在18周岁以上,70周岁以下;2020年11月20日起如果是申请小型汽车、小型自动挡汽车、轻便摩托车驾驶证的年龄上限由70周岁调整为不作限制,但需对70周岁以上人员考领驾驶证的,增加记忆力、判断力、反应力等能力测试;

②申请低速载货汽车、三轮汽车、普通三轮摩托车、普通二轮摩托车或者轮式自行机械车准驾车型的,在18周岁以上,60周岁以下;

③申请城市公交车、大型货车、无轨电车或者有轨电车准驾车型的,在20周岁以上,50周岁以下;

④申请中型客车准驾车型的,在21周岁以上,50周岁以下;

⑤申请牵引车准驾车型的,在24周岁以上,50周岁以下;

⑥申请大型客车准驾车型的,在26周岁以上,50周岁以下。

2020年11月20日起申请大型客车、牵引车驾驶证的年龄下限由26周岁、24周岁降低至22周岁;申请大中型客货车驾驶证年龄上限由50周岁调整至60周岁。同时,缩短增驾时间间隔,对无相应记分周期满分记录,申请大型客车驾驶证的,由取得大型货车驾驶证至少5年缩短至3年;申请牵引车和中型客车驾驶证的,由取得大型货车驾驶证至少3年缩短至2年。

(4)身体条件:

①身高:申请大型客车、牵引车、城市公交车、大型货车、无轨电车准驾车型的,身高为155厘米以上。申请中型客车准驾车

型的,身高为150厘米以上。

②视力:申请大型客车、牵引车、城市公交车、中型客车、大型货车、无轨电车或者有轨电车准驾车型的,两眼裸视力或者矫正视力达到对数视力表5.0以上。申请其他准驾车型的,两眼裸视力或者矫正视力达到对数视力表4.9以上。单眼视力障碍,优眼裸视力或者矫正视力达到对数视力表5.0以上,且水平视野达到150度的,可以申请小型汽车、小型自动挡汽车、低速载货汽车、三轮汽车、残疾人专用小型自动挡载客汽车准驾车型的机动车驾驶证。

③辨色力:无红绿色盲。

④听力:两耳分别距音叉50厘米能辨别声源方向。有听力障碍但佩戴助听设备能够达到以上条件的,可以申请小型汽车、小型自动挡汽车准驾车型的机动车驾驶证。

⑤上肢:双手拇指健全,每只手其他手指必须有三指健全,肢体和手指运动功能正常。但手指末节残缺或者左手有三指健全,且双手手掌完整的,可以申请小型汽车、小型自动挡汽车、低速载货汽车、三轮汽车准驾车型的机动车驾驶证。

⑥下肢:双下肢健全且运动功能正常,不等长度不得大于5厘米。但左下肢缺失或者丧失运动功能的,可以申请小型自动挡汽车准驾车型的机动车驾驶证。

⑦躯干、颈部:无运动功能障碍。

(六)办理机动车保险

在中国境内道路上行驶的机动车的所有人或管理人,应当依法参加机动车交通事故责任强制保险。对未参加强制保险的机动车,车管部门不得予以登记,且不予核发机动车检验合格标志。

(七)交通事故处理

1. 在道路上发生造成人身伤亡或造成道路、供电、通信等设施损毁的交通事故,车辆驾驶人应当立即停车,保护现场。

2. 造成人身伤亡的,车辆驾驶人应当立即抢救受伤人员,因抢救受伤人员变动现场的,应当标明位置。

3. 发生交通事故未造成人身伤亡且当事人对事实及成因无争议的，在记录交通事故的时间和地点、对方当事人的姓名和联系方式、机动车牌号、驾驶证号、保险凭证号、碰撞部位，并共同签名后撤离现场，自行协商损害赔偿事宜。当事人对交通事故事实及成因有争议的，应当迅速报告执勤的交通警察或者公安交通管理部门。

（八）交通违法处理

临时入境的外籍人士驾驶机动车，须向入境地或始发地公安车管部门申领中国临时驾驶证并随身携带，依法驾驶。外籍人士在穗驾驶机动车违章被交通民警现场纠正或执罚的，听取交通民警的告知事项后，有权进行申辩，外籍人士的翻译应当场将交通民警的告知事项向外籍人士陈述，对行政处罚不服的可依法提起行政复议或行政诉讼。临时入境的外国车辆，必须按规定向入境地区或始发地的公安机关申领中国临时专用号牌和临时驾驶证，准确登记在穗的通信地址及电话。外籍人士在穗驾驶机动车违章被电子监控摄录的，在现场或通过邮政收到违章处理通知书后，应按通知书上的告知事项进行办理。

1. 广州市交警大队交通违法处理窗口联系方式

（1）地址：

①越秀大队（兼办理原流花大队、东山大队查处的道路交通违法行为业务）：广州市越秀区豪贤路127号

②荔湾大队（兼办理原芳村大队查处的道路交通违法行为业务）：广州市荔湾区芳村大道西塞坝路1号

③海珠大队：广州市海珠区墩和路195号

④天河大队：广州市天河区棠石路6号之一

⑤白云一大队：广州市白云区广园中路景泰直街西三巷一号二楼

⑥白云二大队：广州市白云区夏花三路400号

⑦巡逻大队：广州市天河区华观路1725号

⑧高速一大队：广州市白云区增槎路461号

⑨高速二大队：广州市白云区广龙路91号

⑩高速三大队：广州市天河区华观路1725号

⑪环城大队：广州市越秀区广园西路340号之一

⑫高速五大队：广州市黄埔区广新路469号

⑬违法处理中心（承办原机动大队查处的道路交通违法行为业务）：广州市越秀区广园西路340号之一

⑭黄埔大队：广州市黄埔区广汕四路3号

⑮南沙大队：广州市南沙区东涌镇市南路107号

⑯增城大队违法处理室：广州市增城区荔城街挂绿路18号

⑰从化大队违法处理室：广州市从化区青云路353号

⑱花都大队违法处理室：广州市花都区狮岭镇新花路10号

⑲番禺大队一中队：广州市番禺区市桥街东环路315号

⑳港航大队：东莞市麻涌镇广麻大道146号

（2）办公电话：020-12345。

（3）办公时间：

①—⑲编号单位周一至周五：9:00—12:00，13:00—17:00，周六日不对外办公，法定节假日按照国务院通知统一排休。

⑳编号单位周一至周五：9:00—12:00，13:30—17:30，周六日不对外办公，法定节假日按照国务院通知统一排休。

2. 外籍人士对交通技术监控记录的违法行为接受处理所需材料

（1）身份证明原件

外国人的身份证明，是其入境时所持有的护照或者其他旅行证件、居（停）留期为三个月以上的有效签证或者停留、居留证件，以及公安机关核发的住宿登记证明。

外国驻华使馆、领馆人员、国际组织驻华代表机构人员的身份证明，是外交部核发的有效身份证件。

（2）驾驶证原件

驾驶证是指"中华人民共和国机动车驾驶证"。

"临时机动车驾驶许可证"应当与所持有境外机动车驾驶证及

其中文翻译文本同时使用。

（3）行驶证原件

行驶证是指"中华人民共和国机动车行驶证"。当事人因违反《广东省交通安全条例》第六十七条规定被扣留行驶证、司法判决等特殊原因无法出示行驶证的，应当出示有关证明材料，民警核实后应予受理。

（4）其他材料

大队根据调查取证工作实际情况需驾驶人或车辆所有人、管理人配合提供的有关材料。违法行为适用一般程序办理的，当事人还需提供违法行为发生时车辆有效的交通事故强制责任保险证明。

六、法律纠纷

（一）法律服务

外国人、外国企业和组织在广州市需要律师提供非诉讼法律服务的，应委托持中华人民共和国律师执业证的律师代理。外国律师事务所驻穗代表机构及其代表只能从事不包括中国法律事务的活动。外国人、外国企业和组织到人民法院起诉、应诉的，可以委托本国人为诉讼代理人，也可以委托本国律师以非律师身份担任诉讼代理人；需要委托律师代理诉讼的，必须委托中华人民共和国律师。

广州市律师协会
地址：广州市越秀区东风中路437号越秀城市广场南塔9楼
电话：020-83550600
网址：http://www.gzlawyer.org
越秀区登峰街外国人法律服务工作室
地址：广州市童心路7—9号
电话：020-83508274

（二）法律援助

根据《中华人民共和国刑事诉讼法》的有关规定，外国籍、无国籍的犯罪嫌疑人、被告人是盲、聋、哑人，或者是尚未完全丧失辨认或者控制自己行为能力的精神病人，没有委托辩护人的；外国籍、无国籍的犯罪嫌疑人、被告人可能被判处无期徒刑、死刑，没有委托辩护人的，人民法院、人民检察院和公安机关应当通知法律援助机构指派律师为其提供刑事辩护。法律援助机构在接到通知后，将派出律师为外国籍、无国籍的犯罪嫌疑人、被告人提供免费的刑事辩护的法律援助服务。申请人需提交的证件和证明材料如下：

1. 护照或其他有效的身份证明，代理申请人还应当提交其有代理权的证明；

2. 家庭经济困难的证明；

3. 与所申请的法律援助事项有关的案件材料。

广州市法律援助处
地址：广州市越秀区仓边路 42 号
电话：020-83562631

（三）通过调解方式解决商事、海事纠纷

若有贸易、投资、金融、证券、知识产权、技术转让、房地产、工程承包、运输、保险以及其他商事、海事等领域的争议，在纠纷双方自愿的基础上，可以采用调解的方式解决。调解应根据合同的规定，依照法律，参照国际惯例，按照客观、公正和公平合理的原则进行，以促进当事人互谅互让，达成和解。中国国际贸易促进委员会/中国国际商会调解中心及其各分会的调解中心，均备有各自的调解员名单，供当事人在个案中指定。

> 中国国际贸易促进委员会、中国国际商会广东调解中心
> 地址：广东省广州市环市东路 450 号广东华信中心首层
> 电话：020-87617779
> 传真：020-87616497
> 邮编：510075

（四）通过仲裁方式解决商事、海事纠纷

外国人在中国境内发生的合同纠纷和其他财产权益纠纷，包括涉外经济贸易、运输和海事中发生的纠纷，可以仲裁。婚姻、收养、监护、扶养、继承等纠纷应当由行政机关依法处理。当事人采用仲裁方式解决纠纷，应当双方自愿，达成仲裁协议。仲裁实行一裁终局的制度。裁决作出后，当事人就同一纠纷再申请仲裁或者向人民法院起诉的，仲裁委员会或者人民法院不予受理。

> 广州仲裁委员会
> 地址：广州市越秀区沿江中路 298 号江湾大酒店 C 座 12-4 楼
> 电话：020-83287919
> 网址：http://www.gzac.org

（五）创新法律服务

1. 运用大数据、云计算和人工智能等现代科技，创新"互联网+公共法律服务"建设，推出"广州微司法行政"、"问律师"、"广州市法律援助"、"羊城慧调解"平台、"广州智慧公证"平台、"广州公共法律服务链"、"广州法视通"、"广州法律地图"等免费智能咨询、查询小程序，方便外籍人士随时随地线上预约申办多种公共法律服务，查阅进度。

2. 完善法律援助服务指引，编制出台英文版广州市法律援助处服务指南（*Guangzhou Legal Aid Service Guide*），帮助外籍人士处理日常法律事项。

第五章
经商投资指引

一、投资环境及商务发展概况

近年来,广州坚持以习近平新时代中国特色社会主义思想为指导,围绕党中央、国务院赋予广州的增强国际商贸中心功能的定位要求,积极推进商务领域改革发展,全力稳外贸、稳外资、促消费,取得了积极成效。"十三五"期间,广州外贸首次跃上万亿元台阶;实际使用外资累计328.3亿美元,占历年累计数30.4%,在穗投资的世界500强企业累计309家、投资项目1166个;社零额连续突破8000亿元、9000亿元。今年第一季度,全市进出口2444.4亿元,增长21.3%;实际使用外资132.07亿元人民币,增长34.0%;社零额2629.57亿元,增长31.7%。

近些年,广州城市核心竞争力和国际影响力大幅跃升。经济实力迈上新台阶,2020年GDP突破2.5万亿元,增长2.7%,人均GDP达到高收入经济体水平,固定资产投资增长10%,外贸出口增长3.2%。广州要素集聚力显著增强,获评全国营商环境标杆城市,政务服务指标排名全国首位。全国性资本市场均在穗设立机构,广州期货交易所获批在南沙设立。广州的全球地位不断跃升,全球创新集群百强排名中,穗、深、港联合排名第2。广州在全球金融中心指数中排名第21,国际航运中心发展指数中排名第13,《世界城市名册》中位列全球一线城市。科技创新策源全面提速,高新技术企业数量5年增长6倍,国家科技型中小企业备案入库数连续3年居全国第1。产业高端化加速推进,战略性新兴产业增加值占地区生产总值比重30%,人工智能与数字经济战略引擎工程稳步推进,新一代信息通信技术、智能与新能源汽车、生物医药与健康产业、新材料、智能装备与机器人等新兴支柱产业蓬勃发展。枢纽地位更加凸显,2020年机场旅客吞吐量登顶全球第1,港口货物、集装箱吞吐量居全球第4、第5,广州南站客流量居全国铁路枢纽站第1,广交会展馆即将建成全球最大的会展综合体。

二、产业扶持政策

（一）服务贸易与服务外包政策

1. 奖励政策

（1）对在广州市注册的，年度开展服务贸易出口（含离岸服务外包）、服务贸易进口业务实绩达到50万美元以上的企业，给予最高不超过100万元奖励；对开展服务外包在岸业务达到50万美元以上的，给予最高不超过100万元奖励。

（2）对广州市企业获得国家级机构认定的服务贸易和服务外包类荣誉项目，给予最高不超过20万元奖励。

（3）对广州市新认定的服务贸易示范企业和重点培育企业分别给予最高不超过50万元和30万元奖励。对已认定为服务贸易重点培育企业的经认定达到服务贸易示范企业标准的，一次性给予最高不超过20万元奖励。

（4）对广州市获得服务贸易和服务外包国际认证的企业，给予最高不超过5万元的奖励。

2. 税收政策

（1）对注册在广州的企业从事离岸服务外包业务取得的收入免征增值税。

（2）对经认定的技术先进型服务企业，减按15%的税率征收企业所得税；企业发生的职工教育经费支出，不超过工资薪金总额8%的部分，准予在计算应纳税所得额时扣除，超过部分，准予在以后纳税年度结转扣除。

3. 总部政策

对被认定为广州市总部企业的，按广州市总部经济政策给予财政奖励。

4. 技术奖励

对广州市医药企业从境外引进先进技术到广州市产业化或由广州市企业主导产业化的，给予技术交易金额的10%奖励，最高不超过1000万元。

（二）会展业促进政策

1. 促进会展企业落户

对新落户广州市、具备独立法人资格的会展企业，其首个完整会计年度年营业收入超过1000万元的，按其首个完整会计年度年营业收入的2%给予最高不超过200万元的一次性奖励。已获得广州市促进总部经济发展、促进企业加快落户等政策奖励补贴的会展企业原则上不适用此扶持措施。

2. 促进展览项目落户

对办展单位首次在广州市举办、展览面积达到6000平方米（含）以上的展览，以3年作为培育期，连续3年每年给予奖励（每年在我市举办两届及以上的，当年只奖励一届，以办展单位自主申报为准）。其中，展览面积3万平方米以下的，奖励30万元；3万（含）至5万平方米的，奖励60万元；5万（含）至10万平方米的，奖励100万元；10万（含）平方米以上的，奖励150万元。专业展览

题材属于IAB（信息技术人工智能、生物医药）、NEM（新能源、新材料）、数字经济等广州市政府明确重点发展产业领域的，奖励额度上浮50%。

3. 支持大型展览稳定发展

在广州市举办、展览面积达到5万平方米（含）以上，处于非培育期的展览，每届给予奖励。其中，面积5万（含）至10万平方米的，奖励20万元；面积10万（含）至20万平方米的，奖励40万元；面积20万（含）至30万平方米的，奖励60万元；面积30万（含）平方米以上的，奖励80万元。

4. 鼓励扩大展览规模

在广州市举办的非培育期展览，展览面积达6000平方米（含）以上，对比上届在广州市举办（在广州市一年举办两届及以上的，与上年同季展比较；两年一届或每两年巡回到广州市举办的，可隔年比较）面积增长达到一定比例的，按展览期不超过5天（以布展不超过2天加展览不超过3天计算）的新增面积场租的一定比例给予补助，具体为：展览面积6000平方米（含）至5万平方米，面积增长20%（含）以上的，按新增面积租金的50%给予补助；展览面积5万平方米（含）至10万平方米的，按新增面积租金的50%给予补助；展览面积10万平方米（含）以上的，按新增面积租金的80%给予补助。单个项目补助最高不超过200万元。

141

5. 鼓励举办高端会议等活动

对在广州市举办的符合条件的国际性会议、行业会议和活动等，按照活动场租的80%给予实际出资的主办或承办单位补助，每届活动的补助金额不超过100万元。其中，国际性会议指与会人员来自5个（含）以上国家或地区（不含港、澳、台地区）或国际性组织，会期1天（含）以上，与会人数50人（含）以上，外国与会人士占20%（含）以上，以服务产业、技术研讨等经济、科技、文化交流为主要目的的会议。行业会议和活动指国家一级商协会和学会学术研究机构在广州市主办或承办全国性年会、论坛、与展览相关赛事、会展讲座等活动，参会、参赛人员达到200人（含）以上的活动。会议项目被纳入国际大会及会议协会（ICCA）、国际协会联盟（UIA）等国际权威机构统计范围的，另行给予一次性奖励15万元。

6. 引导展览品牌化发展

对被评定为广州市重点品牌展会的，给予奖励50万元；被评定为优质品牌展会的，给予奖励30万元；被评定为成长型品牌展会的，给予奖励20万元。上述评定三年进行一次，具体评定办法另行制定。

7. 鼓励展览数字化发展

对办展单位在线下展览项目中实施的应用云计算、大数据、物联网、区块链、5G等技术的创新项目，项目完成后，按照不超过项目投入费用的45%给予一次性补助，补助金额最高不超过30万元。

8. 鼓励进行国际认证

对获得国际展览业协会（UFI）等国际展览机构认证的广州市会展场馆、会展行业组织、会展项目、会展配套服务企业等，给予一次性奖励20万元。

9. 支持企业境外办展

对广州市商协会、企业等机构在境外举办的展览，参展的广州地区企业在20家以上、展览面积在2000平方米（含）以上的，给予奖励。其中，展览面积2000平方米（含）至5000平方米的奖励20万元，面积5000平方米（含）以上的奖励30万元。

10. 支持穗港澳合作办展

由广州市与香港、澳门会展业促进主管部门双方或三方共同在广州市主办的展览,分别对广州市参展市场主体按展位费的50%—80%给予补助。

11. 鼓励港澳机构在广州市独立办展

港澳机构在广州市独立办展,可享受与境内机构在广州市办展同等待遇,由港澳办展单位出具委托函,委托境内相关单位申请和领取本政策措施规定的相关奖补资金。

12. 鼓励引进和培育高端人才

引进优秀高端国际会展人才,按照广州市有关人才安居政策给予落户。对申报国家、省、市人才计划成功的会展人才或团队,按照广州市相关政策标准给予补助。

13. 鼓励社会机构在广州市开展会展专业人才培训

国家一级商协会和学会学术研究机构在广州市举办会展职业技能培训,培训时间3天(含)以上,培训人员达50人(含)以上的,对广州市承办单位实际支出给予专项补助,补助金额不超过20万元。已获得广州市职业技能提升培训补贴等措施培训补贴的会展职业技能培训项目不适用此扶持措施。

(三)外商投资政策

1. 外商投资信息报告

外国投资者直接在中国境内投资设立公司、合伙企业的,外国(地区)企业在中国境内从事生产经营活动的,外国(地区)企业在中国境内设立从事生产经营活动的常驻代表机构等,应按照《外商投资信息报告办法》的规定,通过企业登记系统在线提交初始报告、变更报告。

(1)初始报告

外国投资者在中国境内设立外商投资企业或股权并购境内非外商投资企业,应于办理外商投资企业设立登记或办理被并购企业变更登记时通过企业登记系统提交初始报告。

(2)变更报告

初始报告的信息发生变更,涉及企业变更登记(备案)的,外商投资企业应于办理企业变更登记(备案)时通过企业登记系统提交变更报告。不涉及企业变更登记（备案）的，外商投资企业应于变更事项发生后20个工作日内通过企业登记系统提交变更报告。企业根据章程对变更事项作出决议的，以作出决议的时间为变更事项的发生时间；法律法规对变更事项的生效条件另有要求的，以满足相应要求的时间为变更事项的发生时间。

外商投资的上市公司及在全国中小企业股份转让系统挂牌的公司，可仅在外国投资者持股比例变化累计超过5%或者引起外方控股、相对控股地位发生变化时，报告投资者及其所持股份变更信息。

（3）信息报告方式

登录广州市市场监督管理局网站（网址：http://scjgj.gz.gov.cn）—"政务服务"—"办事服务"—"外资报告"栏目进行初始、变更报告。

2. 外商投资项目奖励政策

自2017至2022年，对在广东设立的年实际外资金额（不含外方股东贷款）超过5000万美元的新项目（房地产业、金融业及类金融业项目除外）、超过3000万美元的增资项目和超过1000万美元的外资跨国公司总部或地区总部，省财政按其当年实际外资金额不低于2%的比例予以奖励，最高奖励1亿元。对世界500强企业（以《财富》排行榜为准）、全球行业龙头企业在广东新设（或增资设立）的年实际外资金额超过1亿美元的制造业项目，以及新设的年实际外资金额不低于3000万美元的IAB（新一代信息技术、智能装备、生物医药）和NEM（新能源、新材料）制造业项目，可按"一项一议"方式给予重点支持。外资跨国公司总部或地区总部对省级财政年度贡献首次超过1亿元的，省财政按其当年对省级财政贡献量的30%给予一次性奖励，最高奖励1亿元。

3. 广州市重点产业促进政策简明手册（修订版）

请扫描下面的二维码了解详情。

三、重点经济开发区简介

（一）南沙区

1. 南沙自贸区最新发展情况

南沙位居粤港澳大湾区的地理几何中心，拥有国家级新区、自贸试验区、粤港澳全面合作示范区等多重国家战略平台，是广州唯一的城市副中心。相继获批国家综合保税区、进口贸易促进创新示范区、国际化人才特区等。"十三五"期间，南沙成为广州发展最快的增长区域，地区生产总值增长超七成，规模以上工业产值跃升至全市第2，税收收入实现翻番，固定资产投资、进出口总值和实际利用外资等主要经济指标实现年均两位数增长。2020年实现地方生产总值1846亿元、同比增长7.1%。固定资产投资922亿元、增长22.2%，规上工业总产值2845亿元、增长6.1%，进出口总值2265亿元、增长6%，税收总额656.5亿元（含关税）、增长5%，一般公共预算收入90亿元、增长7.5%，累计落户企业15.8万家、世界500强企业投资项目201个。今年第一季度，GDP增长20.6%，规上工业总产值增长41.4%，固定资产投资增长30.6%，一般公共预算收入增长23.4%，税收总额（含关税）增长30%，新设企业1.3万家，实际利用外资3.4亿美元，集中签约动工136个项目、总投资额超4900亿元。

南沙区在科技创新、先进制造业、战略新兴产业、航运物流及金融创新等领域产业集聚效应不断壮大。全区高新技术企业数量达到587家，年均增长66.7%。落户华南地区唯一的全球IPv6测试中心实验室。积极推动5G、区块链、大数据、人工智能、物联网等技术"赋能"制造业发展，汽车制造业产值连续3年突破千亿元大关，获批国家级智能网联汽车测试示范区，打造新的千亿级智能网联新能源汽车产业园。集聚300多家人工智能企业、210多家生命健康企业，落户粤港澳大湾区精准医学产业基地项目，中科空天飞行科技

产业化基地启动建设，第三代半导体形成全产业链集聚，新兴产业集群不断壮大。落户广州期货交易所、国际金融论坛（IFF）永久会址等重大金融平台。广州港南沙港区已建成华南最具规模的集装箱、汽车和通用码头群，航线通达全球200多个港口城市，广州航交所交易额稳居全国第2。

2. 南沙区招商引资优惠政策

为支持企业、人才聚集，广州南沙出台了"1+1+10+N"产业政策体系，对总部经济、科技创新、航运物流、金融服务等重点产业以及人才、用地、项目引荐、经济贡献等产业促进要素设置了全面的政策扶持，围绕人工智能、外贸综合服务、旅游、邮轮、种业小镇、生活服务业、港澳青年创新创业、人力资源产业园、生物技术、法律服务业、新一代信息技术等新兴产业设置专项政策。相关政策体系涵盖对外商投资企业、外籍人才的扶持，一方面，既涵盖南沙重点发展产业领域发展，又在人才集聚、用地等要素供给方面为产业发展提供充分保障；另一方面，针对企业落户、增资、研发、经营、上市等不同发展阶段，设置了奖励、补贴或股权投资等政策扶持，为企业提供全生命周期服务。

3. 相关网址

广州南沙新区（自贸片区）"1+1+10+N"产业政策体系：

http://www.gznsnews.com/index.php?m=content&c=index&a=lists&catid=50

南沙区英文门户网站：

http://nansha.guangdong.chinadaily.com.cn/

（二）黄埔区、广州开发区

1. 区情简介

黄埔区、广州开发区位于广州市东部珠江口，管辖面积484平方公里，下辖16街1镇，总人口132万，自古以来是华南门户，有着厚重的文化底蕴和丰富的历史遗存，拥有古代海上丝绸之路重要起点——南海神庙、近代民主革命策源地——黄埔军校、珠江黄金岸线和华南重要港口——黄埔港。作为粤港澳大湾区的"湾顶明珠"，黄埔区加快对接湾区铁路大动脉，主动融入大湾区一小时生活圈。2014年1月，国务院批复同意撤销原黄埔区、萝岗区，设立新的黄埔区；2015年9月，新黄埔区正式挂牌成立，与广州开发区实行深度融合的管理体制。

全区分为四大片区，分别是中新广州知识城、广州科学城、黄埔港、广州国际生物岛。中新广州知识城总规划获国务院批复，打造国家级双边合作新典范，推进知识城开发建设"一号工程"，高起点建设"一核两心多园"，加快建设具有全球影响力的国家知识中心。科学城"双创"示范基地连续两年获国务院督查奖励，围绕粤港澳大湾区制度创新先行区和"中小企业能办大事"先行示范区，高标准提升"一核三区两轴"，建设具有国际影响力的中国智造中心。黄埔港加速发展高端港口经济，加快建设广州人工智能与数字经济试验区（鱼珠片区），打造服务"一带一路"新贸易创新中心。积极创建生物岛国家生物医药政策创新试验区，建设国际高端医疗器械创新产业基地及世界顶尖的生物医药和生物安全研发中心。

2020年全区地区生产总值3662.67亿元，同比增长4.1%，财税总收入超1300亿元、增长11.6%，规上工业总产值突破8000亿元，固定资产投资总额、商品销售总额等7项主要指标居全市第一。累计引进外资企业4100多家，截至2020年底，累计合同利用外资452.32亿美元，实际利用外资294.61亿美元，聚集世界500强投资项目205个，上市企业63家，新三板挂牌企业131家。科技创新实力连续3年保持全国经开区第一，瞪羚企业总数连续5年位列全国高新区前四，建成华南地区最大科技孵化器集群，荣获"中国优秀孵化器集聚区奖"。荣获联合国"2019年度全球杰出投资促进机构大奖"，成为唯一获此奖项的中国机构。2020年获评为"企业家幸福感最强区"，蝉联"中国最具幸福感城市（城区）"，连续两年蝉联全国经开区营商环境指数第一。在2020年第二届中国国际化营商环境高峰论坛中，广州开发区以第一名的成绩荣获"国际化营商环境建设十佳产业园区"。

2. 黄埔区、广州开发区主要政策概览

黄埔区、广州开发区致力打造政策高地，为企业投资创业提供良好的政策助力，陆续出台了"黄金十条""美玉十条"等多个产业扶持政策，目前已形成较为完善的政策体系。

所有政策奖励内容、支持条件、具体奖励细则均以相关规定为准。广州市黄埔区、广州开发区政策兑现服务信息系统网址：https://zcdx.gdd.gov.cn/wedPc/policy，及相关APP如下。

黄埔兑现通　　广州开发区政务

企业服务禾雀花工程　　广州市黄埔区政务服务数据管理局　　黄埔区广州开发区政策兑现服务

四、知识产权保护

（一）知识产权保护政策措施逐步完善

一是印发《广州市关于强化知识产权保护的若干措施》，综合运用法律、行政、经济、技术、社会治理手段，出台25条措施实施最严格的知识产权保护。二是全市39个部门共同签署《关于对知识产权领域严重失信主体及其有关人员开展联合惩戒的合作备忘录》，推出32项惩戒措施，及时公示知识产权违法失信企业，推进对知识产权领域严重失信主体联合惩戒工作。三是出台《广州市市场监督管理局关于优化营商环境加强知识产权保护的若干措施》，从知识产权创造、运用、保护等方面采取12项举措，建立以"信用+监管"为核心的知识产权保护体系。

（二）知识产权保护工作机制日趋健全

一是广州市市场监督管理局先后与深圳市市场监督管理局、广州海关、黄埔海关、广州市中级人民法院签订知识产权保护合作协议，建立知识产权保护跨部门衔接机制，共享知识产权保护执法信息。二是建设中国（广州）知识产权保护中心，打造集快速审查、快速确权、快速维权、高效运营、公共服务、人才培育于一体的国家级知识产权功能性平台，提升广州市知识产权快速保护能力。三是广州市市场监督管理局和广州市工商业联合会共同设立"广州市民营企业知识产权保护指导服务中心"，指导海珠区建立广州海珠区促进琶洲会展和数字经济知识产权保护中心，为广州市企业提供优质高效的知识产权保护服务。四是推动在全市11区全覆盖建立重点产业知识产权维权援助与保护工作站，积极配合推动成立广东省海外知识产权保护维权援助研究院，成立广东企业海外知识产权保护专家委员会，推进企业海外知识产权维权援助服务平台建设。目前,广州市有知识产权调解机构62家、知识产权仲裁机构5家、知识产权快速维权及援助机构28家。

(三)知识产权行政保护能力不断增强

一是在办理知识产权案件中引入知识产权司法鉴定机,为知识产权侵权判断提供司法鉴定服务,为知识产权行政执法提供专业技术支撑。二是加强与国家知识产权局专利审查协作广东中心的合作,为专利侵权纠纷案件的办理提供技术调查服务。

(四)知识产权侵权行为得到遏制

印发《2020年度知识产权保护专项行动方案》,针对重点领域、重点专业市场开展知识产权保护专项行动,大力打击侵犯知识产权违法行为,重点加强对高价值专利、驰名商标、老字号商标和地理标志产品的保护,优化专业市场知识产权保护环境。2020年共办结知识产权行政处罚案件859宗,涉案金额942.46万元,罚没1731.01万元。办理专利侵权纠纷案件1777宗。

(五)严厉打击与疫情相关知识产权违法行为

印发《关于加强疫情防控商品知识产权保护工作的通知》,强化疫情防控关键领域、重点产品执法检查,严厉打击侵犯口罩、防护服等防疫商品商标、专利权违法行为。指导荔湾区市场监管局协调配合公安部门快速查处了价值23万元假冒"3M"注册商标专用权口罩案件,该案经法院审判,以销售假冒注册商标商品罪判处当事人3年徒刑并处4万元罚金。组织相关区局严厉查处恶意申请注册"李文亮""雷神山""火神山""吹哨人"等商标的违法行为,对涉案的9家代理公司立案查处。市场监管局连同荔湾区局对国览城开展了打击医疗器械、用品领域侵犯知识产权专项行动。专项行动重点检查市场内近300家经销的口罩、呼吸机、防护服、红外体温计(额温枪)、新型冠状病毒检测试剂、熔喷布、无纺布、红外传感器等重要防疫物资是否存在商标侵权、假冒专利等违法情况。

附：相关网址

1. 广州出台25项具体措施打造知识产权保护新模式

http://www.gz.gov.cn/xw/jrgz/content/mpost_7107818.html

2. 广州市知识产权工作领导小组办公室关于印发知识产权领域严重失信主体及其有关人员开展联合惩戒的合作备忘录的通知

http://scjgj.gz.gov.cn/zwdt/tzgg/content/post_5449940.html

3. 广州市获批建设中国（广州）知识产权保护中心

http://scjgj.gz.gov.cn/zwdt/tt/content/post_5892141.html

4. 广州市市场监管局广州市工商联共同设立民营企业知识产权保护指导服务中心

http://scjgj.gz.gov.cn/zwdt/gzdt/content/post_5311342.html

with the public security department to rapidly investigate and handle a case of counterfeit masks worth RMB 230,000 infringing the registered trademark "3M". Tried by the court, the person concerned was sentenced to three years' imprisonment and a fine of RMB 40,000 imposed for the sale of counterfeit goods of registered trademark. Relevant district administrations have rigorously investigated and dealt with malicious applications for the registration of "Li Wenliang", "Leishen Mountain", "Huoshen Mountain", "Whistle Blower" and other trademarks. Nine agencies involved in the case were investigated and prosecuted. Guangzhou Market Regulation Administration, together with the Liwan District Market Regulation Administration, have launched a special operation to combat infringement of intellectual property of medical devices and supplies in the Kwoklam Medical City, focusing on trademark infringement, patent counterfeiting and other violations in relation to important epidemic prevention materials such as masks, respirators, protective clothing, infrared thermometers (forehead thermometers), COVID-19 testing reagents, melt-blown fabric, non-woven fabric and infrared sensors sold by nearly 300 companies in the market.

Appendix: Related websites

1. Guangzhou introduces 25 specific measures to create a new model of intellectual property protection http: //www.gz.gov.cn/xw/jrgz/content/mpost_7107818.html

2. *Notice by Guangzhou Municipal Intellectual Property Leading Group Office on the issuance of the Memorandum of Cooperation on Joint Punishment for Seriously Defaulting Subjects and Related Persons in Intellectual Property*

http: //scjgj.gz.gov.cn/zwdt/tzgg/content/post_5449940.html

3. Guangzhou to build China (Guangzhou) Intellectual Property Protection Center http: //scjgj.gz.gov.cn/zwdt/tt/content/post_5892141.html

4. Guidance and Service Center for the Protection of Intellectual Property for Private Enterprises Jointly Established by Guangzhou Municipal Administration for Market Regulation and Guangzhou Federation of Industry and Commerce

http://scjgj.gz.gov.cn/zwdt/gzdt/content/post_5311342.html

protection services for enterprises in Guangzhou. Fourth, we have promoted the establishment of IPR protection assistance workstations for key industries in all 11 districts in the city, actively cooperated with the establishment of the Guangdong Institute for Overseas IPR Protection Assistance, set up an expert committee on overseas IPR protection for Guangdong enterprises, and promoted the development of a service platform for overseas IPR protection assistance for enterprises. At present, Guangzhou has 62 IPR mediation agencies, 5 IPR arbitration agencies and 28 fast-track IPR protection assistance agencies.

(III) Continuous enhancement of administrative protection of intellectual property

First, we have introduced IPR judicial authentication institutions in handling IPR cases to provide judicial authentication services for the determination of IPR infringement and technical support for IPR administrative enforcement. Second, the cooperation with the Guangdong Center for Patent Examination and Collaboration of the State Intellectual Property Office has been strengthened to provide technical investigation services for the handling of patent infringement dispute cases.

(IV) Curbing intellectual property infringement

The *Action Plan for 2020 IPR Protection Special Campaign* has been issued to carry out targeted actions for IPR protection in key areas and key professional markets, vigorously crack down on IPR infringement and violations, focusing on protecting high-value patents, well-known trademarks, long-established trademarks and products of geographical indication, and optimizing IPR protection environment in professional markets. 859 IPR administrative punishment cases, involving a total amount of RMB 9,424,600 and confiscated and fined value of RMB 17,310,100, were settled and 1,777 cases of patent infringement disputes were handled in 2020.

(V) Cracking down on epidemic-related IPR violations

The *Notice on Protecting the Intellectual Property of Epidemic Prevention and Control Commodities* has been issued to strengthen enforcement and inspection of key areas and key products for epidemic prevention and control, and crack down on infringement of trademarks and patents of epidemic prevention commodities such as masks and protective clothing. We have instructed Liwan District Market Regulation Administration to coordinate

IV. Protection of Intellectual Property Right

(I) Gradual improvement of intellectual property protection policies and measures

First, the *Measures of Guangzhou Municipality on Strengthening the Protection of Intellectual Property* has been issued, introducing 25 measures to implement the strictest protection of intellectual property rights through legal, administrative, economic, technological and social governance means. Second, 39 departments of the city have signed the *Memorandum of Cooperation on Joint Punishment against Seriously Defaulting Subjects and Related Persons in Intellectual Property Rights* to introduce 32 punitive measures, promptly publicize enterprises in breach of intellectual property laws or being discreditable, and promote joint punishment against seriously defaulted subjects in intellectual property rights. Third, the *Measures on Optimizing Business Environment and Strengthening the Protection of Intellectual Property by Guangzhou Municipal Administration for Market Regulation* have been issued, which adopts 12 measures in the creation, application and protection of intellectual property to establish a protection system for IPR with "credit + supervision" as the core.

(II) The mechanism for intellectual property protection continues to improve

First, Guangzhou Municipal Administration for Market Regulation has signed IPR protection cooperation agreements with Shenzhen Municipal Administration for Market Regulation, Guangzhou Customs, Huangpu Customs and Guangzhou Intermediate People's Court, establishing an inter-departmental connection mechanism for IPR protection and sharing information on IPR protection enforcement. Second, the China (Guangzhou) Intellectual Property Protection Center has been established to create a national-level IPR functional platform that integrates rapid examination, rapid confirmation and protection of rights, efficient operation, public services and talent cultivation so as to enhance prompt protection of intellectual property in Guangzhou. Third, the Guidance and Service Center for the Protection of Intellectual Property for Private Enterprises has been jointly established by Guangzhou Municipal Administration for Market Regulation and Guangzhou Federation of Industry and Commerce. The Pazhou Intellectual Property Protection Center was also established in Haizhu District to provide quality and efficient intellectual property

Entrepreneurs" and the "Happiest City (Urban District) in China" for the second consecutive year. It was also the second consecutive year GDD ranked No. 1 in the Business Environment Index of Economic Development Districts in China. In 2020, GDD was awarded the first place in the "Top 10 Industrial Parks for International Business Environment" at the second China International Business Environment Summit.

2. Overview of the main policies of Huangpu District/ Guangzhou Development District

Huangpu District/GDD is committed to building a policy highland to support enterprises in their investment and business establishment, and has issued a number of industrial support policies such as the "Ten Golden Articles" and "Ten Jade Articles", forming a relatively comprehensive policy system.

The content of all policies, conditions of support and specific details of awards are subject to relevant regulations. Website: Information System for Policy Delivery Service of Guangzhou Huangpu District and Guangzhou Development District https://zcdx.gdd.gov.cn/wedPc/policy. The relevant apps are as follows:

Huangpu Policy Delivery

Government Service of Huangpu District

"Rice Bird" Business Service Project

Government Service Data Management Bureau of Huangpu District, Guangzhou

Policy Delivery Service of Huangpu District/ GDD

established and has since been under a deeply integrated management system with the Guangzhou Development District.

The district consists of four major zones, namely the Sino-Singapore Guangzhou Knowledge City, Guangzhou Science City, Huangpu Port and Guangzhou International Bio-Island. Approved by the State Council, the Sino-Singapore Guangzhou Knowledge City aims to be a new model of national-level bilateral cooperation, and will advance the "Project One" of the development of the Knowledge City, build "one core, two centers and multiple parks" from a high starting point, and develop a national knowledge center with global influence. The "Double Innovation" demonstration base of the Science City has been awarded by the State Council in its supervision for two consecutive years, and the "one core, three zones and two axes" have been upgraded to be the pioneer zone for mechanism innovation of the Guangdong-Hong Kong-Macao Greater Bay Area and the pilot zone demonstrating "SMEs can do great things". The development of an internationally influential smart manufacturing center in China is underway. Focusing on high-end port economy, Huangpu Port is accelerating the development of the Guangzhou Artificial Intelligence and Digital Economy Pilot Zone (Yuzhu Area), and building an innovation center to serve the new trade of the "Belt and Road". The Bio-Island Innovation Pilot Zone for National Biomedical Policies is also underway, along with the development of an innovative industrial base for high-end medical device and a world-leading R&D center in biomedicine and biosafety.

In 2020, the district's GDP exceeded RMB 366.267 billion, with a year-on-year growth of 4.1%; the fiscal revenue reached over RMB 130 billion, an annual increase of 11.6%; the total output value of industrial enterprises above designated size exceeded RMB 800 billion; and 7 major indicators, including total investment in fixed assets and total merchandise sales, ranked first in the city. By the end of 2020, the district was home to more than 4,100 foreign companies, the accumulative contracted foreign investment reached USD 45.232 billion and the actual utilized foreign investment was USD 29.461 billion. The district has also attracted 205 investment projects from the Fortune Global 500 companies, 63 listed companies and 131 companies list on the NEEQ. The strength of innovation of Huangpu has remained the first in all economic development zones of the country for three consecutive years, and the number of "gazelle enterprises" has ranked among the top four in all high-tech zones in China for five consecutive years. With the largest cluster of technology incubators in South China, the District has won the "Award of Outstanding Incubator Cluster in China". GDD won the UN Investment Promotion Agency Award 2019, becoming the only Chinese organization receiving this award. In 2020, GDD was awarded as the "Happiest District for

2. Preferential policies for attracting investment to Nansha District

To attract enterprises and talents, Nansha has introduced the "1+1+10+N" industrial policy system, laying comprehensive policy support for key industries such as headquarters economy, scientific and technological innovation, shipping logistics and financial services, as well as industrial promotion elements such as talent, land, project attraction and economic contribution. Special policies have been developed for emerging industries including AI, comprehensive services for foreign trade, tourism, cruise ships, seed towns, life services, innovation and start-up by young people of Hong Kong and Macao, industrial parks for human resources, biotechnology, legal services and next generation information technology. The relevant policy system also supports foreign-invested enterprises and foreign talents. On one hand, it covers the development of Nansha's priority industries, and provides sufficient guarantee for industrial development in talent, land and other factors. On the other hand, policy supports such as incentives, subsidies or equity investment are set up for enterprises at different stages of development from their settlement, capital increase, R&D to operation and listing to provide whole life-cycle services for them.

3. Related websites

The "1+1+10+N" industrial policy system of Nansha New Area, Guangzhou (Free Trade Zone): http: //www.gznsnews.com/index.php?m=content&c=index&a=lists&catid=50

English portal of Nansha District: http: //nansha.guangdong.chinadaily.com.cn/

(II) Huangpu District/Guangzhou Development District

1. General information

Huangpu District/Guangzhou Development District is located in the estuary of the Pearl River in eastern Guangzhou, with an area of 484 km^2, 16 sub-districts and a town under its jurisdiction, and a population of 1.32 million. It has been the gateway of South China since ancient times with rich cultural heritage and a wealth of historical relics, such as the Nanhai God Temple, a key starting point of the ancient Maritime Silk Road; the Whampoa Military Academy, the fountainhead of the modern democratic revolution; and Huangpu Port, the golden coastline of the Pearl River and an important port in South China. As the "pearl at the top of the Bay" in the Greater Bay Area, the district has accelerated its connection to the railway arteries of the Bay Area to be part of its one-hour living circle.

In January 2014, the State Council approved the abolition of the former Huangpu District and Luogang District and the establishment of the new Huangpu District; in September 2015, the new Huangpu District was officially of high-tech enterprises in the district has reached 587, with an average annual growth rate of 66.7%. The only global IPv6 testing center and lab in South China was settled here. Nansha has also been driving the development of 5G, blockchain, big data, artificial intelligence, Internet of Things and other technologies to "empower" the manufacturing industry, and the output value of the automobile manufacturing industry has exceeded RMB 100 billion for three consecutive years. Approved as a national demonstrative testing zone for intelligent connected vehicles, Nansha is building a new 100 billion yuan-level industrial park for ICVs and new energy vehicles. The district has gathered more than 300 AI enterprises and 210 life and health enterprises, and has become home to the precision medicine base of the Guangdong-Hong Kong-Macao Bay Area.

With the construction of the industrial base of flight technology by the Aerospace Information Research Institute of the Chinese Academy of Sciences and the third-generation semiconductor industry forming a whole industry chain cluster, the cluster of emerging industries continues to grow. Major financial platforms such as the Guangzhou Futures Exchange and the permanent site of the International Financial Forum (IFF) have settled here. The Nansha Port Area of Guangzhou Port has become the largest container, automotive and general terminal group in South China, with shipping routes to over 200 port cities around the world and the trading volume of Guangzhou Shipping Exchange ranking second in China.

III. Introduction to Key Economic Development Zones

(I) Nansha District

1. Latest development of Nansha Free Trade Zone

Located in the geometric center of the Guangdong-Hong Kong-Macao Greater Bay Area, Nansha has multiple national strategic platforms such as the national new zone, the pilot free trade zone and the demonstration zone for comprehensive cooperation between Guangdong, Hong Kong and Macao, and is the only sub-center of Guangzhou. It has been granted the status of national comprehensive bonded zone, demonstration zone for import promotion and innovation, and a special zone for international talents. During the 13th Five-Year Plan period, Nansha has become the fastest growing region in Guangzhou, with the district GDP growing by over 70%, the output value of industrial enterprises above designated size leaping to the second in the city, tax revenue doubling, and major economic indicators such as fixed asset investment, total import and export volume and actual utilization of foreign investment achieving double-digit growth annually.

The regional GDP was RMB 184.6 billion in 2020, an increase of 7.1% annually; the fixed asset investment reached RMB 92.2 billion, an annual increase of 22.2%; the total output value of industrial enterprises above designated size was RMB 284.5 billion, a growth of 6.1% from 2019; the total import and export volume was RMB 226.5 billion, a 6% growth year-on-year; the tax revenue was RMB 65.65 billion (including tariffs), an increase of 5%; the general budget revenue reached RMB 9 billion, an increase of 7.5%. Accumulatively Nansha has attracted 158,000 enterprises and 201 investment projects by the Fortune Global 500 companies. In the first quarter of this year, the GDP of the district grew 20.6%, the total output value of industrial enterprises above designated size grew by 41.4%, the fixed asset investment increased 30.6%, the general budget revenue grew by 23.4%, the total tax revenue (including tariffs) grew 30%. 13,000 new enterprises were established, the actual foreign investment utilized reached USD 340 million, and 136 projects with a total investment of over RMB 490 billion were signed and commenced.

Nansha District has been strengthening the industrial clustering effect in scientific and technological innovation, advanced manufacturing, strategic emerging industries, shipping logistics and financial innovation. The number contribution of the year and up to RMB 100 million to the corporation.

3. *Handbook on Guangzhou's Promotion Policies for Key Industries* (revised version)

Please scan the QR code below.

(2) Amendment report

If the information in the initial report is changed and involves amendment in the registration (filing) of the enterprise, the foreign-invested enterprise shall submit an amendment report through the enterprise registration system at the time of registration (filing) of the amendment of the enterprise. If the change does not involve the registration (filing) of the enterprise, the foreign-invested enterprise shall submit an amendment report through the enterprise registration system within 20 working days since the occurrence of the changes. If the enterprise makes a resolution on the change according to its articles of association, the time when the resolution is made shall be the time of occurrence of the change. If there are other conditions precedent according to laws and regulations for the change, the time when the conditions are met shall be the time of occurrence of the change.

Foreign-invested listed companies and foreign-invested companies listed on the National Equities Exchange and Quotations may report changes of investors or their shareholding only when the cumulative change in the shareholding of foreign investors exceeds 5% or causes a change in the controlling or relative controlling status of the foreign party.

(3) Information reporting procedure

Log in to the website of Guangzhou Municipal Administration for Market Regulation (http://scjgj.gz.gov.cn), "Administrative Services" – "Civil Services" – "Foreign Investment Report" for the initial report and amendment report.

2. Incentive policy for foreign investment projects

From 2017 to 2022, for new projects (except projects in real estate, financial and quasi-financial industries) with an annual actual foreign investment (excluding loans from foreign shareholders) exceeding USD 50 million, capital increase projects exceeding USD 30 million and foreign multinational corporations' headquarters or regional headquarters projects exceeding USD 10 million established in Guangdong, the provincial government will provide incentives at a rate of not less than 2% of the actual foreign investment in the year, with a maximum amount of RMB 100 million. Manufacturing projects of the Global 500 companies (based on the Fortune ranking) and global industrial leaders with an annual actual foreign investment of more than USD 100 million, and newly established (or capital-increased) IAB (next generation information technology, artificial intelligent equipment, and biomedicine) and NEM (new energy and new materials) manufacturing projects with an annual actual foreign investment of not less than USD 30 million in Guangdong may enjoy key support on a "case by case" basis. If the annual contribution of the headquarters or regional headquarters of a foreign-invested multinational corporation to the provincial fiscal revenue exceeds RMB 100 million for the first time, the provincial government will provide a one-off incentive equal to 30% of its fiscal

11. Supporting Hong Kong and Macao organizations to hold exhibitions independently in Guangzhou

Hong Kong and Macao organizations holding exhibitions independently in Guangzhou shall enjoy the same treatment as mainland organizations holding exhibitions in Guangzhou. The exhibition organizers of Hong Kong and Macao shall issue a letter of entrustment and entrust the relevant mainland organizations to apply for and receive the relevant subsidies as stipulated in relevant policies on their behalf.

12. Attracting and cultivating high-caliber talents

High-caliber talents in international convention and exhibition will be supported in their settlement here according to the relevant talent settlement policies of Guangzhou. Subsidies will be given to individuals or teams in convention and exhibition industry who have successfully applied for national, provincial or municipal talent programs in accordance with the relevant policies of Guangzhou.

13. Encouraging organizations to carry out training for convention and exhibition professionals in Guangzhou

A dedicated subsidy up to RMB 200,000 will be granted to organizers in Guangzhou for the actual expenditure in trainings by national level-one chambers of commerce, associations, academic societies and research institutes in convention and exhibition professional skills in Guangzhou which last for three days or longer and with 50 or more trainees. This supporting measure is not applicable to the exhibition vocational skills training projects already receiving the training subsidy from Guangzhou for vocational skills upgrading or other programs.

(III) Foreign Investment Policies

1. Foreign investment information report

Foreign investors who directly establish companies or partnerships in China, foreign (regional) enterprises engaged in production and operation activities in China, and foreign (regional) enterprises establishing permanent representative offices engaged in production and operation activities in China shall submit initial reports and any amendment reports online through the enterprise registration system in accordance with the provisions of the *Measures for the Reporting of Foreign Investment Information*.

(1) Initial report

Foreign investors establishing foreign-invested enterprises or merging and acquiring domestic non-foreign-invested enterprises in China shall submit the initial report through the enterprise registration system when registering the establishment of the foreign-invested enterprise or registering the amendment of the merged/acquired enterprise.

and cultural exchanges such as industrial services and technical discussions. Industry conferences and events refer to national annual conferences, forums, exhibition-related contests and lectures in Guangzhou held by national first-level chambers of commerce, associations or academic/research institutes with 200 or more participants. A one-off award of RMB 150,000 will be given to events included in the statistics of international authorities such as the International Congress and Convention Association (ICCA) and the Union of International Associations (UIA).

6. Guiding the brand development of exhibition

An award of RMB 500,000 will be given to exhibitions assessed as key brand exhibitions of Guangzhou; an award of RMB 300,000 will be given to exhibitions assessed as quality brand exhibitions; and an award of RMB 200,000 will be given to exhibitions assessed as growing brand exhibitions. These assessments will be conducted once every three years; the specific assessment methods will be formulated separately.

7. Encouraging digital development of exhibition

For innovative projects implemented by organizers in their offline exhibitions applying technologies such as cloud computing, big data, Internet of Things, block chain and 5G, a one-off subsidy equal to a maximum of 45% of the project expenses and up to RMB 300,000 will be given upon completion of the project.

8. Encouraging international certification

A one-off award of RMB 200,000 will be given to Guangzhou exhibition venues, exhibition industry organizations, exhibition projects and exhibition supporting service enterprises certified by international exhibition organizations such as the International Association of the Exhibition Industry (UFI).

9. Supporting enterprises to hold exhibitions abroad

Bonus will be given to exhibitions held abroad by Guangzhou chambers of commerce, associations, enterprises and other organizations participated by more than 20 enterprises from Guangzhou and with an exhibition area of 2,000 m^2 or more. Those with an exhibition area of 2,000 (inclusive) to 5,000 m^2 will be rewarded with RMB 200,000, and those with an area of 5,000 m^2 or more will be rewarded with RMB 300,000.

10. Supporting exhibitions jointly held by Guangzhou, Hong Kong and Macao

For exhibitions in Guangzhou jointly organized by two or all three parties of the exhibition industry promotion authorities of Guangzhou, Hong Kong and Macao, a subsidy equal to 50% to 80% of their booth fees will be given to the participating exhibitors from Guangzhou.

reaches a certain percentage compared to its last session in Guangzhou (for exhibitions held twice or more in Guangzhou in a year, the comparison is made with the same seasonal exhibition of the previous year; for exhibitions held once every two years or touring to Guangzhou every two years, the comparison can be made in alternate years), a subsidy equal to a certain percentage of the rental of the increased space will be granted, calculated on the basis of an exhibition period not exceeding five days (on the basis that move-in is not more than two days and exhibition not more than three days). Specifically: Exhibitions with an area of 6,000 (inclusive) to 50,000 m^2 and an increase in area of 20% (inclusive) or higher will be granted a subsidy equal to 50% of the rental of the increased area; exhibitions of 50,000 (inclusive) to 100,000 m^2 will have a subsidy equal to 50% of the rental of the increased area; exhibitions of 100,000 m^2 (inclusive) or more will have a subsidy equal to 80% of the rental of the increased area. The maximum amount of subsidy for a single project will not exceed RMB 2 million.

5. Encouraging the holding of high-end conferences and events in Guangzhou

For eligible international conferences, industrial conferences and events held in Guangzhou, a subsidy equal to 80% of the venue rental will be given to the actually paying hosts or organizers, with the amount of subsidy not exceeding RMB 1 million per event. International conferences here refer to conferences with participants from five or more countries or regions (excluding Hong Kong, Macao and Taiwan) or international organizations, lasting for a day or more, with 50 or more participants and among whom foreign participants accounting for at least 20%, and whose main purposes are economic, scientific advanced technology from abroad for industrialization in Guangzhou or whose industrialization is led by Guangzhou enterprises, a bonus equal to 10% of the amount of the technological transaction and up to RMB 10 million will be awarded.

(II) Policies to Promote the Convention and Exhibition Industry

1. Attracting convention and exhibition enterprises

For convention and exhibition enterprises with independent legal entity status newly settled in Guangzhou, if their annual business revenue exceeds RMB 10 million in their first full fiscal year, a one-off bonus equal to 2% of the annual revenue of their first full fiscal year and up to RMB 2 million will be awarded. In principle, those already received incentives and subsidies under Guangzhou's policies to promote headquarters economy and accelerate the settlement of enterprises are not eligible for this measure.

2. Attracting exhibition projects

For exhibitions held in Guangzhou for the first time with an exhibition area of 6,000 m^2 or more, an incubation period of three years will be granted during which incentives will be given for each of the three consecutive years (if the exhibition is held twice a year or more in the city, only one session will be rewarded in each year, as applied by the exhibition organizer). An award of RMB 300,000 will be given to exhibitions with an area of less than 30,000 m^2; an incentive of RMB 600,000 will be awarded to exhibitions of 30,000 (inclusive) to 50,000 m^2; RMB 100,000 will be awarded to exhibitions with an area of 50,000 (inclusive) to 100,000 m^2; RMB 1.5 million will be awarded to exhibitions with an area of 100,000 m^2 (inclusive) or more.

For exhibitions in IAB, NEM, digital economy and other key industries specified by Guangzhou Municipal Government, the reward amount will increase 50%.

3. Supporting the stable development of large exhibitions

Exhibitions held in Guangzhou with an exhibition area of 50,000 m^2 or more and not in the incubation period will receive bonus for each session. Exhibitions with an area of 50,000 (inclusive) to 100,000 m^2 will receive an award of RMB 200,000; those with an area of 100,000 (inclusive) to 200,000 m^2 will be awarded RMB 400,000; those with an area of 200,000 (inclusive) to 300,000 m^2 will have a bonus of RMB 600,000; and those with an area of 300,000 m^2 (inclusive) or more will receive a financial support of RMB 800,000.

4. Encouraging the expansion of exhibitions

For exhibitions not in incubation period held in Guangzhou, if the exhibition area reaches 6,000 m^2 (inclusive) or more, and the increase of area

II. Industrial Support Policies

(I) Policies for trade in services and service outsourcing

1. Incentive policies

(1) For enterprises registered in Guangzhou, a maximum reward of RMB 1 million will be awarded to those reaching an annual revenue in service export (including offshore service outsourcing) and/or service import of USD 500,000 or more; the same amount of bonus will be awarded to businesses with an annual revenue in onshore service outsourting of USD 500,000 or more.

(2) An award of up to RMB 200,000 will be given to enterprises in Guangzhou undertaking nationally recognized honorable projects in trade in services and service outsourcing.

(3) A maximum of RMB 500,000 and RMB 300,000 will be awarded to newly recognized demonstrative enterprises and key cultivated enterprises in trade in services in Guangzhou respectively. A one-off award of up to RMB 200,000 will be given to enterprises that have been identified as key cultivated ones and are certified to have met the standards of demonstrative enterprises in trade in services.

(4) A bonus of up to RMB 50,000 will be given to enterprises in Guangzhou that have obtained international certification for trade in services and service outsourcing.

2. Taxation policies

(1) For enterprises registered in Guangzhou, the VAT on income derived from offshore service outsourcing business will be exempted.

(2) The enterprise income tax will be levied at a reduced rate of 15% for those certified as technologically advanced service enterprises; expenses by enterprises for employee education shall be deducted from the calculation of taxable income up to the amount of 8% of total wages and salaries, and any excess shall be allowed to be carried forward for deduction in subsequent tax years.

3. Headquarters policies

Financial incentives will be given to enterprises recognized as headquarters enterprises in Guangzhou in accordance with the Guangzhou headquarters economy policies.

4. Technology incentives

For pharmaceutical enterprises in Guangzhou that have imported economy progressing steadily; and new pillar industries, such as the next generation information and communication technology, intelligent and new energy vehicles, biomedicine and health industry, new materials, intelligent equipment and robotics, flourishing. In 2020, Guangzhou's airport passenger flow ranked first in the world, its seaports ranked fourth and fifth in cargo and container throughputs respectively, Guangzhou South Railway Station ranked first in passenger traffic among the country's railway hubs, and the Canton Fair Complex will soon be built as the world's largest exhibition complex.

I. Investment Environment and Business Development

In recent years, guided by Xi Jinping thought on socialism with Chinese characteristics for a new era and working towards the goal set by the Party Central Committee and the State Council to strengthen Guangzhou's role as an international commercial and trade center, Guangzhou has been actively promoting reform and development of the commercial sector, making every effort to stabilize foreign trade, foreign investment and promote consumption, and has achieved positive results. During the 13th Five-Year Plan period, Guangzhou's foreign trade leaped to over RMB one trillion for the first time; the actual use of foreign investment accumulated USD 32.83 billion, accounting for 30.4% of the total accumulation of all years; 309 Fortune Global 500 companies have invested in a total of 1,166 projects in Guangzhou accumulatively; the total retail sales of consumer goods have exceeded RMB 800 billion and 900 billion in succession. In the first quarter of this year, the city's import and export volume reached RMB 244.44 billion, an increase of 21.3%; the actual use of foreign investment was RMB 13.207 billion, an increase of 34.0%; the total retail sales of consumer goods were RMB 262.957 billion, an increase of 31.7%.

In recent years, Guangzhou's core competitiveness and international influence have grown significantly. Its economic strength has reached a new level, with the GDP exceeding RMB 2.5 trillion in 2020, a 2.7 % growth; GDP per capita reaching the level of that of high-income economies; fixed asset investment growing 10%, and export growing 3.2%. The concentration of key factors has significantly enhanced; the city was awarded the national benchmark city for business environment, and ranked first in the national government service index. All national capital markets have set up institutions in Guangzhou, and the Guangzhou Futures Exchange has been approved to be set up in Nansha. Guangzhou ranked second among the Top 100 Global Innovation Clusters, 21st in the Global Financial Centre Index and 13th in the International Shipping Center Development Index, and was listed as an Alpha city by GaWC. The innovation in science and technology has seen all-round acceleration: the number of high and new-tech enterprises has increased six-fold in five years, and the number of technological SMEs in the national pool has ranked first in China for three consecutive years. High-end industries are developing rapidly, with the added value of the strategic emerging industries accounting for 30% of regional GDP; the strategic engine project of artificial intelligence and digital

Chapter V
Business and Investment Guide

2. To improve the legal aid service, Guangzhou has published the English version of the *Guangzhou Legal Aid Service Guide* to help foreign nationals deal with daily legal matters.

China Council for the Promotion of International Trade, Guangdong Mediation Center of China Chamber of International Commerce
Address: 1F Guandong Huaxin Center,450 Huanshidong Lu, Guangzhou, Guangdong
Tel: 020-87617779
Fax: 020-87616497
Postcode:510075

(IV) Resolving commercial and maritime disputes through arbitration

Contract disputes and other property rights and interest disputes involving foreigners in China, including disputes arising from foreign-related economic and trade, transportation and maritime affairs, may be arbitrated. Disputes over marriage, adoption, guardianship, maintenance and inheritance shall be handled by administrative organs according to law. When the parties settle disputes by arbitration, they shall reach an arbitration agreement voluntarily. Arbitration adopts the system of final ruling. After the award is made, if the parties apply for re-arbitration or bring a lawsuit to the people's court for the same dispute, the Arbitration Commission or the people's court will not accept it.

Guangzhou Arbitration Commission
Address: 12-4F, Building C, Jiangwan Hotel, 298 Yanjiang Zhonglu, Yuexiu District, Guangzhou
Tel: 020-83287919
Website: http://www.gzac.org

(V) Innovating legal services

1. Using modern technologies such as big data, cloud computing and artificial intelligence, Guangzhou has innovated the "internet + public legal services", and launched free smart consultation and inquiry Applets such as "Guangzhou Micro Judicial Administration" "Ask a Lawyer" "Guangzhou Legal Aid", "YangChengHui Mediation" platform, "Guangzhou Smart Notary" platform, "Guangzhou Public Legal Service Chain" "Guangzhou FaShiTong Legal Service" and "Guangzhou Legal Service Map" for foreigners to make appointments for various public legal services and check their progress online anytime and anywhere.

(II) Legal aid

According to the relevant provisions of the *Criminal Procedure Law of the People's Republic of China*, for foreign and stateless criminal suspects and defendants who are blind, deaf or dumb, or mental patients who have not completely lost the ability to identify or control their behaviors and have not entrusted defenders; and foreign and stateless criminal suspects and defendants who may be sentenced to life imprisonment or death penalty and have not entrusted defenders, the people's courts, people's procuratorates and public security organs shall notify legal aid institutions to appoint lawyers to provide criminal defense for them. After receiving the notice, the legal aid institution will appoint lawyers to provide free legal aid services for criminal defense for the foreign or stateless criminal suspects or defendants. Documents and supporting materials to be submitted by the applicant are as follows:

1. Passport or other valid identity certificates, the proxy applicant shall also submit power of attorney proof;
2. Proof of family financial difficulty;
3. Case materials related to the legal aid matters applied for.

Guangzhou Legal Aid Center
Address: 42 Cangbian Lu, Yuexiu District, Guangzhou
Tel: 020-83562631

(III) Settling commercial and maritime disputes through mediation

In case of disputes in trade, investment, finance, securities, intellectual property rights, technology transfer, real estate, engineering project contracting, transportation, insurance and other commercial and maritime fields, mediation can be adopted on the basis of voluntariness of both parties to the dispute. Mediation shall be conducted in accordance with the provisions of the contract, laws, international practices and the principles of objectivity, impartiality, fairness and reasonableness, so as to promote mutual understanding and accommodation between the parties and reach a settlement. The Mediation Center of China Council for the Promotion of International Trade/China Chamber of International Commerce and its branches all have their own lists of mediators for the parties to designate in their cases.

VI. Legal Disputes

(I) Legal services

If foreign nationals, foreign enterprises and organizations need lawyers to provide non-litigation legal services in Guangzhou, they shall entrust lawyers with practicing licenses of lawyers of the People's Republic of China to represent them. The representative offices of foreign law firms in Guangzhou and their representatives can only engage in activities not involving Chinese legal affairs. If foreign nationals, foreign enterprises and organizations go to the people's court to sue or respond to lawsuits, they may entrust persons from their home country as agents ad litem, or they may entrust lawyers from their home country to act as agents ad litem as non-lawyers; If they need to entrust a lawyer to represent the lawsuit, they must entrust a lawyer of the People's Republic of China.

> **Guangzhou Lawyers Association**
> Address: 9F, South Tower, Yuexiu City Plaza, 437 Dongfeng Zhonglu, Yuexiu District, Guangzhou
> Tel: 020-83550600
> Website: http://www.gzlawyer.org
> Legal Service Office for Foreigners of Dengfeng Sub-district, Yuexiu District
> Address: 7-9 Tongxin Lu, Guangzhou
> Tel: 020-83508274

Panyu District, Guangzhou

T. Port and Maritime Brigade: 146 Guangma Dadao, Mayong Town, Dongguan

(2) Tel: 020-12345

(3) Office Hours:

Brigades numbered A-S open from Monday to Friday: 9:00-12:00, 13:00-17:00. Saturdays and Sundays are closed to the public, and legal holidays are scheduled in accordance with the notice of the State Council as other public institutions.

Brigade numbered T opens from Monday to Friday: 9:00-12:00, 13:00-17:00. Saturdays and Sundays are closed to the public, and legal holidays are scheduled according to the notice of the State Council as other public institutions.

2. Materials required for foreigners to accept handling of their road traffic violations recorded by traffic monitoring system

(1) The original identity certificates

The identity certificates of foreigners are passports or other travel documents held by them at the time of entry, valid visas or stay or residence certificates with a residence (stay) period of more than three months, and accommodation registration certificates issued by public security organs;

The identity certificates of members of foreign embassies and consulates in China and members of representative offices of international organizations in China are valid identity documents issued by the Ministry of Foreign Affairs.

(2) Original driving license

The driving license refers to the Motor Vehicle Driving License of the People's Republic of China;

Temporary Motor Vehicle Driving Permit, which shall be used simultaneously with the overseas motor vehicle driving license held by the driver and its Chinese translation document.

(3) Original vehicle license

The vehicle license refers to the Vehicle License of the People's Republic of China. If a person is unable to produce the vehicle license due to special reasons such as the license being detained as the person has violated Article 67 of the *Regulations on Traffic Safety of Guangdong Province*, or the person is subject to judicial decisions, etc., he or she shall produce relevant proof materials, which shall be accepted after verification by the police.

(4) Other materials

Relevant materials required by the traffic police brigade for investigation and evidence collection, which shall be provided by the driver, vehicle owner or manager. When the illegal act can be handled according to the general procedure, the parties shall also provide the valid certificate of compulsory liability insurance for traffic accidents of the vehicle when the illegal act occurs.

Chapter IV Safety Rules and Regulations

entry or the departing place of the vehicle as required, and accurately register their correspondence address and telephone number in Guangzhou. Foreigners who drive a motor vehicle in violation of regulations and are recorded by the electronic monitoring system, shall follow the procedure as informed after receiving the Notice of Violation on the spot or through post.

1. Contact information of traffic violation processing window of Guangzhou Traffic Police Brigade

(1) Address

A. Yuexiu Brigade (also handle road traffic violations of the former Liuhua Brigade and Dongshan Brigade): 127 Haoxian Lu, Yuexiu District, Guangzhou

B. Liwan Brigade (also handle road traffic violations of former Fangcun Brigade): 1 Xisaiba Lu, Fangcun Dadao Xi, Liwan District, Guangzhou

C. Haizhu Brigade: 195 Dunhe Lu, Haizhu District, Guangzhou

D. Tianhe Brigade: 6 Zhiyi Tangshi Lu, Tianhe District, Guangzhou

E. Baiyun First Brigade: 2F,1 Xisanxiang, Jingtaixi Jie, Guangyuanzhong Lu, Baiyun District, Guangzhou

F. Baiyun Second Brigade: 400, Xiahua 3 Lu, Baiyun District, Guangzhou

G. Patrol Brigade: 1725 Huaguan Lu, Tianhe District, Guangzhou

H. High-speed First Brigade: 461 Zengchu Lu, Baiyun District, Guangzhou

I. High-speed Second Brigade: 91 Guanglong Lu, Baiyun District, Guangzhou

J. High-speed Third Brigade: 1725 Huaguan Lu, Tianhe District, Guangzhou

K. Huancheng Brigade: 340 Zhiyi Guangyuan Xilu, Yuexiu District, Guangzhou

L. High-speed Fifth Brigade: 469 Guangxin Lu, Huangpu District, Guangzhou

M. Traffic Violation Processing Center (replace the former Motor Brigade to handle road traffic violations): 340, Guangyuan Xilu, Yuexiu District, Guangzhou

N. Huangpu Brigade: 3 Guangshan 4 Lu, Huangpu District, Guangzhou

O. Nansha Brigade: 107 Shi Nanlu, Dongchong Town, Nansha District, Guangzhou

P. Road Traffic Violation Centre of Zengcheng Brigade: 18 Gualv lU, Licheng Jie, Zengcheng District, Guangzhou

Q. Road Traffic Violation Centre of Conghua Brigade: 353 Qingyun Lu, Conghua District, Guangzhou

R. Road Traffic Violation Centre of Huadu Brigade: 10 Xinhua Lu, Shiling Town, Huadu District, Guangzhou

S. First Squadron of Panyu Brigade: 315 Donghuan Lu, Shiqiao Jie,

G. Trunk and neck: Applicants should have no impediment in their moving functions.

(VI) Handling motor vehicle insurance

Owners or managers of motor vehicles traveling on roads within the territory of China shall buy compulsory traffic accident liability insurance for motor vehicle according to law. For motor vehicles not covered by the compulsory insurance, the vehicle administration department shall not register them or issue motor vehicle inspection mark.

(VII) Handling traffic accidents

1. When a traffic accident occurs on the road that causes personal injury or death or damages to road, power supply or communication facilities, the driver shall immediately stop the vehicle and keep the scene intact;

2. If the accident causes casualties, the driver shall immediately rescue the injured persons. If the scene of the accident is changed due to rescue of the injured persons, the location of the scene shall be marked out clearly.

3. Where a traffic accident that occurs on the road does not cause casualties and the parties have no objections to the facts and causes of the accident, they shall evacuate the site after recording the time and place of the accident, the name and contact information of the other party, the motor vehicles' license plates, the drivers' license numbers, the insurance certificate numbers and the colliding parts and signing together, and negotiate the damage compensation by themselves. If the parties have objections to the facts and causes of the accident, they shall promptly report to the traffic police officer on duty or the traffic administrative department of the public security organ.

(VIII) Handling traffic violations

Foreign nationals who enter the country temporarily and wish to drive motor vehicles shall apply for a temporary driving permit from the vehicle administrative department of the public security organ at the place of entry or the place of origin to drive a motor vehicle, carry it with them and drive according to law. Foreigners who drive motor vehicles illegally in Guangzhou and are corrected or punished by the traffic police officer on the spot have the right to defend themselves after listening to the matters informed by the traffic police officer. The foreigners' translators should translate the matters informed to the foreign nationals on the spot. Those who are dissatisfied with the administrative punishment may bring an administrative reconsideration or administrative lawsuit according to law. Foreign vehicles temporarily entering the country shall apply for a Chinese temporary special license plate and a temporary vehicle license from the public security authorities in the area of who do not have a full deduction record in the corresponding scoring period, the minimum period of 5 years to have driving license for large bus after obtaining license for large goods vehicle will be shortened to 3 years, and for those who apply for driving license for tractor and medium-sized bus, the minimum period of 3 years after having driving license for large goods vehicle will be shortened to 2 years.

(4) Physical status:

A. Stature: The stature of applicants for the driving license of permitted models of large bus, tractor, city bus, large goods vehicle, or trolley bus shall be 155 cm or above. The stature of applicants for the driving license of permitted models of medium-sized bus shall be 150 cm or above;

B. Eyesight: The naked vision or corrected vision of both eyes of the applicants for the driving license of permitted models of large bus, tractor, city bus, medium-sized bus, large goods vehicle, trolley bus or tramcar shall reach 5.0 or above in the logarithmic visual acuity chart. The naked vision or corrected vision of both eyes of the applicants for the driving license of other permitted models of vehicle shall reach 4.9 or above in the logarithmic visual acuity chart. Those with monocular visual impairment, if the naked eye vision or corrected vision of the other eye reaches 5.0 or above in the logarithmic visual acuity chart, and its horizontal visual field reaches 150 degrees, they can apply for motor vehicle driving license for permitted models of small vehicle, small automatic shift vehicle, low-speed goods vehicle, three-wheeled car and small automatic passenger vehicle for the disabled;

C. Color discrimination: The applicants shall have no red-green color-blindness;

D. Audition: Applicants should be able to identify the direction of sound source when both ears are 50 cm from the tuning fork respectively. Those with hearing impairment but can meet the above conditions by wearing hearing aid equipment can apply for motor vehicle driving license of permitted models of small vehicle or small automatic shift vehicle;

E. Upper limbs: The applicants' both thumbs should be sound, either of their hands must have three other sound fingers, and the moving functions of their limbs and fingers should be normal. Those who have mutilated distal fingers or three sound fingers on the left hand but both palms are intact may apply for motor vehicle driving license for permitted models of small vehicle, small automatic shift vehicle, low-speed goods vehicle and three-wheeled car;

F. Lower limbs: The applicants' both lower limbs should be sound and their moving functions normal, the length difference of both lower limbs should not exceed 5 cm. Those who lose their left lower limbs or lose its moving functions may apply for motor vehicle driving license for permitted models of small automatic shift car;

a crime;

D. Those committing a crime in a major traffic accident after drinking or drunk driving a motor vehicle;

E. Those who have driven a motor vehicle under the influence of alcohol or driven a commercial motor vehicle after drinking and whose motor vehicle driving licenses have been revoked within five years;

F. Those who have drunk driven a commercial motor vehicle and whose driving licenses have been revoked according to law within ten years;

G. Those whose motor vehicle driving licenses have been revoked within two years due to other circumstances;

H. Those whose motor vehicle driving licenses were revoked within three years;

I. Other circumstances prescribed in laws and regulations.

Anyone who drives a motor vehicle without obtaining a motor vehicle driving license and commits one of the acts in Items E to G stated above shall not apply for a motor vehicle driving license within the prescribed time limit.

(3) Age conditions:

A. People aged between 18 and 70 are eligible to apply for the driving license of permitted models of small vehicle, small automatic shift vehicle, small automatic shift passenger vehicle for the disabled and light motorcycle; starting from November 20, 2020, the 70 years' upper age limit for the driving licenses for small vehicle, small automatic shift vehicle and light motorcycle is lifted, but people over 70 should receive additional tests in abilities such as memory, judgment and responsiveness when they take the driving test;

B. People aged between 18 and 60 are eligible to apply for the driving license of permitted models of low-speed goods vehicle, three-wheeled motor vehicle, common three-wheeled motorcycle, common two-wheeled motorcycle or wheeled automatic car;

C. People aged between 20 and 50 are eligible to apply for the driving license of permitted models of city bus, large goods vehicle, trolley bus or tramcar;

D. People aged between 21 and 50 are eligible to apply for the driving license of permitted models of medium-size bus;

E. People aged between 24 and 50 are eligible to apply for the driving license of permitted models of tractor;

F. People aged between 26 and 50 are eligible to apply for the driving license of permitted models of large bus;

Starting from November 20, 2020, the minimum age of drivers for licenses for large bus and tractor will be lowered from 26 and 24 respectively to 22, and the upper age limit for driving licenses for large and medium-sized buses and goods vehicles will be adjusted from 50 to 60. At the same time, the time interval for increasing types of vehicle driven will be shortened. For those

People's Republic of China issued by the Ministry of Foreign Affairs.

B. The Passport of the People's Republic of China is the entry and exit identification document for overseas Chinese.

C. The entry and exit identification documents of foreigners refer to their passports or other valid entry and exit certificates, valid visas or stay/residence certificates held at the time of entry. For those who are exempted for visa, their entry and exit identification documents shall be their passports or other valid entry and exit certificates held at the time of entry.

D. "Overseas motor vehicle driving license" refers to the license for qualification to drive motor vehicles alone issued by foreign countries, Hong Kong or Macao Special Administrative Region or Taiwan.

E. "Permitted Entry Period" refers to the permitted entry period endorsed on the entry and exit identity documents of temporary entrants.

F. Hong Kong, Macao and Taiwan residents who apply for a temporary driving permit with a Hong Kong, Macao or Taiwan Resident's Residence Permit do not need to provide their entry and exit identification documents.

G. When temporary entrants apply for a temporary driving permit or a temporarily-entering motor vehicle's license plate, if the overseas motor vehicle driving license and the motor vehicle registration certificate issued by the overseas competent department are not in Chinese, a Chinese translation document shall be provided.

H. The temporary motor vehicle driving permit shall be used together with the overseas motor vehicle driving license and its Chinese translation.

4. Relevant provisions

(1) Applicants holding an overseas motor vehicle driving license who apply for a motor vehicle driving license in China should take Subject One of the driving test. Applicants for driving license for large buses, tractors, city buses, medium-sized buses and large trucks should also take Subject Three.

Applications made by members of foreign embassies and consulates in China and representative offices of international organizations in China shall be handled under the principle of diplomatic reciprocity.

(2) Whoever is under any of the following circumstances shall not apply for a motor vehicle driving license:

A. Those with organic cardiopathy, epilepsy, Meniere's syndrome, vertigo, hysteria, parkinsonism, mental disease, aphrenia, or nervous system disease that affects the movement of limbs, or any other disease that impedes safe driving;

B. Those who have taken or injected drugs or been released from compulsory isolation and detoxification measures within three years, or have long-term addiction to dependent psychotropic substances and not been abstinent;

C. Those who escaped after causing a traffic accident and thus constituting

(4) Original and photocopy of the overseas motor vehicle driving license within the validity period (Chinese translation is required if it is in a foreign language).

(5) Four recent color bareheaded photos (size: 1 inch) at white background with the head taking about two-thirds of the photo's length.

(6) In addition to the above requirements, foreign consuls, consular staff and administrative staff in Guangzhou shall also provide the original and photocopy of their consular officer's certificate or civil servant's certificate, and the photocopy of their passport or its Chinese translation should bear the signature of the head of consulate and the official seal of consulate. The Notice for Handling Consular Vehicles Related Certificates issued by the Foreign Affairs Office of Guangdong Provincial People's Government shall also be provided.

Address: General Business Hall B, Vehicle Administration Office of Traffic Police Detachment of Guangzhou Public Security Bureau (1732 Huaguan Lu, Tianhe District, Guangzhou).

3. Temporary driving permit:

Applicable to motor vehicle drivers who temporarily enter the People's Republic of China

(1) Materials required for applying for a temporary driving permit:

A. Entry and exit identity document;

B. Overseas motor vehicle driving license. If it is not in Chinese, a Chinese translation shall also be provided;

C. Two recent color bareheaded photos (size: 1 inch) of the applicant at white background with the head taking about two-thirds of the photo's length.

(2) The validity period of the temporary driving permit. For temporary entrants who stay in China for a short time, the temporary driving permit is valid for three months; if the persons' residence/stay period exceeds 3 months, the validity period of the temporary driving permit shall be consistent with the permitted residence/stay period, but not exceed one year; the temporary driving permit can be used for multiple times without re-application if the persons enter China repeatedly within the validity period.

(3) Time limit. Upon receipt of the application materials, the examination will be conducted on the same day. If the application meets the requirements, the temporary motor vehicle driving permit will be issued on the same day after providing three hours' training on road traffic safety laws and regulations to the applicant.

(4) Other information

A. The entry and exit identity documents of Hong Kong, Macao and Taiwan residents are Mainland Travel Permit for Hong Kong and Macau Residents, Mainland Travel Permit for Taiwan Residents or Travel Permit of the

1. Materials required for foreign nationals without overseas driving license to apply for Chinese driving license for the first time:

(1) Fill out the Motor Vehicle Driving License Application Form (provided by the driving training school).

(2) The original and photocopy of the applicant's identity certificate. The identity certificates of foreign nationals are passports or other travel documents held by them at the time of entry, valid visas or residence permits with a residence (stay) period of more than three months, or the Foreign Permanent Resident ID Card of the People's Republic of China, as well as accommodation registration certificates issued by public security organs. The identity certificates of the personnel of foreign embassies and consulates in China and the personnel of representative offices of international organizations in China are valid identity documents issued by the Ministry of Foreign Affairs.

(3) Provide the Certificate of Motor Vehicle Driver's Physical Conditions from a qualified medical institution at county level or above, or a military medical institution at or above regiment level.

(4) Four recent color bareheaded photos (size: 1 inch) at white background with the head taking about two-thirds of the photo's length.

[Note] Applicants should be trained in a driving school. The driving schools shall go to the Vehicle Administration Office of the Traffic Police Detachment of Guangzhou Public Security Bureau (1732 Huaguan Lu, Tianhe District, Guangzhou) to handle relevant procedure.

2. Materials required for foreign nationals who apply to convert their driving license of their home country to a Chinese one:

(1) Motor Vehicle Driving License Application Form (provided by the Vehicle Administration Office, no need to fill out).

(2) The original and photocopy of the applicant's identity certificate. The identity certificates of foreign nationals are passports or other travel documents held by them at the time of entry, valid visas or residence permits with a residence (stay) period of more than three months, or the Foreign Permanent Resident ID Card of the People's Republic of China, as well as accommodation registration certificates issued by public security organs. The identity certificates of the personnel of foreign embassies and consulates in China and the personnel of representative offices of international organizations in China are valid identity documents issued by the Ministry of Foreign Affairs.

(3) The Certificate of Motor Vehicle Driver's Physical Conditions from a qualified medical institution at county level or above, or a military medical institution at or above regiment level (if applicants are members of foreign embassies or consulates in China or representative offices of international organizations in China, their Certificate of Motor Vehicle Driver's Physical Conditions will not be examined).

Guangzhou (Driving test ground)
Address: Dongbian Cun, Furong Dadao, Huadu District, Guangzhou (Vehicle Administration)

Nansha Vehicle Administration Office
Address: 513 Guangzhu Lu, Hengli Town, Nansha District, Guangzhou

Zengcheng Vehicle Administration Office
Address: 1 Zhucun Dadao Dong, Zhucun Jie, Zengcheng District, Guangzhou (Integrated vehicle management services, Vehicle Administration and Subject1 Examination Place)

Conghua Vehicle Administration Office
Address:106Huanshidong Lu,ConghuaDistrict, Guangzhou
Address: 353 Qingyun Lu, ConghuaDistrict, Guangzhou (Integrated vehicle management services)
Address: Hengkeng Cun, Aotou Town, ConghuaDistrict, Guangzhou (Driving test GroGunuadn)gzhou Public Security Bureau: 110Inquiry and Complaint

Inquiry and Complaint
Guangzhou Public Security Bureau: 110
Traffic Police Detachment of Guangzhou Public Security Bureau: 020-83118400
Vehicle Administration Department of Traffic Police Detachment of Guangzhou Public Security Bureau: 020-12345

(V) Applying for motor vehicle driving license

Foreign nationals applying for motor vehicle driver's license shall meet the requirements for driver's license specified by the department for public security under the State Council; and after passing the examination, the applicant shall be issued by the traffic control department of the public security organ the driver's license commensurate with the type of the motor vehicle.

Foreign nationals holding a motor vehicle driver's license of another country who meet the requirements for driver's license specified by the department for public security under the State Council and pass the examination by the traffic control department of the public security organ shall be issued a Chinese motor vehicle driver's license.

registration certificate issued by public security organs.

3. The identity certificates of personnel of foreign embassies, consulates and representative offices of international organizations in China are valid proof of identity issued by the Ministry of Foreign Affairs.

The motor vehicle origin certificate refers to the national unified invoice for motor vehicle sales or used car transaction if it is purchased in China. If purchased abroad, the origin certificate is the sales invoice issued by the sales organization of the motor vehicle and its translation, but the origin certificate is not required for the motor vehicles under customs supervision.

List of Guangzhou Vehicle Administration Office

CencunHeadquarter
Address: 1732HuaguanLu, Cencun, Tianhe District, Guangzhou

Tianhe VehicleAdministration Sub-station
Address: 1732 Huaguan Lu, Cencun, Tianhe District, Guangzhou

Yuexiu VehicleAdministration Sub-station
Address: 34 Chengang Lu,Liwan District, Guangzhou

Liwan VehicleAdministration Sub-station
Address: 563 Fangcun Dadao West, Liwan District, Guangzhou

Hualong VehicleAdministration Sub-station
Address: 18 Chuangzhan Dadao, Hualong Town, Huangpu District, Guangzhou

Baiyun VehicleAdministration Sub-station
Address: 97 Helongsi Lu, Taihe Town, Baiyun District, Guangzhou

Panyu Vehicle Administration Office
Address: 500 Yayun Dadao, Panyu District, Guangzhou (Integrated vehicle management services)
Address:359 Fubei Lu, Fuyong Cun, Shawan Town, Panyu District, Guangzhou (Vehicle Administration and Driving Test Ground)

HuaduVehicle Administration Office
Address: 101 Tiantui Lu, Huadu District, Guangzhou
Address: Mingzhu cun, Sijiao Wei, Tanbu Town, Huadu District,

customer service number: 12580, Telecom customer service number: 114) to make an appointment.

2. Required materials

(1) Application Form of Vehicle Registration, Transferring, Cancellation Registration/ Transferring;

(2) Original and photocopied identity certificate of vehicle owner;

(3) Original certificate of vehicle source;

(4) The original third page of compulsory vehicle insurance certificate of traffic accident. If the original is lost, the photocopy of any other page affixed official seal of insurance company or the reissue certificate provided by insurance company could be accepted;

(5) Original quality certificate of whole China-made vehicle; original import certificate of imported vehicle; original chassis quality certificate;

(6) Tax Payment Certificate of Tax on Buying Vehicles or tax exemption certificate;

(7) Original Vehicle Examination Record issued by the police after confirming the vehicle;

(8) Permit for Quota of the Fixed Vehicle Allocation shall be provided if governments, enterprises or institutions purchase buses under 19 seats (including 19 seats); Original and photocopy of Capital Verification Report shall be provided if wholly foreign-owned enterprises, Sino-foreign joint ventures, collective enterprises or private-owned enterprises purchase buses under 19 seats (including 19 seats);

(9) Vehicle and vessel tax payment or tax exemption certificate;

(10) Small and medium-sized vehicles shall also submit the certificate of quota for the small and medium-sized vehicles in Guangzhou;

(11) Ambulance, fire engine and engineering emergency vehicles shall provide Certificate of Vehicle Using Character issued by local administration at county level or above. Other vehicle using character can be reported by the vehicle owner on his/her freewill;

(12) Original and photocopy of other certificates shall be provided according to concerning laws and regulations.

Proof of identity means:

1. The identity certificates of foreign embassies and consulates in China, foreign offices in China and representative offices of international organizations in China are the certificates issued by the embassies and consulates or the offices and representative offices and the identity documents of relevant personnel.

2. The identify certificate of foreigners refers to their passports or other travel documents held at the time of entry (notarized translation in Chinese is required for registration in a foreign language), valid visa or residence permit with residence (stay) period of more than six months, and accommodation

sure there is no vehicle approaching before getting out. Do not stay on the motorway after getting off, walk to the sidewalk immediately.

7. When taking a car, passengers should fasten their seat belts, do not put their heads or hands out of the car, do not throw objects out of the window, watch for other vehicles when opening the door and getting off the car, and do not stop or get off within 50 meters to intersections or on forbidden sections.

(IV) Registration of motor vehicles

1. Relevant provisions

(1) The country applies a system of registration to motor vehicles. A motor vehicle is not allowed to run on road until it has been registered by the traffic administrative department of the public security organ.

(2) To apply for a motor vehicle license plate or a vehicle license for the first time, the motor vehicle owner shall apply for initial registration to the vehicle management station at the place of his domicile.

(3) The vehicle applies to be registered should meet the regulations on discharge standard of vehicle pollutant stipulated by Guangzhou Municipality and the state.

(4) There are five ways to determine the vehicle number: 1) use the original vehicle number; 2) selected by computer automatically; 3) selected or compiled by the vehicle owner according to vehicle number standard regulations (only valid for small-scale automobiles); 4) issue the small-scale automobile number by bidding; 5) pre-selected online.

(5) Imported vehicle, dangerous chemical materials transportation vehicle, school bus or medium-scale bus or above should only be registered in the sub-stations or service stations of vehicle registration in urban area of Guangzhou city. Small and micro-scale passenger vehicles can only be registered in the sub-stations or service stations of vehicle registration in urban area of Guangzhou city or in Zengcheng, Huadu and Panyu.

(6) The agent who applies for vehicle registration or other affairs shall provide the identity certificate and the written power of attorney of the vehicle owner.

(7) The application for registration of small and medium-sized passenger cars shall also comply with the relevant provisions of the *Measures for the Control and Management of the Total Volume of Small and Medium-sized Passenger Cars in Guangzhou*.

(8) Those who apply for registration of small and medium buses should first apply through the Online Traffic Management Office (www.gzjd.gov.cn/cgs), mobile APP (China Mobile users - Guangzhou JingMinTong, Unicom users - Wo JingMinTong, Telecom user - Tianyi JingMinTong) or customer service hotlines (Unicom customer service number: 116114, China Mobile

lane, always try to drive on the right side of the road and do not enter the motor vehicle lane.

2. On roads with signs prohibiting non-motorized traffic, cyclists shall get off their bikes/electric bikes and walk them on the sidewalk.

3. When crossing a road, cyclists shall strictly follow the rule of "stop on red, go on green", pass according to the traffic lights on the sidewalk, get off the bike/electric bikes and push them on the pedestrian crossing.

4. At intersections with crosswalk, cyclists shall pass according to the traffic lights of the motor vehicle lane and always try to stay at the right side of the motor vehicle lane.

5. Slow down, look backward, stretch out your hand and signal before turning at the intersection, do not compete for the road or make a sharp turn.

6. If the road is fenced by guardrails, cyclists shall follow the traffic signs and push the bike/electric bike through the pedestrian tunnel or overpass.

7. When riding a non-motor vehicle, one shall not carry goods exceeding the prescribed size and weight, and shall not take passengers on urban roads. Notes: Pedestrians and non-motor vehicle drivers who violate road traffic safety regulations can be fined up to RMB 50; those who refuse to accept the fine punishment may have their non-motor vehicles detained; those who obstruct police officers from performing official duties may be sentenced to administrative detention for less than 15 days according to law. If the circumstances are serious, they shall be investigated for criminal responsibility.

(III) General knowledge of safe travel on foot and by car

1. At intersections with crosswalks and traffic lights, pedestrians shall strictly follow the rule of "stop on red, go on green". When crossing the road, use the crosswalk, do not cross the fencing guardrail. It is strictly forbidden to run a red light or cross the road indiscriminately.

2. When the green light is on, pedestrians should quickly pass the crosswalk. If they have not entered the crosswalk when the green light flashes, they should stay and wait at the roadside or on the safety island.

3. When crossing the road at intersections with no crosswalk, pedestrians should watch traffic from both directions and pass quickly when safe.

4. When the road is fenced with guardrail, pedestrians shall pass through the pedestrian tunnel or overpass as indicated by the traffic signs.

5. When taking a bus, passengers should wait at the bus stop, do not stand on the bus lane. When the bus has stopped steadily, get on in turn. When taking a taxi, do not hail a taxi in a place or lane where taxi parking is prohibited. After the taxi has stopped steadily, get on from the right.

6. When getting off a car, passengers should look behind the car and make

V. Traffic Laws and Regulations

(I) Traffic safety codes to be observed when driving a motor vehicle

1. The driver of motor vehicles shall hold a valid motor vehicle driving license issued by the traffic administrative department of the public security organ.

2. It is forbidden to use altered, forged, misappropriated or fraudulently obtained motor vehicle license plate, driving license, pass or other traffic management certificates.

3. No motor vehicles with incomplete license plates or illegible words/numbers on the license plates caused by coverage or defacement are allowed to be driven.

4. When driving a motor vehicle, the driver shall not answer or make mobile phone calls or check on the mobile phone, and shall not throw objects out of the vehicle to affect traffic safety.

5. No use of invalid documents related to traffic management is allowed.

6. No temporary parking on road sections with no-parking signs; in case of temporary parking on non-forbidden sections, drivers shall not leave the cab, and shall not affect the traffic or impede traffic safety. If there is a police officer on site, obey the command of the police officer.

7. No motor vehicle driving training on roads.

8. Avoid buses and trolley buses entering and departing from the station.

9. Equip motor vehicles with effective fire extinguishing tools.

10. Abide by other traffic safety laws and regulations of governments of various levels of the People's Republic of China.

Guangzhou has banned motorcycles from roads in the urban area, but the number of other motor vehicles is still increasing and traffic congestion is inevitable between 7:00-9:00 am and 5:00-8:00 pm. Therefore, foreign nationals are advised to familiarize themselves with the complex road conditions before driving on their own and try to use public transportation such as taxi or metro during rush hours.

(II) General knowledge of safe travel by non-motor vehicles

1. Non-motor vehicles shall take the non-motor vehicle lane and do not go beyond the parking line when parking; on roads without non-motor vehicle

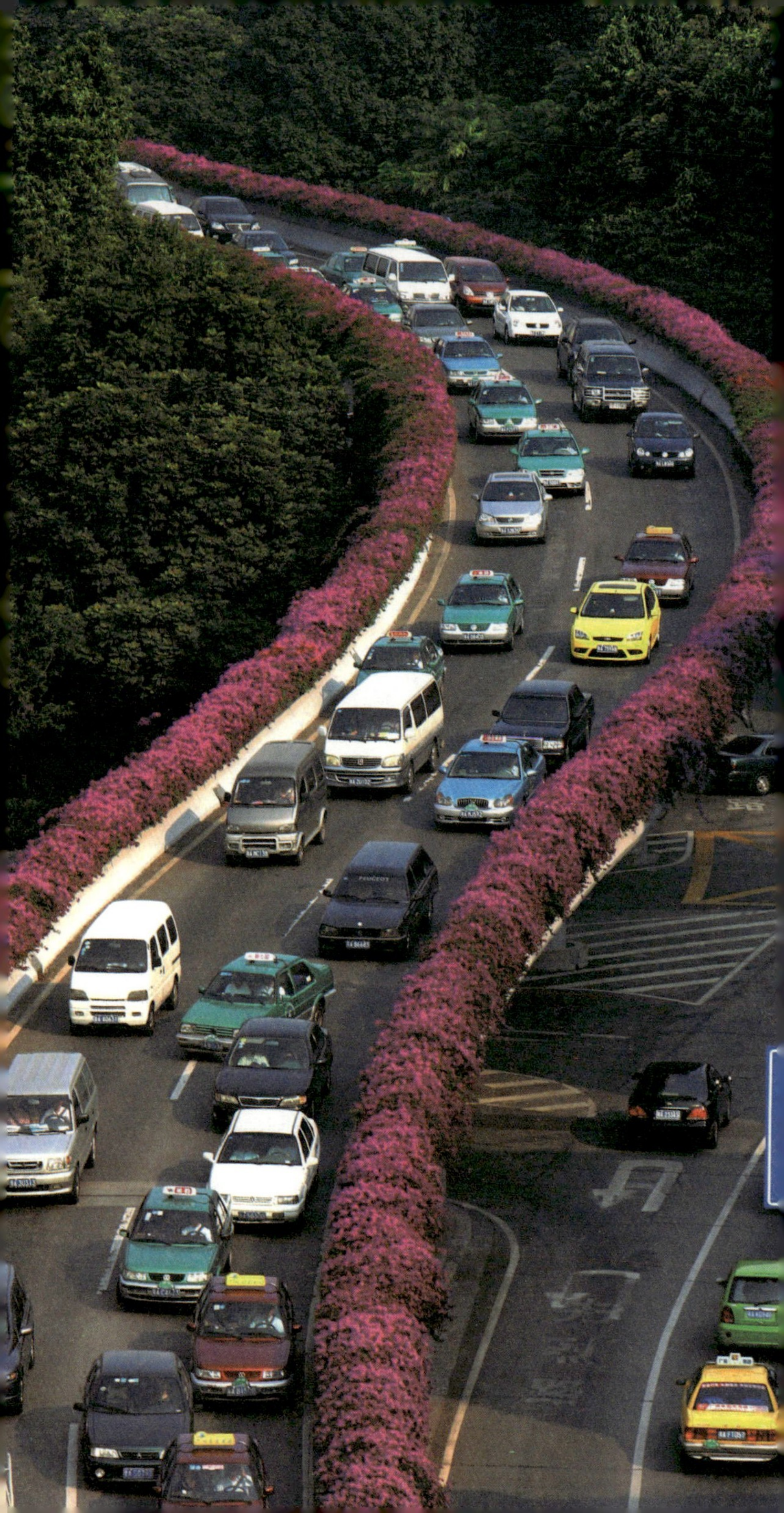

Chapter IV Safety Rules and Regulations

Tax Item		Taxable Unit	Applicable Tax Amount (yuan / year)	Note
Motorcycles		per vehicle	36	
Vessels	Motorized Vessels	Net tonnage ≤ 200 tons per ton	3	
		Net tonnage 201 tons - 2000 tons per ton	4	
		Net tonnage 2,001 tons - 10,000 tons per ton	5	
		Net tonnage ≥ 10,001 tons per ton	6	Tugboats, non-motorized barges are calculated in accordance with 50% of the tax on motorized vessels
	Yachts	Length ≤ 10 meters per meter	600	Length means the total length of the yacht
		Length 11-18 meters per meter	900	
		Length 19-30 meters per meter	1300	
		Length ≥ 31 meters per meter	2000	
	Auxiliary power sailing	per meter	600	

2. Vehicles & Vessels of the foreign embassies and consulates in China, the representative institutions of international organizations in China and their personnel, shall be exempted from tax in accordance with the relevant provisions of law.

3. The places for vehicle and vessel tax payment shall be the places where Vehicles & Vessels have been registered or the withholding agents for vehicle and vessel tax are located. With respect to any Vehicles & Vessels that are not required to be registered, the places for vehicle and vessel tax payment shall be the places where the owners or managers of such Vehicles & Vessels are located.

4. The time when the taxpayer undertakes vehicle and vessel tax liability is the month when the ownership or right to management of Vehicles & Vessels is obtained.

5. The vehicle and vessel tax is declared annually, calculated monthly and paid one-off. The tax year is from January 1 to December 31.

IV. Vehicles and Vessels Tax

1. Within the territory of the People's Republic of China, the owners or managers of vehicles and vessels as prescribed in the Schedule of Vehicle and Vessel Tax Items and Amounts shall be the payers of vehicle and vessel tax, who shall pay vehicle and vessel tax in accordance with the law.

Schedule of Vehicle and Vessel Tax Items and Amounts in Guangdong Province (effective from 2018)

Tax Item		Taxable Unit	Applicable Tax Amount (yuan / year)	Note
Passenger Cars [according to the engine cylinder capacity (exhaust volume) grade]	10 liters (inclusive) below	per vehicle	60	Authorized number of passengers: 9 people (inclusive) or less
	10 liters to 1 6 liters (inclusive)		300	
	16 liters to 20 liters (inclusive)		360	
	20 liters to 25 liters (inclusive)		660	
	25 liters to 30 liters (inclusive)		1200	
	30 liters to 40 liters (inclusive)		2400	
	40 liters or more		3600	
Commercial Vehicles	Medium-sized buses (approved to carry 10-19 passengers)	per vehicle	480	Authorized number of passengers: 9 people or more, including trams
	Large buses (approved to carry ≥ 20 passengers)		510	
	Lorry	Curb weight per ton	16	Including semi-trailer tractors, three-wheeled vehicles and low-speed cargo vehicles, etc.
Trailer		Curb weight per ton	8	
Other Vehicles	Specialized work vehicles	Curb weight per ton	16	Excluding tractors
	Wheeled special machinery vehicles		16	

(IV) Declaration methods of individual income tax

Table 5 Declaration Methods

Income Items	Resident Individuals	Non-resident Individuals	
Income from salary and wages, income from remuneration for personal services, income from royalties, and income from author's remuneration	Comprehensive Income	Where the individual income tax is calculated on an annual basis and there is a withholding agent, the withholding agent shall withhold and prepay tax on a monthly basis or when the taxable income arises. If the income is subject to tax reconciliation return, the tax payer shall handle the tax reconciliation return at the end of the year.	Where the individual income tax is calculated on a monthly basis, or when taxable income arises, the withholding agent shall withhold and pay tax. Reconciliation return is not required. Where a non-resident individual obtains salary and wages from two or more sources within China, he shall declare such income on his own.
Income from interest, dividends or bonuses, income from the lease of property, income from the conveyance of property, or contingent income		On a monthly basis or when the taxable income arises, the withholding agent shall withhold and pay the tax in full for all its employees in according with the provisions of the law. Where the withholding agent has failed to withhold and pay tax, the taxpayer shall make the tax declaration before June 30 of the year following that in which the income was obtained. Where the tax authorities specify a time limit for tax payment, the taxpayer shall pay the tax within the given time.	
Income from business operation		The individual income tax shall be calculated on an annual basis, be pre-paid on a monthly (quarterly) basis, and the reconciliation return be handled after the end of the year.	

In any of the following circumstances, taxpayers shall make the tax declaration in accordance with the law:

1. Where the taxpayer obtains comprehensive income for which the annual tax reconciliation return is required;

2. Where the taxpayer obtains taxable income but there is no withholding agent;

3. Where the taxpayer obtains taxable income but the withholding agents has failed to withhold and pay the tax;

4. Where the taxpayer obtains income from overseas;

5. Where the taxpayer emigrates to another country and cancels his Chinese household registration;

6. Where a non-resident individual obtains salary and wages from two or more sources within China;

Taxpayers can use the mobile APP for individual income tax or the WEB terminal of the Electronic Tax Bureau for Natural Persons to make the declaration, or use postal declaration, or visit the tax service center to handle the declaration.

expenses, advertising expenses, necessary social expenses for business operations), living allowance (housing expenses, travel expenses), where the above-mentioned incomes can be clearly classified, then only income obtained from salary and wages is subject to individual income tax in accordance with the regulations.

3. Tax benefits for dividends

The incomes gained by individual foreigners (including Hong Kong, Macao and Taiwan compatriots) from dividends and bonuses of foreign-invested enterprises are exempted from individual income tax.

4. Tax exemptions for foreign experts' wage and salary income

The wage and salary incomes gained by foreign experts (including Hong Kong, Macao and Taiwan compatriots) who conform with one of the following conditions may be exempt from individual income tax:

(1) Foreign experts directly sent by the World Bank to work in China in accordance with a special loan agreement;

(2) Experts directly sent by the United Nations' Organizations to work in China;

(3) Experts coming to work in China for the UN aid projects;

(4) Experts sent by an aid-granting country to China to work specially for the project granted gratis by the country;

(5) Cultural and educational experts coming to China to work for up to two years on the cultural exchange project under an agreement signed between two governments, with their wages and salaries being borne by the country concerned;

(6) Cultural and educational experts coming to China to work for up to two years on the international exchange projects of China's universities and colleges, with their wages and salaries being borne by the country concerned;

(7) Experts coming to work in China through a non-government scientific research agreement, with their wages and salaries being borne by the government organization of the country concerned.

5. Tax exemptions for income from stock transfer

Starting from November 17, 2014, the income of individual investors in the Hong Kong market derived from the transfer difference obtained from investing in A shares listed on the Shanghai Stock Exchange is temporarily exempted from individual income tax; Starting from December 5, 2016, the income of individual investors in the Hong Kong market derived from the transfer difference obtained from investing in A shares listed on the Shenzhen Stock Exchange is temporarily exempted from individual income tax.

Starting from December 18, 2015, the income of individual investors in the Hong Kong market derived from the transfer difference between the shares of Chinese mainland funds bought and sold through mutual recognition of funds is temporarily exempted from individual income tax.

(6) The six subsidies enjoyed by foreigners residing in Hong Kong or Macao for family reasons prescribed as special circumstances.

Starting from January 1, 2004, with regard to the foreign individuals hired by enterprises within China (excluding individual residents of Hong Kong or Macao) who live in Hong Kong or Macao for family or any other reason, come and go between the Mainland and Hong Kong or Macao, the housing, food, laundry and move subsidies given to them by the enterprises within China (including their connected enterprises) in non-cash form or in the form of actual reimbursement for actual costs may, if supported by valid voucher, and upon examination and confirmation of the competent tax organ, be exempted. With respect to the subsidies obtained by any of the foreign individuals as mentioned above for the expenses of his (her) language training and children education in Hong Kong or Macao, if they can provide valid payment voucher and other materials, the subsidies determined as reasonable by the competent tax organ upon examination and confirmation shall be exempted from the individual income tax.

From January 1, 2019 to December 31, 2021, foreign individuals who meet the criteria of resident individuals can enjoy the special additional deduction of personal income tax; or according to the provisions of the preferential tax policies, they can enjoy the subsidies and tax exemptions such as housing allowance, language training fees, children's education fees. They can choose to enjoy either of the above two policies. Once selected, it cannot be changed within a tax year. From January 1, 2022, foreign individuals will no longer enjoy subsidies and tax exemptions such as housing allowance, language training fees, children's education fees, and shall enjoy special additional deductions in accordance with the regulations.

2. Lump sums paid by foreign employers

For foreign staff coming to China with a lump sum paid by their foreign employers, which includes personal salary, public expenses (postage, office

Income from business operation is subject to a five-grade progressive tax rates in excess of specific amount ranging from 5% to 35%.

Table 4 Tax Rates for Income from Business Operation

Grade	Annual Taxable Income (RMB)	Tax Rate (%)	Quick Deduction Amount (RMB)
1	The portion under 30,000 (inclusive) ≤30,000	5	0
2	The portion between 30,000 and 90,000 (inclusive) 30,000-90,000	10	1500
3	The portion between 90,000 and 300,000 (inclusive) 90,000-300,000	20	10 500
4	The portion between 300,000 and 500,000 (inclusive) 300,000-500,000	30	40 500
5	The portion above 500,000 >500,000	35	65 500

3. Interest, dividend and bonus income, property leasing income, property transfer income and incidental income are subject to a proportional tax rate of 20%.

(III) Tax benefits for foreigners

1. Tax exemptions for foreign individuals' allowances and subsidies

The following allowances and subsidies obtained by foreign individuals (including Hong Kong, Macao and Taiwan compatriots) are exempted from personal income tax presently:

(1) Housing subsidies, food allowances, moving fees and laundry fees gained by foreign individuals in the non-cash form or in the form of being reimbursed for what they spend;

(2) Relocation expenses obtained in the form of actual reimbursement for actual costs in connection with employment or dis-employment in China, excluding monthly or regular payments made by the employer to the foreign employee in the name of relocation expenses;

(3) Allowances for business travelling at home and abroad gained with reasonable standards;

(4) Family visiting expense within a reasonable amount, which is defined as only the cost of transportation between the individual's place of employment in China and his or her home location (including the residence of spouse or parents) for not more than twice a year;

(5) The portion of language training fees and children's education fees occurred in China that is considered reasonable;

(II) Individual Income Tax Rates

In China, different taxable income items are subject to different individual income tax rates. 1. The seven-grade progressive tax rates in excess of specific amount ranging from 3% to 45% are applicable for comprehensive income.

Table 2 Annual Tax Rate for Comprehensive Income
(applicable to resident individuals)

Grade	Annual Taxable Income (RMB)	Tax Rate (%)	Quick Deduction Amount (RMB)
1	The portion under 36,000 (inclusive) ≤36,000	3	0
2	The portion between 36,000 and 144,000 (inclusive) 36,000-144,000	10	2520
3	The portion between 144,000 and 300,000 (inclusive) 144,000-300,000	20	16 920
4	The portion between 300,000 and 420,000 (inclusive) 300,000-420,000	25	31 920
5	The portion between 420,000 and 660,000 (inclusive) 420,000-660,000	30	52 920
6	The portion between 660,000 and 960,000 (inclusive) 660,000-960,000	35	85 920
7	The portion above 960,000 >960,000	45	181 920

Table 3 Monthly Converted Comprehensive Income Tax Rates
(applicable to non-resident individuals)

Grade	Monthly Taxable Income (RMB)	Tax Rate (%)	Quick Deduction Amount (RMB)
1	The portion under 3,000 (inclusive) ≤3,000	3	0
2	The portion between 3,000 and 12,000 (inclusive) 3,000-12,000	10	210
3	The portion between 12,000 and 25,000 (inclusive) 12,000-25,000	20	1410
4	The portion between 25,000 and 35,000 (inclusive) 25,000-35,000	25	2660
5	The portion between 35,000 and 55,000 (inclusive) 35,000-55,000	30	4410
6	The portion between 55,000 and 80,000 (inclusive) 55,000-80,000	35	7160
7	The portion above 80,000 >80,000	45	15 160

Income Items	Scope
(2) Income from remuneration for personal services	Income obtained by individuals from personal services incluldeing income from design, decoration, installation, mapping, chemical examination, testing, medical treatment, law, accounting, consulting, lecturing, translation, proof-reading, painting and calligraphy, sculpture, film and television, audio and video recording, performance, advertisement, exhibition, technical service, go-between service, brokerage, agency service and other labor services.
(3) Income from author's remuneration	Income obtained by individuals from written workers after publication in books, newspapers or other forms.
(4) Income from royalties	Income obtained by individuals from providing patent rights, trademark rights, copyrights, rights to use non-patented technologies and rights to use other proprietary rights. Income from providing copyright rights does not include income from author's remuneration.
(5) Income from business operation	1. Income from production and business operations by individual households engaging in industry and commercial activity, and income of owners and investors in sole proprietorships and individual partners of partnership enterprises derived from the production and business activities of sole proprietorships and partnerships registered inside China; 2. Income obtained by individuals from running schools or providing medical treatment, consulting or other paid services; 3. Income obtained by individuals from the contracted operation and leased operation of enterprises and public institutions and subcontracting and subleasing; 4. Income obtained by individuals from engaging in other production and business activities.
(6) Income from interest, dividends or bonuses	The income of interest, dividends and bonuses obtained by individuals from their ownership of creditor's rights and equities.
(7) Income from the lease of property	Income obtained by individuals from leasing of their real estate, machinery and equipment, motor vehicles and ships and other property.
(8) Income from the conveyance of property	Income obtained by individuals from transfer of negotiable securities, equities, property shares in partnership enterprises, real estate, machinery and equipment, motor vehicles and ships and other property.
(9) Contingent income	Income obtained by individuals from getting awards, winning prizes in lotteries and other windfalls.

For forms of income (1) through (4) in the preceding table (hereinafter collectively referred to as "Comprehensive Income") earned by a resident individual, they shall be aggregated on a tax year basis to calculate the individual income tax payable while the same earned by a non-resident individual shall be calculated separately on a monthly or transaction basis. For forms of income (5) through (9) in the preceding table, the individual income tax payable shall be calculated separately pursuant to the provisions of *Individual Income Tax Law*.

III. Individual Income Tax

The individual income tax shall be paid by the income earner, i.e. the individual who has the direct tax obligation according to the tax law.

Taxpayers are divided into resident individuals and non-resident individuals, who bear different tax obligations. An individual who is domiciled in China, or an individual who is not domiciled in China but has resided in China for an aggregate of 183 days or more within a tax year, shall be regarded as a resident individual. Income received by a resident individual from within China or overseas shall be subject to individual income tax. However, if an individual who is not domiciled in China has resided in China for less than six consecutive years during which he or she has resided for an aggregate of 183 days or more every year, he or she is exempt from individual income tax on income derived from outside China and paid by an entity or individual outside China, upon filing with the competent tax authority.

An individual who is not domiciled in China and does not reside in China, or an individual who is not domiciled in China but has resided in China for less than an accumulated 183 days within a tax year, shall be regarded as a non-resident individual. Income received by a non-resident individual from within China shall be subject to individual income tax. However, if an individual who is not domiciled in China resides in China for not more than 90 days in a tax year, the portion of his or her income derived from within China that is paid by an overseas employer and is not borne by this employer's institution or site in China is exempt from individual income tax.

(I) Incomes subject to individual income tax

Individual Income Tax Law and its Implementation Regulations stipulate the nine forms of income and the corresponding scope of individual income tax. Individuals shall calculate and pay individual income tax according to the corresponding requirements when they obtain these incomes.

Table 1 Scope of Income Items

Income Items	Scope
(1) Income from salary and wages	Income obtained by individuals from wages, salaries, bonuses, year-end salary bonuses, labor dividends, allowances, subsidies and other income from their job or related to their employment

II. Tax Payment and Exemption

The Guangzhou Municipal Taxation Bureau of the State Administration of Taxation are responsible for the implementation of the laws, regulations, rules and mandatory documents on taxation, social security fees and related non-tax revenues, execution of tax preferential policies stipulated by the State, and the collection and management of taxes, social security fees and related non-tax revenues in the area under its jurisdiction.

Foreigners who set up enterprises in Guangzhou shall go to the tax authorities for taxpayer identity information confirmation or taxpayer (withholding agent) identity information reporting when engaging in production and operation or when tax-related matters occur. Enterprises that have received business license containing unified social credit code can use the business license in the place of tax registration certificate, with no need to register for taxation or collect tax registration certificate.

> **The Guangzhou Municipal Taxation Bureau of the State Administration of Taxation**
> Tel: 020-12366
> Website: http://guangdong.chinatax.gov.cn/gdsw/gzsw/gzsw_index.shtml

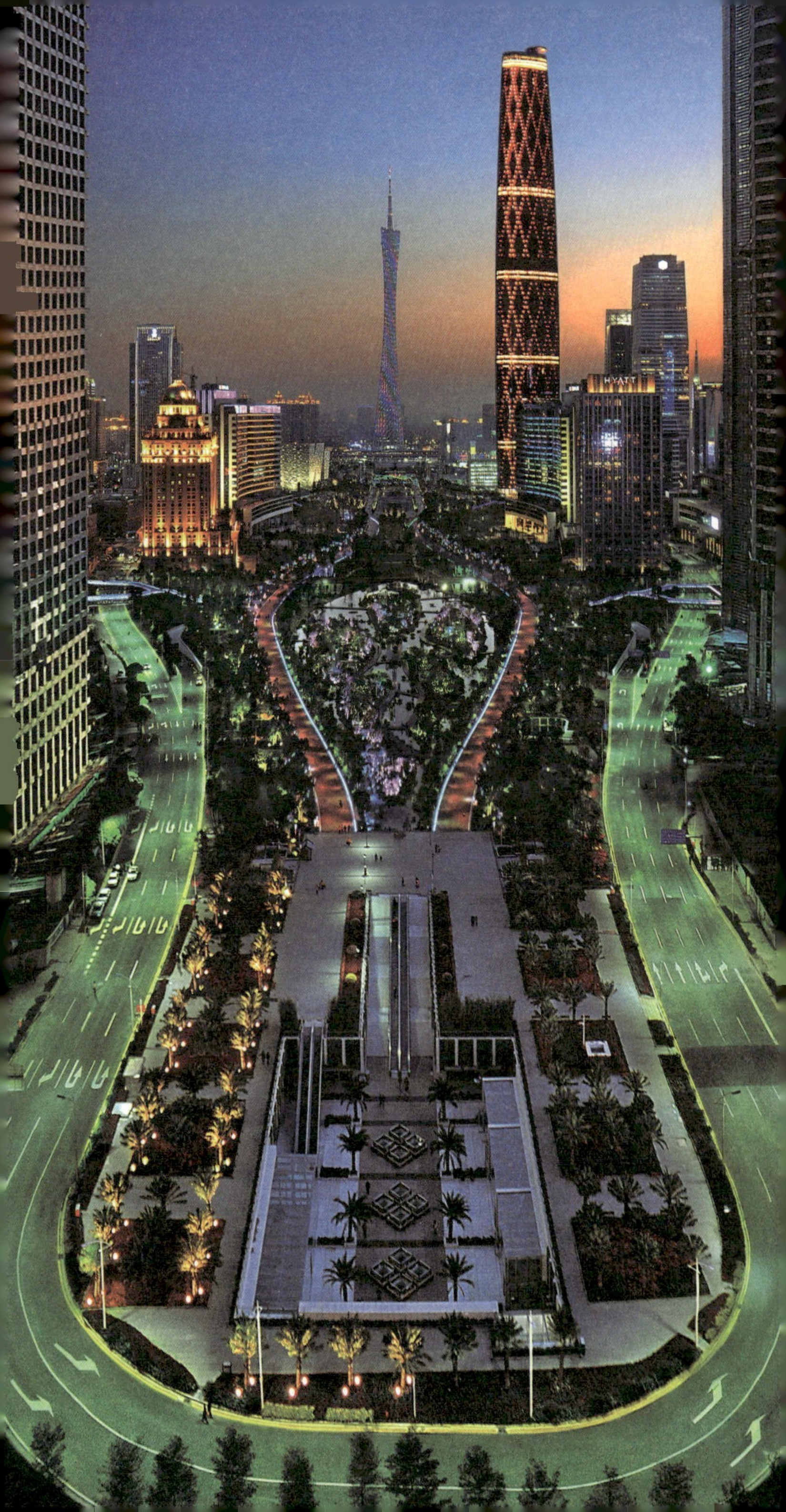

I. Safety

(I) Security

1. Foreigners staying in hotels or guesthouses shall present their original identity documents to the hotel staff and register for temporary accommodation as required.

2. Foreigners visiting hotels or guesthouses shall register their visits as required.

3. Drug use, prostitution, whoring and fighting are all violations of Chinese law.

(II) Emergencies

Foreigners who are involved in traffic accidents or emergencies shall call the following numbers for help promptly. The police and emergency centers are able to handle calls in English.

> Police: 110
> Fire: 119
> Ambulance: 120
> Traffic accident: 122

Police stations and duty points could be found in all sub-districts and busy roads of Guangzhou. The police stations are on duty and police cars patrolling 24 hours a day to deal with requests for help and perform the tasks assigned by 110 police hotline.

Chapter IV
Safety Rules and Regulations

Contact the course advisor on WeChat for free experience vouchers:

Download CHIease APP to learn easily anytime, anywhere.

X. Learning Chinese

5Idea is the expert in workplace Chinese training.

Its self-developed 6+N textbook series General Chinese in International Workplaces provide 60+ themes, 100+ work scenarios and 1000+ practical sentences.

Focusing on listening and speaking while also enhancing reading and writing, 5Idea quickly improves your Chinese expression ability and helps you communicate in workplace without barriers. Plus the CHIease APP, you can learn at ease whenever and wherever you want.

Online self-study + offline reinforcement, 5Idea allows you to use what you learn immediately, saving time and money.

10 minutes a day, learn useful Chinese!

In 3 months, you will be able to go for high salary jobs in the workplace and live more comfortably in China!

Contact Us
Tel: +86(20)80502829 WeChat: 18144892155
E-mail: info@5dieachinese.com
Twitter: 5dieachinese
Facebook: 5ideaAPP
Add: 1F, Building 6, 48 Chenjiaci Lu, Liwan District, Guangzhou

Funeral Association and its commissioned institutions. The international corpse transportation service station of Guangzhou is in Guangzhou Funeral Home. Service number: 87087506.

4. Contact information of Guangzhou funeral management service organizations

(1) Policy inquiry

Guangzhou Funeral Management Office

Address: 394 Yanling Lu, Tianhe District

Tel: 87053456

(2) Business service (to report death)

Guangzhou Funeral Home

Address: 418 Yanling Lu, Tianhe District

Tel: 87744444

Huadu District Funeral Home

Address: 164 Nongxin Lu, Xinhua Jie, Huadu District

Tel: 86863490

Panyu District Funeral Home

Address: Pingshan 2 Cun, Shibi Jie, Panyu District

Tel: 84774444

Conghua District Funeral Home

Address: Xialuo Cun, Jiangpu Jie, Conghua District

Tel: 87980145

Zengcheng District Funeral Home

Address: 19 Gongye Lu, Zengjiang Jie, Zengcheng District

Tel: 82742322

IX. Funeral Service

1. Policy for the reduction and exemption of funeral costs

For non-Guangzhou household registration holders who pass away in Guangzhou administrative jurisdiction after September 28, 2016 and whose remains are cremated in the funeral service organizations in the jurisdiction, their family member or assignee can apply for reduction or exemption of the following six basic service fees, up to a maximum reduction of RMB 1,330.

(1) Reduction of the cost of receiving and transporting the remains up to RMB 180 per body.

(2) Reduction of the cost of remains disinfection up to RMB 100 per body.

(3) Reduction of the cost of refrigeration and embalming (not more than 3 days) up to RMB 300 per body.

(4) Reduction of the rental fee of the body farewell hall up to RMB 400 per body.

(5) Reduction of the cost of cremation of up to RMB 250 per body.

(6) Reduction of the cost of the regular ashes cup up to RMB 100 each.

2. Procedure and documents needed:

The funeral assignee can directly handle the fee reduction and exemption procedure in the funeral service organization by producing the following documents:

(1) The Application Form for the Reduction and Exemption of Basic Funeral Service Fees (provided by the funeral parlor);

(2) The Medical Certificate of (Inferred) Death of Residents issued by the public security authority or medical institution;

(3) The ID Card of the funeral assignee.

The funeral service organization will verify the above materials provided by the funeral assignee (photocopies of materials are kept for record except the application form) and give reduction/exemption of fees accordingly.

3. Funeral service information

All five funeral homes in Guangzhou can handle the transportation and cremation of remains of foreign nationals. One may inform his request for the transportation of remains by calling "12349" or the funeral home's telephone number or by logging in to Suihaoban app. When the body has arrived at the funeral home, go to the funeral home to handle relevant procedures. Remains or ashes of foreign nationals that need to be shipped abroad will be handled by the International Corpse Transportation Network Service Center of China

and pay close attention to your health condition, stay home and reduce going out. If you are asked about your condition by government staff, community workers or medical staff, please cooperate with them. If you develop fever, cough, chest tightness, weakness or other symptoms, you must wear a mask and go to the fever clinic of a nearby hospital and tell the doctor truthfully about your travel history of the last 14 days. Please comply with epidemic prevention regulations and accept arrangements for PCR testing.

(5) Vaccination. Several types of Covid-19 vaccines developed and produced in China have had hundreds of millions of safe inoculations and have been proven safe and effective in many countries and regions around the world. WHO has recognized and recommended them. Receiving vaccination is in your best interest. Since April 2021, the health authorities of Guangdong Province have included foreign nationals in China in the vaccination target group. As long as they are of the suitable age (18 years old and above as currently stipulated) and fit for vaccination, they can receive the payable vaccination. If you have joined the provincial or municipal social security health insurance scheme, you will be eligible for the same treatment as the insured Chinese citizens in Guangzhou. If you wish to receive the vaccination, please make an appointment. All districts of the city have designated medical institutions to provide vaccination to expatriates.

Note:

There are currently 114 medical institutions with fever clinics in all 11 districts of Guangzhou.

(III) Inoculation for children

For children born or living in Guangzhou, their parents or guardians shall take them to the inoculation site in their place of residence (the health service center of the street (town)) to receive vaccination and obtain an inoculation certificate according to the prescribed immunization procedure and time. Children who have not completed the required immunizations due to migration, long-term traveling or living in other places may continue the required vaccinations at the inoculation site in their new places of residence by presenting their inoculation certificates. Guardians shall keep the inoculation certificates for checking if the children are enrolled in daycare or school.

Please click "Cancel" if one is unable to keep the appointment.

5. Health guide for foreign nationals in Guangzhou

To ensure daily prevention and control against Covid-19, we suggest these health guidelines for expatriates in Guangzhou:

(1) Pay attention to authoritative information. Please follow the official media such as the WeChat public account "Guangzhou Health Commission" for official notification of the Covid-19 and preventive and control measures, or call the Guangzhou Health Hotline 12320 for advice. If you need services in English, Japanese or Korean, you can call the Guangzhou multilingual public service platform at 960169, an interpreter will connect you to 12320 for a three-way call to answer your questions. Do not be misled by rumors or spread them.

(2) Protect yourself. Maintain personal hygiene, wash your hands frequently, cover your nose and mouth with tissue or elbow when coughing or sneezing, do not spit, and discard used masks as required. Open windows regularly for ventilation and maintain a clean indoor environment. Avoid contact with any wild animals or poultries; cook meat and eggs thoroughly before eating.

(3) Minimize unnecessary outings. Do not travel to medium or high-risk areas and other cities where outbreaks are occurring. Avoid going to crowded places, minimize group activities such as parties and dining together, and keep social distance. If you must attend, wear a mask properly (medical surgical masks are preferred) and refresh your health code on your cell phone.

(4) Cooperate with the work of medical and epidemic prevention staff. If you have visited a medium or high-risk area within 14 days, you shall promptly report to your local disease control institution or the designated organization,

Fill in name and cell phone number, obtain and fill in the verification code, then click "Confirm Appointment".

The appointment time, the clinic's address, map and phone number for consultation can be found on the appointment page.

Guide for Foreigners in Guangzhou (2021)

Select a consultation and test clinic in the list or map.

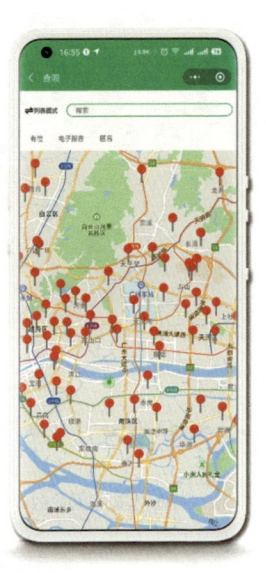

Click "Available times" and select a suitable time.

Chapter III Living in Guangzhou

To make an appointment:

Open WeChat to scan the QR code or search "Chabei" to enter the Chabei Applet.

Click on the "HIV test appointment" button.

Procedure for Foreign Nationals to Receive Covid-19 Vaccination in Guangzhou

Foreign nationals of suitable age for vaccination in Guangzhou

↓

Making an appointment: Scan the "sunflower code" to enter the appointment page for foreign nationals to fill in information and make an appointment

Notes:
The city has started inoculation of Covid-19 vaccines for foreign nationals in Guangzhou under the principle of "informed, voluntary, self-paid and at one's own risk". Guangdong currently uses domestic inactivated Covid-19 vaccines, which include two doses. Foreign nationals who haven't joined the social security medical insurance scheme of Guangdong and are not covered by relevant national regulations for free vaccination can receive the vaccination at their own expense for RMB 100 per dose; foreign nationals joining the scheme or covered by relevant national regulations for free vaccination will enjoy the same free treatment as Chinese nationals.

Before vaccination: A foreigner shall sign the Informed Consent and Disclaimer of Liability, take personal protection and inform his health status; the medical personnel on site will determine whether he is eligible for the vaccination.

During vaccination: "three checks, seven comparisons and one verification"

After vaccination: Vaccination proof will be provided; a foreigner shall stay for 30 minutes' observation and make sure he has no unusual symptoms before leaving; monitor his own health within 14 days and seek medical advice immediately in case of discomfort.

4. Guideline for HIV voluntary consultation and testing appointment for foreign nationals in Guangzhou

Guangzhou provides free and voluntary HIV consultation and testing to all expatriates.

List of Covid-19 Vaccination Institutions for Foreign Nationals in Guangzhou

No.	Vaccination Institution	Address	Telephone
1	Yuexiu District Hospital of Traditional Chinese Medicine	6 Zhengnan Lu, Yuexiu District	83330808-8124 83331597
2	Guangdong Second Provincial General Hospital	466 Xingang Zhong, Haizhu District, Guangzhou	89168015
3	Liwan Central Hospital of Guangzhou	35 Liwan Lu, Guangzhou	81349306
4	Guangzhou Twelfth People's Hospital	1 Tianqiang Lu, Tianhe District, Guangzhou	38981247
5	Baiyun Branch, Nanfang Hospital of Southern Medical University	23 Yuanxiadi Lu, Huangshi Jie, Baiyun District, Guangzhou	4000201120
6	The Third Affiliated Hospital of Sun Yat-sen University Lingnan Hospital	2693 Kaichuang Dadao, Huangpu District	82179413
7	Huadu District People's Hospital (Vaccination point at Huadu Gymnasium)	41 Xiuquan Dadao, Huadu District, Guangzhou	020-62935411
8	Guangdong Clifford Hospital	3 Hongfu Lu, Zhongcun Jie, Panyu District	020-84518222 extention70700
9	Nansha Hospital, Guangzhou First People's Hospital	105 Fengze Donglu, Nansha District, Guangzhou	020-28698677
10	The Fifth Affiliated Hospital of Southern Medical University	566 Congcheng Dadao, Conghua District, Guangzhou	020-61780566
11	Guangdong Hydropower Group Hospital (Fenghuang area)	4-6 Qichecheng Donglu, Yongning Jie, Zengcheng District	66266953

"informed, voluntary, self-paid and at one's own risk", the city has designated one vaccination institution in each of the 11 districts for foreign nationals. According to the current national policy, foreign nationals between 18 and 59 years old in Guangdong Province, and those aged 60 or above who need to take the vaccination for special reasons and are in good physical conditions can register for vaccination online through the GD Healthcare WeChat service platform. Guangdong currently uses domestic inactivated Covid-19 vaccines, which include two doses. Foreign nationals who have joined the social security medical insurance scheme of Guangdong will be treated the same as the insured Chinese nationals upon presentation of valid medical insurance certificate on site. Those not covered by the scheme can receive the vaccination at their own expense at RMB 100 per dose.

Appointment procedure: Scan the QR code (attached) to log on to the "Covid-19 vaccination service for foreign nationals" page on the Guangdong Healthcare WeChat platform to fill in the information and make an appointment. After successfully making the appointment, bring Foreign Permanent Resident ID card of PRC or passport with valid resident/visitor documents and proof of medical insurance to the designated place at the appointed time. Before receiving the vaccination, one shall sign the informed consent and disclaimer of liability according to the procedure, take personal protection and inform his health status, then the medical staff will determine whether he is eligible for the vaccination. One shall pay close attention to his own health condition within 14 days of vaccination, and seek medical advice if he feels unwell.

QR code for the appointment app

Guangzhou Zengcheng District People's Hospital
Address: 28 Chuangxin Dadao, Ningxi Jie, Zengcheng District, Guangzhou
Tel: 020-62707024

(II) Seeking treatment for infectious disease or major epidemic

1. Those who are bitten or scratched by animals (dogs, cats, rats, etc.) should visit the nearest medical institution immediately to clean and treat the wounds, and then go to the Guangzhou Eighth People's Hospital (Dongfeng Area or Jiahe Area, 24-hour service) for rabies vaccination, or a nearby designated rabies vaccination site (log on to the "Guangzhou Disease Prevention and Control Center" website → "Service Guide" → "Immunization" → "Locations of Rabies Vaccination Clinics in Guangzhou") for vaccination.

2. Those who are diagnosed with a statutory infectious disease or suspected infectious disease by a medical institution shall cooperate with medical and health institutions for examination, isolation, epidemiological investigation and other measures, and be transferred to a designated medical institution for treatment in accordance with relevant regulations.

Guangzhou Center for Disease Control and Prevention
Address: 1 Qide Lu, Baiyun District, Guangzhou
Tel: (8620) 36052333, 83822400
Website: http://www.gzcdc.org.cn

Guangzhou Chest Hospital
Address: 62 Hengzhigang Lu, Yuexiu District, Guangzhou
Tel: (8620) 83595977

Guangzhou Eighth People's Hospital
Address: (Dongfeng area) 627 Dongfeng Donglu, Yuexiu District, Guangzhou;
(Jiahe area) 8 Huaying Lu, Jiahe, Baiyun District, Guangzhou
Tel: (8620) 838386888, 83800419 (Dongfeng area)
(862) 36549012 (Jiahe hospital area)

3. Guideline for foreign nationals of suitable age to take Covid-19 vaccination

The city has started inoculation of Chinese Covid-19 vaccines for foreign nationals of suitable age in Guangzhou. With the principle of

Guangdong Clifford Hospital
Address: 3 Hongfu Lu, Panyu District, Guangzhou
Tel: 020-84518222

Guangzhou Huadu District People's Hospital
Address: 48 Xinhua Lu, Xinhua Jie, Huadu District; 60 Gongyuanqian Lu, Xinhua Jie, Huadu District, Guangzhou; 10 Shuguang Lu, Xinhua Jie, Huadu District, Guangzhou
Tel: 020-86838973

Guangzhou Hospital of Integrated Chinese and Western Medicine, Guangzhou Hospital of Integrated Chinese and Western Medicine Internet Hospital
Address: 87 Yingbin Dadao, Xinhua Jie, Huadu District; 8 Funing Lu, Xinhua Jie, Huadu District;
Shop 5, 6, 7, 8, 10-1, 17, 18, 19, 26, 34 and No.1 middle shopping mall on 1F, Duhui Yayuan, 7 Meigui Lu, Huacheng Jie, Huadu District
Tel: 020-86888997

Huadu District Maternal and Neonatal Healthcare Hospital of Guangzhou (Hu Zhong Hospital)
Address: 51 Jianshe Lu, Xinhua Jie, Huadu District; 7 Songyuan Lu, Xinhua Jie, Huadu District; 17 Gongye Dadao, Xinhua Jie, Huadu District; 35 Gongyi Lu, Xinhua Jie, Huadu District
Tel: 020-86825072

Zengcheng District People's Hospital of Guangzhou
Address: 1 Guangming Donglu, Zengjiang Jie, Zengcheng District, Guangzhou; 26, Fangzhi Lu, Zengjiang Jie, Zengcheng District, Guangzhou; 120 Zengzheng Lu, Zengjiang Jie, Zengcheng District, Guangzhou
Tel: 020-82735052

Zengcheng Hospital of Traditional Chinese Medicine of Guangzhou
Address: 50 Minsheng Lu, Licheng Jie, Zengcheng District, Guangzhou; 31 Heping Lu, Licheng Jie, Zengcheng District, Guangzhou; Room 301, North Building, 22 Heping Lu, Licheng Jie, Zengcheng District, Guangzhou

Foresea Life Insurance Guangzhou General Hospital
Address: 703 Xincheng Dadao, Zengcheng District, Guangzhou
Tel: 020-32632102

Guangdong 999 Brain Hospital
Address: 578 Shatai Lu Nanlu, Guangzhou
Tel: 020-87736999

Baiyun Psychiatric Rehabilitation Hospital
Address: 17 Woshan Xincun, Tonghe Jie, Baiyun District, Guangzhou
Tel: 020-36314381

Guangzhou Xinshi Hospital
Address: 79 Zhiyi and Zhier, Xinshi Xinjie, Xinshi Jie, Baiyun District, Guangzhou
Tel: 020-86307051

Baiyun Jingkang Hospital
Address: 2 Helong 5 Xiang, Bei Cun, Longgui Jie, Baiyun District, Guangzhou
Tel: 020-37379393, 37386065

Guangzhou Development District Hospital
Add: 196 Youyi Lu, Guangzhou Economic and Technological Development District
Tel: 020-82215578

Panyu Hospital of Chinese Medicine
Address: 65 and 93 Qiaodong Lu, Shiqiao Jie, Panyu District
Tel: 020-84822332

Guangzhou Panyu Central Hospital
Address: 8 Fuyu Donglu, Qiaonan Jie Panyu District, Guangzhou
Tel: 020-84826647

Guangzhou Panyu Maternal and Child Care Service Centre of Guangzhou (Guangzhou Panyu He Xian Memorial Hospital, Internet Hospital of Guangzhou Panyu He Xian Memorial Hospital)
Address: 2 Qinghe Dongli, Panyu District, Guangzhou;
12 Maoyuan Dajie, Shawan Town, Panyu District, Guangzhou;
99, 101, 103, 105, 107 Huancheng Donglu, Shiqiao Jie, Panyu District, Guangzhou;
101, 102 Shiqiao Xincun 1 Zuo, Shiqiao Jie, Panyu District, Guangzhou
Tel: 020-84629993

Guangzhou Women and Children's Medical Center
Address: 9 Jinsui Lu, Zhujiang New Town, Tianhe District, Guangzhou
Tel: 020-87036039

Guangzhou Red Cross Hospital
Address: 396 Tongfu Zhonglu
Tel: 020-34403815

Guangzhou Chest Hospital
Address: 62, Hengzhigang Lu, Guangzhou
Tel: 020-83595977

Liwan Central Hospital of Guangzhou
Address: 35 Liwan Lu, Liwan District, Guangzhou
Tel: 020-81346935

Guangzhou Aier Eye Hospital
Address: 191 Huanshi Zhonglu, Yuexiu District, Guangzhou
Tel: 020-87313480

Fuda Cancer Hospital, Guangzhou Fuda Medical Co., Ltd.
Address: 2 and 2 Zhier, Tangde Xilu, Tianhe District, Guangzhou; 91 and 93 Jude Zhonglu, Chigang, Haizhu District, Guangzhou
Tel: 020-3899396

Mental Hospital of Bureau of Civil of Guangzhou Municipality
Address: 143 Dongxiu Lu, Shijing Jie, Baiyun District, Guangzhou
Tel: 020-86441601

Guangzhou Baiyun District Maternal and Childcare Hospital
Address: 1128 Jichang Lu, Baiyun District;
344 Guangyuan Xilu, Guangzhou; 4 Huangyuan 1 Jie, Huangshi Lu; 1148 Sanyuanli Dadao
Tel: 020-86329682

Guangzhou Baiyun District Second People's Hospital
Address: 16 Zhiyi, Beisheng Jie, Jianggao Town, Baiyun District; 80 Shengli Lu, Baiyun District
Tel: 020-86601231

Guangzhou Twelfth People's Hospital
Address: 1 Tianqiang Lu, Huangpu Dadao Xi, Guangzhou; 35 Jingtai Zhijie, Guangyuan Zhonglu; Huangpo Cave, Baiyun Mountain; 1F, Ruida Building, 43 Huangpu Dadao Xi, Guangzhou
Tel: 85591881-3332

The First Affiliated Hospital of Guangzhou Medical University
Address: 151 Yanjiang Lu, Guangzhou
Tel: 020-83337616

The Second Affiliated Hospital of Guangzhou Medical University
Address: 250 Changgang Donglu
Tel: 020-34152464

The Third Affiliated Hospital of Guangzhou Medical University
Address: 63 Duobao Lu, Guangzhou
Tel: 020-81292135

The Fifth Affiliated Hospital of Guangzhou Medical University
Address: 621 Gangwan Lu, Huangpu District, Guangzhou
Tel: 020-82279975-2462

Affiliated Cancer Hospital and Institute of Guangzhou Medical University
Address: 78 Hengzhigang, Luhu Lu, Guangzhou
Tel: 020-83595032

Affiliated Stomatology Hospital of Guangzhou Medical University
Address: 31 Huangsha Dadao, Guangzhou
Tel: 020-61359477

The Affiliated TCM Hospital of Guangzhou Medical University
Address: 16 Zhuji Lu, Liwan District, Guangzhou
Tel: 020-81886504

The Affiliated Brain Hospital of Guangzhou Medical University
Address: 36 Mingxin Lu, Liwan District, Guangzhou
Tel: 020-81891425

Guangzhou Eighth People's Hospital of Guangzhou Medical University
Address: 627 Dongfeng Donglu, Guangzhou; 8 Huaying Lu, Baiyun District, Guangzhou
Tel: 020-83816453

The Third Affiliated Hospital of Guangzhou University of Chinese Medicine (The Third Clinical Medical College of Guangzhou University of Chinese Medicine, Affiliated Orthopaedic Hospital of Guangzhou University of Chinese Medicine)
Address: 261 and 263 Longxi Dadao, Liwan District, Guangzhou
Tel: 020-22292888

Jinshazhou Hospital of Guangzhou University of Chinese Medicine
Address: 1 Lichuan Dongjie, Baiyun District, Guangzhou
Tel: 020-81330999

The First Affiliated Hospital of Jinan University
Address: 613 Huangpu Dadao Xi, Tianhe District, Guangzhou
Tel: 020-38688036

The First Affiliated Hospital of Guangdong Pharmaceutical University
Address: 19 Nonglin Xialu, Guangzhou
Tel: 020-61325637

Women and Children Hospital of Guangdong Province
Address: 13 Guangyuan Xilu, Guangzhou
Tel: 020-61118777

Guangdong Provincial Hospital for Occupational Disease Prevention Treatment
Address: 165 Haikang Jie, Xingang Xilu
Tel: 020-89022988

Guangdong Provincial Family Planning Specialized Hospital
Address: 17 Meidong Lu, Guangzhou
Tel: 020-87776784

Guangdong Work Injury Rehabilitation Hospital
Address: 68 Qide Lu, Baiyun District, Guangzhou; 117 Wenquan Donglu, Wenquan Town, Conghua District, Guangzhou
Tel: 020-87830238

Guangzhou First People's Hospital
Address: 1 Panfu Lu, Guangzhou
Tel: 020-81048808

Taihe Branch of Nanfang Hospital
Address: 53 Taihe Zhonglu, Taihe Town, Baiyun District, Guangzhou
Tel: 020-87429013

Zhujiang Hospital of Southern Medical University
Address: 253 Gongye Dadao Zhong, Haizhu District
Tel: 020-84339888-43022

The Third Affiliated Hospital of Southern Medical University
Address: 183 Zhongshan Dadao Xi, Guangzhou
Tel: 020-62784240

The Fifth Affiliated Hospital of Southern Medical University
Address: 566 Congcheng Dadao, Chengjiao Jie, Conghua District, Guangzhou
Tel: 020-61780008

Traditional Chinese Medicine-Integrated Hospital of Southern Medical University
Address: 13 Shiliugang Lu, Haizhu District
Tel: 020-61650057

Dermatology Hospital of Southern Medical University, Guangdong Provincial Dermatology Hospital
Address: 2 Lujing Lu, Yuexiu District, Guangzhou
Tel: 020-83027506

Stomatological Hospital of Southern Medical University
Address: 366 Jiangnan Dadao Nan
Tel: 020-84427034

The First Affiliated Hospital of Guangzhou University of Chinese Medicine
Address: 14 and 16 Jichang Lu, Guangzhou
Tel: 020-36591730

Baiyun Hospital of The First Affiliated Hospital of Guangzhou University of Chinese Medicine
Address: 2 Helong 7 Lu, Renhe Town, Baiyun District, Guangzhou
Tel: 020-86452816

The First Affiliated Hospital, Sun Yat-sen University
Address: 58 Zhongshan 2 Lu, Guangzhou
Tel: 020-87755766-8504

Sun Yat-sen Memorial Hospital, Sun Yat-sen University
Address: 107 Yanjiang Xilu, Guangzhou
Tel: 020-81332199

The Third Affiliated Hospital, Sun Yat-sen University
Address: 600 Tianhe Lu, Guangzhou
Tel: 020-85253210

The Third Affiliated Hospital of Sun Yat-sen University Lingnan Hospital
Address: 2693 Kaichuang Dadao, Huangpu District, Guangzhou
Tel: 020-82111376

The Sixth Affiliated Hospital, Sun Yat-sen University
Address: 26 Erheng Lu, Yuancun, Tianhe District, Guangzhou;
17 Shougouling Lu, Tianhe District, Guangzhou
Tel: 020-38254000

Hospital of Stomatology, Sun Yat-sen University
Address: 56 Lingyuan Xi, Guangzhou
Tel: 020-83862558

Zhongshan Ophthalmic Center, Sun Yat-sen University
Address: 54 Xianlie Nanlu, Guangzhou
Tel: 020-87333209

Sun Yat-sen University Cancer Center
Address: 651 Dongfeng Donglu, Guangzhou
Tel: 020-87343088

Nanfang Hospital of Southern Medical University
Address: 1838 Guangzhou Dadao Bei, Guangzhou
Tel: 020-61641888

Baiyun Branch, Nanfang Hospital of Southern Medical University
Address: 23 Yuanxiadi Lu, Huangshi Jie, Baiyun District, Guangzhou;
1305 Guangzhou Dadao Zhong, Guangzhou; 8-12 Xi 2 Xiang, Shuiyin Zhijie, Shuiyin Lu, Yuexiu District, Guangzhou
Tel: 020-87240021

Guangdong Provincial Traditional Chinese Medicine Hospital
Address: 111 Dade Lu, Guangzhou
Tel: 020-81887233

University Town Hospital of Guangdong Provincial Traditional Chinese Medicine Hospital
Address: Neihuan Xilu, University Town, Panyu District, Guangzhou
Tel: 020-81887233-31228

Er'shadao Branch of Guangdong Provincial Traditional Chinese Medicine Hospital
Address: 261 Datong Lu, Guangzhou
Tel: 020-87351238

Guangzhou Charitable Hospital (Fangcun Branch of Guangdong Provincial Traditional Chinese Medicine Hospital)
Address: 36 Yongan Jie, Huadi, Fangcun District, Guangzhou
Tel: 020-81499866

Guangdong Second Traditional Chinese Medicine Hospital
Address: 60 Hengfu Lu, Guangzhou
Tel: 020-83585617

VIII. Medical Service

(I) Medical treatment

Guangzhou has a well-developed health care network, with general and specialized hospitals in every administrative district of the city. Foreign nationals can go to the hospital by themselves. Those who cannot may call the emergency number 120 or the number of a designated hospital for an ambulance to take them to a nearby hospital. This service is payable; the fee usually ranges from RMB one hundred to several hundreds, depending on the distance and medication used.

Hospitals offer various types of appointment services (e.g. through Guangzhou Health Link app, hospitals' official websites, WeChat public account, telephone hotline 12320 etc.).

Patients can also go to the outpatient clinic to register on their own. The procedure to see a doctor is: registration and triage → waiting for your turn → doctor's consultation → fee payment, and then examination/test (If needed. Some examinations need to be booked separately) → prescribing directly or prescribing after having examination/test results → fee payment → collecting medicine.

When visiting the hospital during the Covid-19 pandemic, one shall provide one of the following health certificates as required by local authorities: Sui Kang code (blue or green code), Yue Kang code (green code), notice of fulfillment of medical observation period, nucleid acid test report, and proof of identity.

List of Grade III Hospitals in Guangzhou (As of March, 2021)

Guangdong Provincial People's Hospital
Address: 106 Zhongshan 2 Lu, Guangzhou
Tel: 020-83827812-2507

Guangdong Second Provincial General Hospital
Address: 466 Xingang Zhong, Haizhu District, Guangzhou, Guangdong Province
Tel: 020-84219338-20007

Venues of Religious Activity	Address	Telephone
Renwei Taoist Temple	22 Renwei Zumiao Qianjie, Pantang Lu, Liwan Distict	81705462
Guangzhou City God Temple	48 Zhongyou Dajie, Zhongshan Silu, Yuexiu District	83378036

Christianity

Christian Dongshan Church	9 Sibei Tongjin, Yuexiu District	87776305 87305377
Zion Christian Church	392 Renmin Zhonglu, Yuexiu District	81889054
The Christian Church of Our Savior	184 Wanfu Lu, Yuexiu District	83335778
Guangxiao Christian Church	29 Guangxiao Lu, Yuexiu District	81087837
Henan Christian Church	23 Hongde Wuxiang, Hongde Lu, Haizhu District	84422935

Catholicism

Sacred Heart Cathedral (the "Stone House")	56 Yide Lu, Yuexiu District	83334180
The Church of Our Lady of Lourdes	14 Shamian Dajie, Liwan District	81217858

Islam

Huangsheng Mosque (Lighthouse Mosque)	56 Guangta Lu, Yuexiu District	83333593
Haopan Mosque	378 Haopan Jie, Haizhu District	81091123
Abi Waqqas Mosque and Tomb (Muslim Sage's Tomb)	901 Jiefang Beilu, Yuexiu District	86692743

Notes: venues of Islamic religious activities are generally not open to the public.

Ten historical buildings of five major religions, including temples, abbeys, mosques and churches, rise on the traditional central axis of the old quarters of Guangzhou, contributing to the unique cultural spectacle of religious harmonization. At present, among all 84 registered venues of religious activity that open to the public in the city, 6 of them are key protected cultural relic units at national level, 2 at provincial level and 10 at municipal level. These religious buildings are living evidence of the city's profound heritage of religious culture and witnesses of the its evolution as a renowned historic city.

Venues of Religious Activity	Address	Telephone
Buddhism		
Liurong Temple (The Temple of the Six Banyan Trees)	87 Liurong Lu, Yuexiu District	83392843 83357754
Guangxiao Temple (Bright Filial Piety Temple)	109 Guangxiao Lu, Yuexiu District	81088867
Dafo Temple (Big Buddha Temple)	21 Huixin Zhongjie, Huifu Donglu, Yuexiu District	83393455
Hualin Temple	31 Hualin Temple, Xiagiu Lu, Liwan District	81387849
Hoi Tong Monastery	188 Nanhua Zhonglu, Haizhu District	84399172
Taoism		
Sanyuan Palace	11 Yingyuan Lu, Yuexiu District	83551548
Chunyang Taoist Temple	268 Ruikang Lu, Haizhu District	84189071
Wong Tai Sin Temple	1 Wong Tai Sin Dao, Baihua Lu, Liwan District	81561855

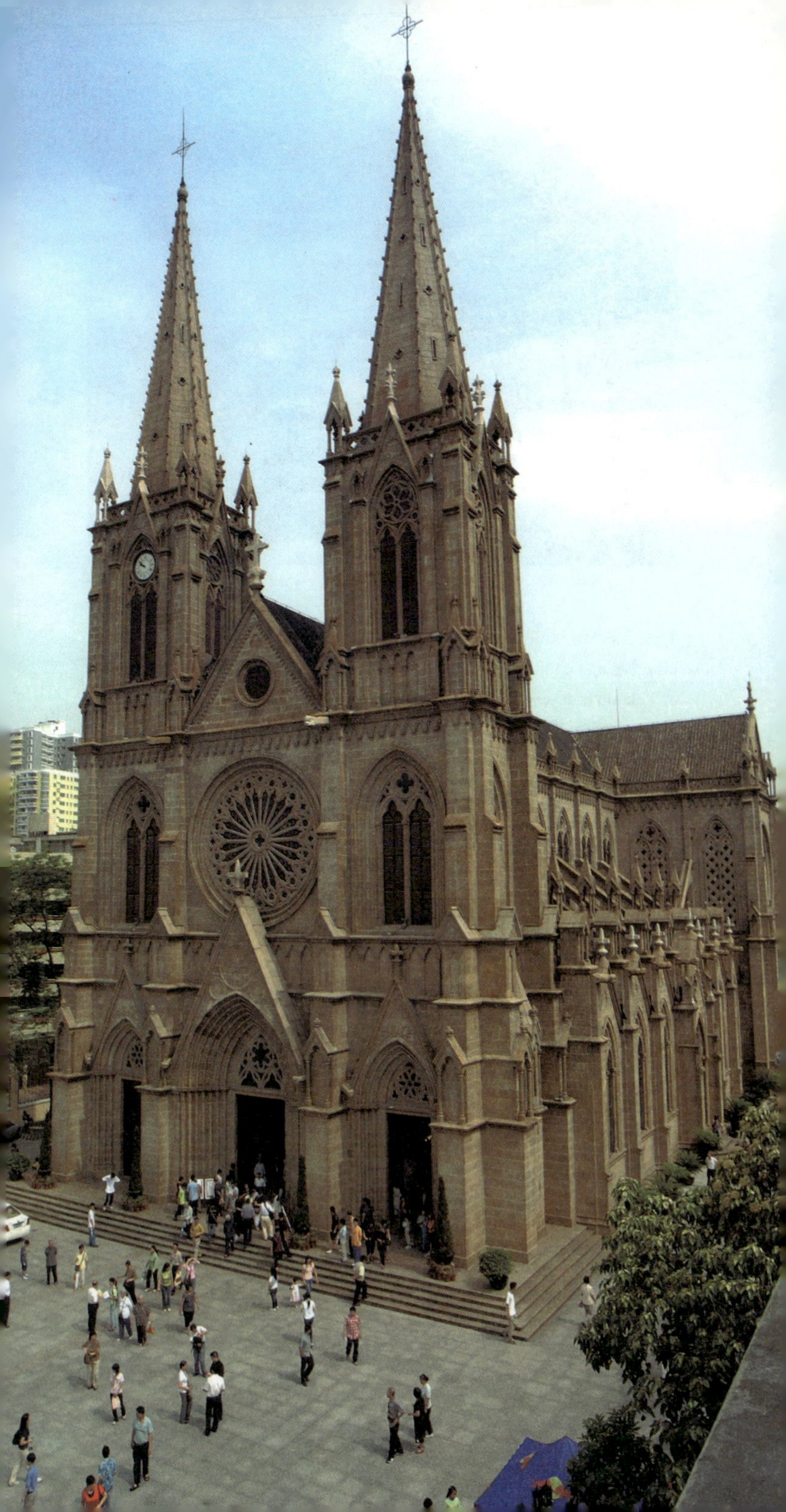

at a temporary venue designated by the religious affairs authority of the people's government at or above the level of province, autonomous region and municipalities directly under the Central Government.

The quota or funds provided by foreign organizations or individuals to support Chinese students studying abroad for the purpose of training religious practitioners shall be accepted according to actual need by the national religious groups of China, which shall coordinate the selection of Chinese students studying abroad.

Without due approval, foreign organizations or individuals are not allowed to recruit Chinese students studying abroad for the purpose of training religious practitioners in China.

Foreigners studying in religious colleges in China shall comply with the relevant provisions of the Regulations on the Administration of Acceptance of Foreign Students by Higher Learning Institutions and be approved by a national religious group and filed with the State Bureau of Religious Affairs.

Foreigners lecturing at religious colleges in China are subject to provisions of the Measures for the Employment of Foreign Professionals in Religious Colleges.

Foreigners performing religious activities in China shall abide by Chinese laws and regulations. Foreigners shall not interfere with the establishment and changes of Chinese religious groups or venues of religious activity, or the selection and changes of religious practitioners by Chinese religious groups, or any other internal affairs of Chinese religious groups.

Foreigners are not allowed to establish religious organizations, offices, venues of religious activity, religious colleges or religious training courses in any name or form in China; nor appoint religious practitioners among Chinese citizens, develop religious followers, or preach in venues of religious activity without due approval; nor preach in premises other than legally registered venue of religious activity or hold religious gathering without approval; nor hold religious activity with the participation of Chinese citizens at temporary location of religious activity (except for Chinese religious practitioners invited to preside over such religious activity); nor produce or sell religious books, audio-visual religious products, electronic religious publications or any other religious articles, or distribute religious propaganda materials.

(II) Venues of religious activities open to the public

Guangzhou has a long history of diversified religious traditions, including five major religions: Buddhism, Taoism, Islam, Catholicism, and Christianity. Among them, Buddhism, Taoism and Islam have been introduced into Guangzhou for thousands of years, and Catholicism and Christianity for more than two or three hundred years. The city enjoys profound cultural heritage.

VII. Religions and Venues of Religious Activity

(I) Regulations on religious activities in China

Foreigners are allowed to bring printed or audio-visual religious products and other religious articles for personal use when entering China. Relevant formalities are required with the China Customs for bringing those other than self-used ones into the country. It is forbidden to bring into China the printed or audio-visual religious products which contain contents that could jeopardize public interests of the country.

Foreigners are allowed to participate in religious activities in temples, Taoist abbeys, mosques and churches in China. At the invitation of religious groups at or above the level of province, autonomous region or municipality directly under the Central Government, foreigners may preach at venues of religious activity in China.

At the invitation of religious groups at or above the level of province, autonomous region or municipality directly under the Central Government, foreigners who visit China as religious practitioners may preach at venues of religious activity registered in accordance with the law in China.

At the invitation of religious groups at or above the level of province, autonomous region or municipality directly under the Central Government and with the prior consent of the religious affairs department of the people's government at or above the provincial level, foreign religious practitioners who visit China in other identities may preach at venues of religious activity registered in accordance with the law in China.

Foreign religious practitioners invited to preach at a venue of religious activity registered in accordance with the law in China shall abide by the regulations governing such venue and respect the religious beliefs and traditions of people in such venue.

With the consent of religious group in China, foreigners in China may invite Chinese religious practitioners to perform baptism, wedding, funeral and other religious rites and ceremonies for them according to their religious doctrines and traditions. Among them, religious wedding ceremony held for foreigners must be held between a man and a woman who have entered into a marriage relationship in accordance with the law. Group religious event of foreigners in China shall be held in a monastery, Taoist abbey, mosque or church approved by the religious affairs authority of the people's governments at or above the county level and registered in accordance with the law, or comes to Guangdong to register the adoption.

Tel.: 020-83318577, 83368441

E-mail:gd_adoption@163.com

(2) Handover Ceremony: The adopter meets the adoptee and a handover ceremony is held at the Guangdong Adoption Registration Center. Handover in private at hotels is strictly prohibited.

(3) Signing Integration Agreement. The foreign adopter and the person placing out the child for adoption shall sign an Agreement of Entrusted Custody during Integration Period. The period of integration shall be within 48 hours and any abnormalities occurring during this period shall be reported to the Guangdong Adoption Registration Center in a timely manner.

(4) Adoption Registration: Upon expiration of the integration period, if neither the adopter nor the adoptee has any objection, the adopter, the person placing out the child for adoption and the adoptee shall go to the Guangdong Adoption Registration Center in person for adoption registration, and the documents and materials submitted by the adopter are as follows (all documents shall be in A4 format with photocopies being clear and neat and the text being handwritten with a signature pen):

a. One original copy of the Notice of Travelling to China for Adoption;

b. Passport of the adopter and one photocopy of the passport;

c. The Application Form for Adoption Registration filled in by the adopter (attached with one-inch photo, i.e. 33mm×48mm, of each of the husband and the wife of the adopting couple)

d. One original copy of each of the Adoption Agreement and the Agreement of Entrusted Custody during Integration Period between the adopter and the person placing out the child for adoption.

e. When a married couple adopt a child together, if one party is not present, one original copy of the authorization letter on adoption, which is notarized by the notary office of the adopter's resident country and certified by the Chinese embassy (consulate) in that country shall be provided. When the above documents and materials are complete and valid and conform to the provisions of the *Civil Law of the People's Republic of China* and the *Measure for Registration of Adoption of Children by Foreigners in the People's Republic of China*, the registrar shall go through registration formalities for eligible adopters and, upon approval by the Guangdong Provincial Department of Civil Affairs, issue the Adoption Registration Certificate within 7 days. The adoption relationship is established as of the date of registration.

Marriage Registration Offices	Address	Office Hours	Telephone
Marriage Registration Office, Civil Affairs Bureau of Baiyun District	6F, Block A, Anhua Mall, 880 Baiyun Dadao Bei, Baiyun District, Guangzhou	Monday to Friday 9:00am~12:00pm 13:00pm~17:00pm Saturday 9:00am~12:00pm	36637461
Marriage Registration Office, Civil Affairs Bureau of Huangpu District	1F, Building A5, Lefei Homeland, 77 Kaida Lu, Huangpu District, Guangzhou		82112103
Marriage Registration Office, Civil Affairs Bureau of Huadu District	1F, 35 Gongyi Lu, Xinhua Jie, Huadu District, Guangzhou		36897638
Marriage Registration Office, Civil Affairs Bureau of Panyu District	3F, Building C3, Jisheng Vanke Plaza, 274 Xingtai Lu, Shiqiao Jie, Panyu District, Guangzhou		84834583
Marriage Registration Office, Civil Affairs Bureau of Nansha District	19 Huanshi Dadao Zhong, Nansha District, Guangzhou	Monday to Friday 9:00am~12:00pm 13:00pm~17:00pm Saturday 9:00am~12:00pm	34689076 84941999 Marriage and family counseling and legal advice: 84998789
Marriage Registration Office, Civil Affairs Bureau of Conghua District	1F, Building 2-3, 2 Mingyue Shanxi Dadao, Wenquan Town, Conghua District, Guangzhou		87839333
Marriage Registration Office, Civil Affairs Bureau of Zengcheng District	Marriage Registration Hall, Area B, District Government Service Center, 7 Jingguan Dadao Bei, Lihu Jie, Zengcheng District, Guangzhou		82655833 82655838

(VI) Adoption registration

1. Registration authority

Guangdong Adoption Registration Center is entrusted by the Guangdong Provincial Department of Civil Affairs for the registration of foreign-related adoptions.

Office address: 8F, Fuhua Trade Building, 233 Dade Lu, Yuexiu District, Guangzhou

2. Procedures of application for adoption registration in Guangdong by foreign adopters

(1) Appointment of Registration Time: Upon receipt of the Notice of Travelling to China for Adoption issued by the China Center for Children's Welfare and Adoption, the foreign adoptive parent shall make an appointment with the Guangdong Adoption Registration Center ten days before he or she

(3) Photos

When applying for replacement of marriage registration certificates, three couple photos in the size of 2 inches of the concerned parties taken within 6 months (bare-headed, full face, red background) shall be provided; when applying for replacement of divorce registration certificates, two single photos in the size of 2 inches of the concerned parties taken within 6 months (bare-headed, full face, red background) shall be provided.

(IV) Miscellaneous

(1) Any proof document submitted by the concerned party in a foreign language shall be accompanied with a full-text Chinese translation in the same format. Otherwise the said proof document shall be deemed not submitted at all.

The marriage registration authority accepts translated text issued by the embassies (consulates) of the concerned party's resident country in China or a qualified local translation agency.

(2) If neither concerned party applying for marriage registration or replacement of marriage registration certificates speaks Chinese, or if either concerned party applying for divorce registration or replacement of divorce registration certificates does not speak Chinese, a translator shall be brought along with them.

The translator shall submit his/her own valid identity documents, translate truthfully and ensure that the concerned parties have been informed correctly. He/she shall also sign and date the documents/materials that require signature.

(V) Marriage Registration Offices in Guangzhou and Office Hours

Marriage Registration Offices	Address	Office Hours	Telephone
Marriage Registration Office, Civil Affairs Bureau of Yuexiu District	110 Shuiyin Lu, Guangzhou (near West Entrance of Dongfeng Park)	Monday to Friday 9:00am~12:00pm 13:00pm~17:00pm Saturday 9:00am~12:00pm	83814282
Marriage Registration Office, Civil Affairs Bureau of Haizhu District	302 Nantian Lu, Haizhu District, Guangzhou (Marriage and Childbirth Service Center of Haizhu District)		34073601
Marriage Registration Office, Civil Affairs Bureau of Liwan District	1F, 26 Fengyuan Beijie, Fengyuan Lu, Liwan District, Guangzhou		81379313
Marriage Registration Office, Civil Affairs Bureau of Tianhe District	1F, Heng'an Building, 256 Huangpu Dadao Zhong, Tianhe District, Guangzhou		37127127

(3) The concerned party has his/her marriage registration certificate lost or damaged.

(4) The concerned party holds valid identity documents and relevant proof documents.

(5) The concerned party holds a proof document of marriage registration record issued by the marriage registration archiving authority or the handling marriage registration office or a stamped photocopy of the marriage registration record.

2. List of application materials for replacement of marriage registration certificate

(1) Valid identity documents

Chinese Mainland Residents: Valid permanent residence registration booklet and ID card (If the party concerned has collectively registered permanent residence and is not able to provide the original copy of the first page of the collective permanent residence registration booklet, he/she may provide a photocopy of the first page stamped with the official seal of that organization that holds custody of the said booklet and the original copy of his/her own page). If his/her ID card has expired or been lost, a valid temporary ID card can be used.

Foreigners: Valid passport or other valid international travel documents. If overseas Chinese or foreigners have had their passports replaced when they apply for replacement of marriage registration certificate, the old passports used for the purpose of marriage registration shall be submitted along with the new ones. If they are unable to submit their old passports, a proof document on change of passport number issued by a competent authority shall be submitted. Where the old passport number appears in the new passport, the above documents or materials can be exempted.

(2) Proof documents

a. A photocopy of the marriage registration record stamped with the official seal of the original handling marriage registration office or the marriage registration archiving authority, or a proof document on the lost record.

b. If the personal information of the applicant on the marriage(divorce) registration certificate is inconsistent with that on his/her valid identity documents now held due to the change of identity or personal information, a proof document on such change issued by a competent authority shall be provided.

c. When marriage registration record is lost or the personal information on the valid identity documents is inconsistent with that on the marriage registration record, please consult the local marriage registration authority of the registered residence or the marriage registration office previously handling the formalities for details on required documents.

5. Divorce registration procedures

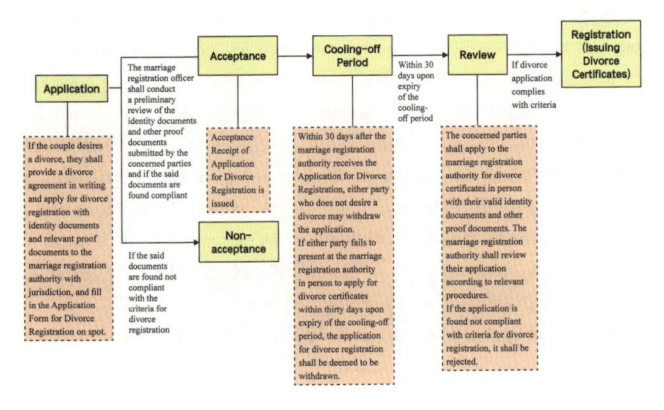

```
Application → Acceptance → Cooling-off Period → Review → Registration (Issuing Divorce Certificates)
```

- **Application**: If the couple desires a divorce, they shall provide a divorce agreement in writing and apply for divorce registration with identity documents and relevant proof documents to the marriage registration authority with jurisdiction, and fill in the Application Form for Divorce Registration on spot.

- **The marriage registration officer shall conduct a preliminary review of the identity documents and other proof documents submitted by the concerned parties and if the said documents are found compliant.**

- **Acceptance**: Receipt of Application for Divorce Registration is issued.
  - **Non-acceptance**: If the said documents are found not compliant with the criteria for divorce registration.

- **Cooling-off Period**: Within 30 days upon expiry of the cooling-off period. Within 30 days after the marriage registration authority receives the Application for Divorce Registration, either party who does not desire a divorce may withdraw the application. If either party fails to present at the marriage registration authority in person to apply for divorce certificates within thirty days upon expiry of the cooling-off period, the application for divorce registration shall be deemed to be withdrawn.

- **Review**: The concerned parties shall apply to the marriage registration authority for divorce certificates in person with their valid identity documents and other proof documents. The marriage registration authority shall review their application according to relevant procedures. If the application is found not compliant with criteria for divorce registration, it shall be rejected.

- **If divorce application complies with criteria** → Registration (Issuing Divorce Certificates)

(III) Replacement of Marriage Registration Certificate

When either concerned party has his/her marriage registration certificate lost or destroyed, or when the personal information on the marriage registration certificate is inconsistent with that on his/her valid identity documents now held, he/she may apply for a replacement of marriage registration certificate.

1. Criteria for acceptance of replacement of marriage registration certificate

(1) The application shall be filed with a marriage registration authority in whose jurisdiction the applicant has been residing.

(2) The concerned party has registered marriage or divorce with the marriage registration authority of Chinese Mainland or the Chinese embassy (consulate) outside of Chinese Mainland and still maintains that status.

(2) Valid identity documents and relevant proof documents

Chinese Mainland Residents: Valid permanent residence registration booklet and ID card (If the party concerned has collectively registered permanent residence and is not able to provide the original copy of the first page of the collective permanent residence registration booklet, he/she may provide a photocopy of the first page stamped with the official seal of the organization that holds custody of the said booklet and the original copy of his/her own page). If his/her ID card has expired or been lost, a valid temporary ID card can be used.

Foreigners: Valid passport or other valid international travel documents.

(3) The Application Form for Divorce Registration shall be filled in on spot in the marriage registration authority.

4. List of application materials for divorce certificates

(1) Marriage certificates issued by marriage registration authority of Chinese Mainland or the Chinese embassies and consulates outside of Chinese Mainland.

(2) Valid identity documents and relevant proof documents

Chinese Mainland Residents: Valid permanent residence registration booklet and ID card (If the party concerned has collectively registered permanent residence and is not able to provide the original copy of the first page of the collective permanent residence registration booklet, he/she may provide a photocopy of the first page stamped with the official seal of the organization that holds custody of the said booklet and the original copy of his/her own page). If his/her ID card has expired or been lost, a valid temporary ID card can be used.

Foreigners: Valid passport or other valid international travel documents. If overseas Chinese or foreigners have had their passports replaced when they apply for divorce registration, the old passports used for the purpose of marriage registration shall be submitted along with the new ones. If they are unable to submit their old passports, a proof document on change of passport number issued by a competent authority shall be submitted. Where the old passport number appears in the new passport, the above documents or materials can be exempted.

(3) Three copies of a divorce agreement signed by the concerned parties in the presence of a marriage registration officer.

(4) Two single photos of the concerned parties taken within 6 months (bare-headed, full face, red background), size: 2 inches

(5) If the identity and personal information of either concerned party are changed, a proof document issued by the competent authority or department shall be provided.

(6) Acceptance Receipt of Application for Divorce Registration or any proof document on missing or lost receipt.

(2) Acceptance: The marriage registration authority shall conduct a preliminary review of the identity documents and other proof documents submitted by the concerned parties and the Acceptance Receipt of Application for Divorce Registration shall be issued if the preliminary review finds all documents appropriate. If the application is found not to conform with criteria for divorce registration, it shall not be denied. When a concerned party requests the Notice on Non-Acceptance of Application for Divorce Registration, the said notice shall be issued.

(3) Cooling-off Period: Within 30 days after receiving the Acceptance Receipt of Application for Divorce Registration (from the next day of the date of receiving the application for registration of divorce by the marriage registration authority, to the 30th day that is not a public holiday or the working day immediately after the public holiday if the 30th day falls on a public holiday), either party who does not desire a divorce may withdraw the application from the registration office by presenting his/her own valid identity documents and filling in the Application Form for Withdrawing Divorce Registration. The Confirmation Form for Withdrawing Application for Divorce Registration shall be issued by the marriage registration authority if it finds all documents appropriate. If either party fails to present at the marriage registration office in person to apply for divorce certificates within thirty days upon the expiry of the cooling-off period, the application for divorce registration shall be deemed to be withdrawn.

(4) Review: Within 30 days after the cooling-off period (from the next day of the last day of the cooling-off period, to the 30th day that is not a public holiday or the working day immediately after the public holiday if the 30th day falls on a public holiday), the concerned parties shall apply to the marriage registration authority for divorce certificates in person by presenting their valid identity documents and other proof documents. The marriage registration authority shall review their true intention, identity documents and other proof documents as well as divorce agreement. If the application is found not compliant with criteria for divorce registration, it shall not be approved. When a concerned party requests the Notice on Disapproval of Application for Divorce Registration, the said notice shall be issued.

(5) Registration (issuing divorce certificates): The marriage registration authority shall go through the registration procedures and issue divorce certificates pursuant to the relevant laws and regulations.

3. List of application materials for divorce registration

(1) Marriage certificates issued by marriage registration authority of Chinese Mainland or the Chinese embassies and consulates outside of Chinese Mainland.

Republic of China in that country or by the embassy (consulate) of that country in China, or the document stating the same as issued by the embassy (consulate) of that country in China.

If the certificate is issued by a country that has not established diplomatic relations with China, it shall be then certified by the embassy (consulate) in that country of a third country with which China has established diplomatic relations, or by the embassy (consulate) of a third country in China.

(II) Divorce registration

If the husband and the wife both desire a divorce, they shall sign a divorce agreement in writing and apply to the marriage registration authority in person for divorce registration. Within thirty days from the date of receiving the application for registration of divorce by the marriage registration authority, either party who does not desire a divorce may withdraw the application from the marriage registration authority. Within thirty days upon the expiry of the cooling-off period, they shall apply to the marriage registration authority in person for divorce certificates. Failure to apply for divorce certificates shall be deemed as a withdrawal of the application for divorce registration.

1. Criteria for acceptance of divorce registration

(1) The application of divorce registration shall be filed with a marriage registration authority in whose jurisdiction either party has been residing;

(2) Divorce must be based upon the complete willingness of both the man and the woman;

(3) The man and the woman desiring a divorce shall register in person with the marriage registration authority;

(4) Both the man and the woman are with full capacity for civil conduct;

(5) Appropriate arrangements have been agreed by and between the man and the woman regarding the care of children and the disposition of property and debt;

(6) Both the man and the woman hold marriage certificates issued by marriage registration authority of Chinese Mainland or the Chinese embassy (consulate) outside of Chinese Mainland;

(7) Neither party commits bigamy;

(8) Both the man and the woman hold valid identity documents and relevant proof documents.

2. Procedures of divorce registration

(1) Application: If the couple desires a divorce, they shall provide a divorce agreement and apply for divorce registration with their identity documents and relevant proof documents to the marriage registration authority in whose jurisdiction either party has been residing. The Application Form for Divorce Registration shall be filled in on spot.

VI. Marriage and Adoption

(I) Marriage registration

The man and the woman desiring to contract a marriage shall register in person with the marriage registration authority. If the proposed marriage is found to conform with relevant laws and regulations, they shall be approved to register and issued marriage certificates. The marriage relationship shall be established as soon as they acquire the marriage certificates.

1. Criteria for acceptance of marriage registration

(1) The application of marriage registration shall be filed with a marriage registration authority in whose jurisdiction either party has been residing;

(2) Marriage must be based upon the complete willingness of both man and woman;

(3) No marriage may be contracted before the man has reached 22 years of age and the woman 20 years of age;

(4) The man and the woman desiring to contract a marriage shall register in person with the marriage registration authority;

(5) The man and the woman shall have no spouse (they shall be either unmarried, divorced or widowed);

(6) The man and the woman are not lineal relatives by blood, or collateral relatives by blood up to the third degree of kinship;

(7) Both the man and the woman hold valid identity documents and relevant proof documents.

2. List of application materials for marriage registration

(1) Three couple photos taken within 6 months (bare-headed, full face, red background), size: 2 inches;

(2) Valid identity documents and relevant proof documents.

Chinese Mainland Residents: Valid permanent residence registration booklet and ID card (If the party concerned has collectively registered permanent residence and is not able to provide the original copy of the first page of the collective permanent residence registration booklet, he/she may provide a photocopy of the first page stamped with the official seal of the organization that holds custody of the said booklet and the original copy of his/her own page). If his/her ID card has expired or been lost, a valid temporary ID card can be used.

Foreigners: Valid passport or other valid international travel documents; single status certificate, issued by a notary public or the local authority of their resident country, then certified by the Embassy (Consulate) of the People's

Chapter III Living in Guangzhou

>>> Tips

1. The applicant or the handler (the Employer's Power of Attorney is required if the handler is not the authorized person in the system) may collect the certificate with his/her valid identification document and *Acceptance Notice on FWP Application* at the accepting agency; or, the employer applies to deliver the certificate by EMS while working on the application, and the accepting agency will mail the FWP to the employer upon approval (freight collect).
2. Foreign graduates may apply for the residence permit at local public security authorities with the FWP.

Scan the QR Code for full version

Service Center

Guangzhou Service Center of Foreigner's Work Permit (Huangpu District and Nansha District are not included)
Address: Counter 517-518, 5th Floor, No.61 Huali Rd, Zhujiang New Town, Tianhe District, Guangzhou

Foreign-related Comprehensive Service Platform, Guangzhou Nansha Government Affairs Service Center (only for Nansha District)
Address: Counter 4-5, Comprehensive Service Platform for Foreign Affairs, Guangzhou Nansha Government Affairs Service Center, 1st Floor, No.1 Fenghuang Avenue, Nansha District, Guangzhou

Service Center of Science and Technology Bureau of Huangpu District (only for Huangpu District)
Address: Counter 401-402, Zone A, 4th Floor, Government Affairs Service Center, No.3 Xiangxue 3rd Rd, Huangpu District, Guangzhou

Office Hours: Monday to Friday
9:00-12:00, 13:00-17:00 (national statutory holidays excluded)

Hotline: 020-12345

Guide to Apply for Foreigner's Work Permit
by Foreign Graduates

For Foreigner's Work Permit related issues, please log in the Service System for Foreigners Working in China at https://fwws.most.gov.cn/lhg/web/

For Service Guide of Foreigner's Work Permit application, please visit the website of Guangzhou Municipal Science and Technology Bureau and refer to Service for Foreign Talents and Talents from Hong Kong, Macao and Taiwan at http://kjj.gz.gov.cn/attachment/6/6777/6777216/7230754.pdf

>>> Application Criteria

Foreigners obtaining master degrees or above from renowned overseas universities for less than one year, or international students obtaining master degrees or above from the universities in China for less than one year.

Approval Criteria:
1. Being at least 18 years old and healthy;
2. With no criminal record;
3. Excellent academic performance, with an average score of no less than 80 (hundred mark system or equivalent), or above B+/B (grade systems), with no record of misconduct at school;
4. Obtained corresponding academic qualifications and degrees;
5. Having a certain employer and the job that fits in with his/her major. The salary shall be no less than the average income of the local employees. The standards are determined by the provisions of the provincial bureau resources and social security departments in accordance with the labor market and the needs for introducing talents;
6. With valid passports or international travel documents.

>>> Checklist

- **(Before entering China)**
- [ ] Application Form for FWP
- [ ] Curriculum Vitae (Resume)
- [ ] Certificate of the highest academic degree
- [ ] Certificate of no criminal record (issued in the last 6 months)
- [ ] Physical examination certificate or Commitment Letter (issued in the last 6 months)
- [ ] The offer of employment
- [ ] The applicant's passport or international travel documents
- [ ] A full-face photo of the applicant taken in the last 6 months
- [ ] Other documents (including certificate of no misconduct record, academic transcript, proof of publishing recruitment at local public HR market and the HR service agencies for over 30 days)

- **(After entering China)**
- [ ] (Z or R) visa or valid Residence Permit held by the applicant
- [ ] Employment contract (no need to re-submit if provided before entering China)
- [ ] Physical examination certificate (no need to re-submit if provided before entering China)

Notes

1. Foreign graduates obtaining degrees from overseas universities apply for FWP according to the procedures of Applying for FWP from outside China, submit the documents as listed in " Before entering China" above to apply for *Notification Letter of FWP*, and submit the documents as listed in " After entering China" above to apply for FWP.
Foreign graduates obtaining degrees from the universities in China apply for FWP according to the procedures of Applying for FWP from within China and submit a full set of documents as listed in " Before entering China" and " After entering China" above;
2. All the scanned or photographed documents must be uploaded in original version of full color;
3. The original documents of No.1,2,4,5 and 12 should be submitted and will not be retained once collected;
4. The original documents of No.3,6,7,8,9,10 and 11 should be verified and submitted in photocopy (affixed with the employer's official seal).

>>> Procedures

The employer registers as account entities, the applicant applies online and provides relevant documents. — 5 working days — Online check

- Failed: If the application fails to meet the requirements, the employer will be informed all the problems and the application will be rejected. → Submit the proper documents
- Passed: Pass if the application meets the requirements.

Accepted Online — 5 working days — Review

- Disapproved
- Approved: Print out the *Notification Letter of FWP* online → *Notification Letter of Foreigner's Work Permit*
- A disapproval decision will be made with the reasons

The information of the Notification Letter will be sent to the Foreign Affairs Department.

Upon granted the Z or R visa, the information of the visa will be sent to the administrative departments for foreigners employed in China.

The applicant should apply for FWP online within 15 days after entering China. — 1 working day — Online check

- Failed: If the application fails to meet the requirements, the employer will be informed all the problems and the application will be rejected. → Submit the proper documents
- Passed: Pass if the application meets the requirements.

If mistakes are found in the documents, the employer will be asked to submit the correct ones.

Documents in paper form verified and collected at the Service Window, the *Acceptance Notice* will be issued immediately. — 3 working days — **Foreigner's Work Permit**

Review and Decide

- Disapproved: A disapproval decision will be made with the reasons
- Approved: An administrative permission will be granted and the FWP can be collected immediately.

The seal

The FWP information will be sent to public security departments, the *Residence Permit* can be applied.

Guangzhou Municipal Science and Technology Bureau © 2021

075

Guide for Foreigners in Guangzhou (2021)

>>> Tips

The *Notification Letter of FWP* will become invalid upon approval of the cancellation and there is no need go to the accepting agency to submit the documents. The applicant may submit a new application in the System according to the procedures of *Applying for FWP from Outside China*.

Scan the QR Code for full version

Service Center

Guangzhou Service Center of Foreigner's Work Permit (Huangpu District and Nansha District are not included)
Address: Counter 517-518, 5th Floor, No.61 Huali Rd, Zhujiang New Town, Tianhe District, Guangzhou

Foreign-related Comprehensive Service Platform, Guangzhou Nansha Government Affairs Service Center (only for Nansha District)
Address: Counter 4-5, Comprehensive Service Platform for Foreign Affairs, Guangzhou Nansha Government Affairs Service Center, 1st Floor, No.1 Fenghuang Avenue, Nansha District, Guangzhou

Service Center of Science and Technology Bureau of Huangpu District (only for Huangpu District)
Address: Counter 401-402, Zone A, 4th Floor, Government Affairs Service Center, No.3 Xiangxue 3rd Rd, Huangpu District, Guangzhou

Office Hours: Monday to Friday
9:00-12:00, 13:00-17:00 (national statutory holidays excluded)

Hotline: 020-12345

Guide for Cancellation of FWP or Notification Letter of FWP

For Foreigner's Work Permit related issues, please log in the Service System for Foreigners Working in China at https://fwws.most.gov.cn/lbgzweb/

For Service Guide of Foreigner's Work Permit application, please visit website of Guangzhou Municipal Science and Technology Bureau and refer to Service for Foreign Talents and Talents from Hong Kong, Macao and Taiwan at http://kjj.gz.gov.cn/attachment/6/6777/6777216/7230754.pdf

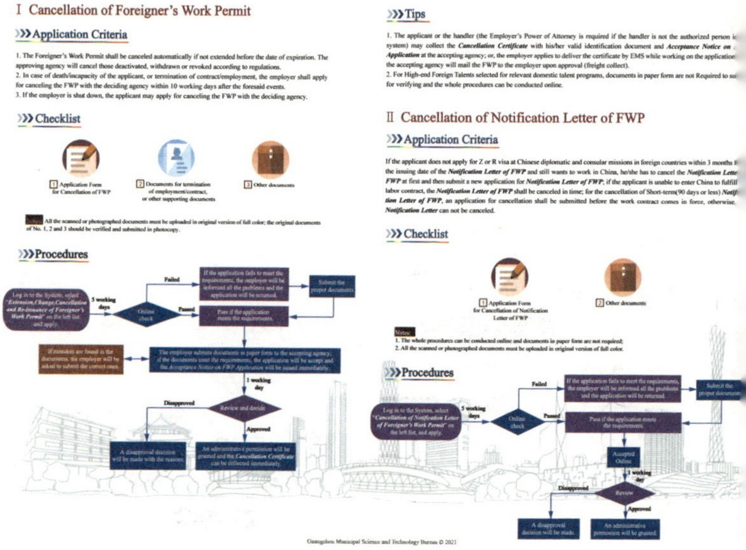

I Cancellation of Foreigner's Work Permit

>>> Application Criteria

1. The Foreigner's Work Permit shall be canceled automatically if not extended before the date of expiration. The approving agency will cancel those deactivated, withdrawn or revoked according to regulations.
2. In case of death/incapacity of the applicant, or termination of contract/employment, the employer shall apply for canceling the FWP with the deciding agency within 10 working days after the foresaid events.
3. If the employer is shut down, the applicant may apply for canceling the FWP with the deciding agency.

>>> Checklist

1. Application Form for Cancellation of FWP
2. Documents for termination of employment/contract, or other supporting documents
3. Other documents

All the scanned or photographed documents must be uploaded in original version of full color; the original documents of No. 1, 2 and 3 should be verified and submitted in photocopy.

>>> Procedures

[Flowchart: Log in to the System, select "Extension/Change/Cancellation and Re-issuance of Foreigner's Work Permit" on the left list and apply → Online check → 3 working days → Failed/Passed → If the application fails to meet the requirements, the employer will be informed all the problems and the application will be returned / Pass if the application meets the requirements → Submit the project documents / The employer submits documents in paper form to the accepting agency; if the documents meet the requirements, the application will be accepted and the *Acceptance Notice on FWP Application* will be issued accordingly → 1 working day → Review and decide → Disapproved/Approved → A disapproval decision will be made with the reasons / An administrative permission will be granted and the *Cancellation Certificate* can be collected immediately.]

>>> Tips

1. The applicant or the handler (the Employer's Power of Attorney is required if the handler is not the authorized person in system) may collect the *Cancellation Certificate* with his/her valid identification document and *Acceptance Notice on FWP Application* at the accepting agency; or, the employer applies to deliver the certificate by EMS while working on the application, the accepting agency will mail the FWP to the employer upon approval (freight collect).
2. For High-end Foreign Talents selected for relevant domestic talent programs, documents in paper form are not Required to submit for verifying and the whole procedures can be conducted online.

II Cancellation of Notification Letter of FWP

>>> Application Criteria

If the applicant does not apply for Z or R visa at Chinese diplomatic and consular missions in foreign countries within 3 months from the issuing date of the *Notification Letter of FWP* and still wants to work in China, he/she has to cancel the *Notification Letter of FWP* at first and then submit a new application for *Notification Letter of FWP*; if the applicant is unable to enter China to fulfill the labor contract, the *Notification Letter of FWP* shall be cancelled in time; for the cancellation of Short-term (90 days or less) *Notification Letter of FWP*, an application for cancellation shall be submitted before the work contract comes in force, otherwise, *Notification Letter* can not be cancelled.

>>> Checklist

1. Application Form for Cancellation of Notification Letter of FWP
2. Other documents

Notes:
1. The whole procedures can be conducted online and documents in paper form are not required;
2. All the scanned or photographed documents must be uploaded in original version of full color.

>>> Procedures

[Flowchart: Log in to the System, select "Cancellation of Notification Letter of Foreigner's Work Permit" on the left list, and apply → Online check → 3 working days → Failed/Passed → If the application fails to meet the requirements, the employer will be informed all the problems and the application will be returned / Pass if the application meets the requirements → Submit the project documents / Accepted Online → 1 working day → Review → Disapproved/Approved → A disapproval decision will be made / An administrative permission will be granted.]

Guangzhou Municipal Science and Technology Bureau © 2021

Chapter III Living in Guangzhou

>>> Tips

1. If the changes do not involve any information printed on the FWP card, the information will be automatically updated in the system and the applicant or employer may scan the QR code for confirmation; If the changes involve the information (including the name and category) printed on the card, the former FWP will be returned to the accepting agency while the new FWP and the *Approval Letter on Administrative Permission* are collected. The former FWP will be cut by the staff of the accepting agency and then return to the applicant.
2. The applicant or the handler (the Employer's Power of Attorney is required if the handler is not the authorized person in the System) may collect the *Approval Letter on Administrative Permission* in the accepting agency with his/her valid identification document and relevant original documents.
3. The relevant documents above can also be applied to be delivered by EMS while working on the application (freight collect).

Scan the QR Code for full version

Service Center

Guangzhou Service Center of Foreigner's Work Permit
(Huangpu District and Nansha District are not included)
Address: Counter 517-518, 5th Floor, No.61 Huali Rd, Zhujiang New Town, Tianhe District, Guangzhou

Foreign-related Comprehensive Service Platform, Guangzhou Nansha Government Affairs Service Center (only for Nansha District)
Address: Counter 4-5, Comprehensive Service Platform for Foreign Affairs, Guangzhou Nansha Government Affairs Service Center, 1st Floor, No.1 Fenghuang Avenue, Nansha District, Guangzhou

Service Center of Science and Technology Bureau of Huangpu District (only for Huangpu District)
Address: Counter 401-402, Zone A, 4th Floor, Government Affairs Service Center, No.3 Xiangxue 3rd Rd, Huangpu District, Guangzhou

Office Hours: Monday to Friday
9:00-12:00, 13:00-17:00 (national statutory holidays excluded)

Hotline: 020-12345

Guide for Extension, Change or Re-issuance of Foreigner's Work Permit

For Foreigner's Work Permit related issues, please log in the Service System for Foreigners Working in China at https://fuwu.most.gov.cn/lgzwfw/

For Service Guide of Foreigner's Work Permit application, please visit the website of Guangzhou Municipal Science and Technology Bureau and refer to Service for Foreign Talents and Talents from Hong Kong, Macao and Taiwan at http://kjj.gz.gov.cn/attachment/6/6/6777/6777216/7230754.pdf

---

I Extension of Foreigner's Work Permit

>>> Application Criteria

The applicant who already holds a FWP and intends to extend his/her employment for a period of more than 90 days should follow this guide. The application shall be made 30-90 days prior to the expiry date of FWP.

>>> Checklist

- Application Form for Extension of FWP
- Employment contract or proof of employment
- Visa or valid Residence Permit
- Other documents

Scope:
All the scanned or photographed documents must be uploaded in original version of full color; the original document of No.1 should be submitted and will not be returned once collected; the original documents of No. 2,3 and 4 should be verified and submitted in photocopy. (affixed with the employer's official seal)

>>> Procedures

Log in to the System, Select "Extension, Change, Cancellation and Re-issuance of Foreigner's Work Permit" on the left list, and apply.

3 working days → Online check → Failed: If the application fails to meet the requirements, the employer will be informed of the problems and the application will be returned. → Submit the missing documents

Passed → Pass if the applicants meets the requirements → The prompt to submit documents in paper form in the accepting agency, if the documents need to be submitted, the applicant will be notified by the *Acceptance Notice on FWP Application* and the email information

If mandates are listed in the documents, the employer will be asked to submit the correct ones → 3 working days → Review and decide → Approval: The FWP information on the System will be automatically updated / Disapproval: A disapproval statement will be made with the reason

If a FWP is issued by the former trial system and the data cannot be found with the ID number of the FWP in the current system, Select "*Applying for FWP from within China*" on the left list of web page and "*Eligible as Identified by Other Administrative*" on the right list.

>>> Tips

1. The applicant or the handler (the Employer's Power of Attorney is required if the handler is not the authorized person in the System) may collect the Approval Letter on Administrative Permission in the accepting agency with his/her valid identification document and *Acceptance Notice on FWP Application*. If, due to personal information change, a new FWP is required, the new one shall be collected at the accepting agency. The relevant documents above can also be applied to be delivered by EMS while working on the application (freight collect).
2. The employer shall submit an application for extension in the online system 30-90 days prior to the expiry date of the applicant's FWP (Otherwise, applicants of Category A have to re-apply according to the procedures of *Applying for FWP from Within China*, and applicants of category B or C have to re-apply according to the procedures of *Applying for Notification Letter of FWP from Outside China*).

---

4. Where an applicant changes his/her position/job or nationality, a new application must be made for FWP (applicants of Category A have to re-apply according to the procedures of *Applying for FWP from Within China*, and applicants of category B or C have to re-apply according to the procedures of *Applying for Notification Letter of FWP from Outside China*).

II Change or Re-issuance of Foreigner's Work Permit

>>> Application Criteria

Change: For any change with the personal information (name, passport, position and category) of a foreigner with a FWP, an application for change shall be made within 10 working days since the change occurs.
Re-issuance: In case of loss/damage of a FWP, the applicant shall make an application for re-issuance since the date of loss/damage.

>>> Checklist

Change
- Application Form for Change of FWP
- Proofs of change
- Other documents

Notes:
1. The whole procedures can be conducted online and documents in paper form are not required.
2. All the scanned or photographed documents must be uploaded in original version of full color.

Re-issuance
- Application Form for Re-issuance of FWP
- Applicant's statement
- Other documents

Notes:
1. The whole procedures can be conducted online and documents in paper form are not required.
2. All the scanned or photographed documents must be uploaded in original version of full color.

>>> Procedures

Log in to the System, Select "Extension, Change, Cancellation and Re-issuance of Foreigner's Work Permit" on the left list, and apply. → 3 working days → Online check → Failed: If the application fails to meet the requirements, the employer will be informed of the problems and the application will be returned. → Submit the proper documents

Passed → Pass if the application meets the requirements → 1 working day → Disapproval / Review / Approval → An administrative permission will be granted and the FWP can be collected immediately

Guangzhou Municipal Science and Technology Bureau © 2021

073

Guide for Foreigners in Guangzhou (2021)

Scan the QR Code for full version

Service Center

Guangzhou Service Center of Foreigner's Work Permit (Huangpu District and Nansha District are not included)
Address: Counter 517-518, 5th Floor, No.61 Huali Rd, Zhujiang New Town, Tianhe District, Guangzhou

Foreign-related Comprehensive Service Platform, Guangzhou Nansha Government Affairs Service Center (only for Nansha District)
Address: Counter 4-5, Comprehensive Service Platform for Foreign Affairs, Guangzhou Nansha Government Affairs Service Center, 1st Floor, No.1 Fenghuang Avenue, Nansha District, Guangzhou

Service Center of Science and Technology Bureau of Huangpu District (only for Huangpu District)
Address: Counter 401-402, Zone A, 4th Floor, Government Affairs Service Center, No.3 Xiangxue 3rd Rd, Huangpu District, Guangzhou

Office Hours: Monday to Friday
9:00-12:00, 13:00-17:00 (national statutory holidays excluded)

Hotline: 020-12345

Guide to Apply for Confirmation Letter for High Level Foreign Talents

For Foreigner's Work Permit related issues, please log in the Service System for Foreigners Working in China at https://fuwu.most.gov.cn/lhgzweb/

For Service Guide of Foreigner's Work Permit application, please visit the website of Guangzhou Municipal Science and Technology Bureau and refer to Service for Foreign Talents and Talents from Hong Kong, Macao and Taiwan at http://kjj.gz.gov.cn/attachment/6/6777/6777216/7230754.pdf

>>> Application Criteria

High Level and urgently needed talents in China's economic and social development who meet the conditions for High-end Foreign Talents (Category A) set forth in the Evaluation Criteria for Foreigners Employed in China (Trial), as well as high-end scientists, science and technology leading talents, international entrepreneurs, special talents and high-skilled talents fulfilling the demand, may apply for the *Confirmation Letter for High Level Foreign Talents* and may apply for the Talent Visa (R visa) with the *Confirmation Letter for High Level Foreign Talents*.

>>> Checklist

1. Application Form for Confirmation Letter for High Level Foreign Talents
2. Invitation Letter or work contract (including project contract and cooperation agreement)
3. The applicant's passport or international travel documents
4. Proof of meeting the conditions for Category A set forth in the Evaluation Criteria for Foreigners Employed in China (Trial)
5. Other documents

>>> Procedures

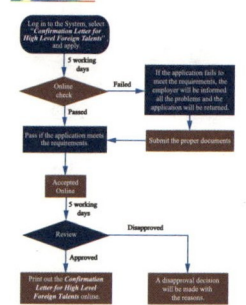

Log in to the System, select "Confirmation Letter for High Level Foreign Talents" and apply.

↓ 5 working days

Online check
- Failed → If the application fails to meet the requirements, the employer will be informed all the problems and the application will be returned.
- Passed ↓

Pass if the application meets the requirements.

↓ Submit the proper documents

Accepted Online

↓ 5 working days

Review
- Disapproved → A disapproval decision will be made with the reasons.
- Approved ↓

Print out the *Confirmation Letter for High Level Foreign Talents* online.

>>> Tips

The *Confirmation Letter for High Level Foreign Talents* may be downloaded and printed out online. No need to collect it at the accepting agency.

Chapter III Living in Guangzhou

Service Center

Guangzhou Service Center of Foreigner's Work Permit (Huangpu District and Nansha District are not included)
Address: Counter 517-518, 5th Floor, No.61 Huali Rd, Zhujiang New Town, Tianhe District, Guangzhou

Foreign-related Comprehensive Service Platform, Guangzhou Nansha Government Affairs Service Center (only for Nansha District)
Address: Counter 4-5, Comprehensive Service Platform for Foreign Affairs, Guangzhou Nansha Government Affairs Service Center, 1st Floor, No.1 Fenghuang Avenue, Nansha District, Guangzhou

Service Center of Science and Technology Bureau of Huangpu District (only for Huangpu District)
Address: Counter 401-402, Zone A, 4th Floor, Government Affairs Service Center, No.3 Xiangxue 3rd Rd, Huangpu District, Guangzhou

Office Hours: Monday to Friday
9:00-12:00, 13:00-17:00 (national statutory holidays excluded)

Hotline: 020-12345

Guide to Apply for Short-term FWP in Guangzhou
(90 days or less)

For Foreigner's Work Permit related issues, please log in the Service System for Foreigners Working in China at https://fuwu.most.gov.cn/lhgzweb/

For Service Guide of Foreigner's Work Permit application, please visit the website of Guangzhou Municipal Science and Technology Bureau and refer to Service for Foreign Talents and Talents from Hong Kong, Macao and Taiwan at http://kjj.gz.gov.cn/attachment/6/6777/6777216/7230754.pdf

>>> Application Criteria

Foreigners intending to work for a short term (90 days or less) in Guangzhou shall apply for Notification Letter of FWP (90 days or less).
Applicants should fit in with one of the following circumstances:
* To complete technical, science research, management, advisory jobs, etc. with their partner within Mainland China
* To conduct trial training for sports within Mainland China (including coaches and athletes)
* Photographing (including advertisements and documentaries)
* Modelling (including models for car shows and print ads)

>>> Checklist

1. Application Form for FWP or Application Form for Invitation Letter for Foreign Experts
2. Work contract (including project contract and cooperation agreement), invitation letter of the employer
3. The applicant's passport or international travel documents
4. Other documents

>>> Procedures

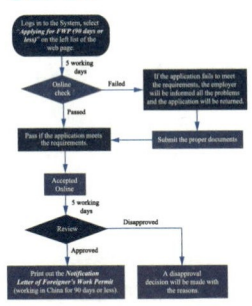

Logs in to the System, select *Applying for FWP (90 days or less)* on the left bar of the web page.

↓ 5 working days

Online check → Failed → If the application fails to meet the requirements, the employer will be informed all the problems and the application will be returned.

↓ Passed

Pass if the application meets the requirements. → Submit the proper documents

↓

Accepted Online

↓ 5 working days

Review → Disapproved → A disapproval decision will be made with the reasons.

↓ Approved

Print out the *Notification Letter of Foreigner's Work Permit* (working in China for 90 days or less)

>>> Tips

1. For those applying for the *Notification Letter of Foreigner's Work Permit*, the *Notification Letter* will be automatically issued in the System. The employer may print it out and send it to the applicant. With the *Notification Letter of FWP* and other required documents, the applicants may apply for Z or F visa at the very Chinese diplomatic or consular missions in foreign countries.
2. Applicants with Z visa who stay for less than 30 days do not need to apply for work-type residence permits; those who stay for more than 30 days (included) shall apply for work-type residence permits.

Guangzhou Municipal Science and Technology Bureau © 2021

Guide for Foreigners in Guangzhou (2021)

Scan the QR Code for full version

Service Center

Guangzhou Service Center of Foreigner's Work Permit (Huangpu District and Nansha District are not included)
Address: Counter 517-518, 5th Floor, No.61 Huali Rd, Zhujiang New Town, Tianhe District, Guangzhou

Foreign-related Comprehensive Service Platform, Guangzhou Nansha Government Affairs Service Center (only for Nansha District)
Address: Counter 4-5, Comprehensive Service Platform for Foreign Affairs, Guangzhou Nansha Government Affairs Service Center, 1st Floor, No.1 Fenghuang Avenue, Nansha District, Guangzhou

Service Center of Science and Technology Bureau of Huangpu District (only for Huangpu District)
Address: Counter 401-402, Zone A, 4th Floor, Government Affairs Service Center, No.3 Xiangxue 3rd Rd, Huangpu District, Guangzhou

Office Hours: Monday to Friday
9:00-12:00, 13:00-17:00 (national statutory holidays excluded)

Hotline: 020-12345

Guide to Apply for Foreigner's Work Permit from Within China (over 90 days)

For Foreigner's Work Permit related issues, please log in the Service System for Foreigners Working in China at https://fuwu.most.gov.cn/lhgzweb/

For Service Guide of Foreigner's Work Permit application, please visit the website of Guangzhou Municipal Science and Technology Bureau and refer to Service for Foreign Talents and Talents from Hong Kong, Macao and Taiwan at http://kjj.gz.gov.cn/attachment/6/6777/6777216/7230754.pdf

>>> Application Criteria

1. Being at least 18 years old and healthy, with no criminal record, employed by a certain employer in Mainland China and obtaining the professional skills or certain level of knowledge necessary for the job.
2. Being a professional which is urgently needed in China and employed for a job which is in line with the social and economic development in China.
3. Complying with the provisions of other laws and regulations on employment of foreigners in China, if any.

(For details of categories, please see Evaluation Criteria for Foreigners Employed in China (Trial) at http://kjj.gz.gov.cn/attachment/6/6777/6777216/7230754.pdf)

4. Fitting in with one of the following circumstances:

(1) A foreigner working in China and intending to work for a different company, with the job position (occupation) remaining the same and valid work-type residence permit;
(2) The foreign spouse or children of a Chinese citizen or a foreigner permanently residing or working in China with valid visas or residence permits;
(3) Being in line with the relevant preferential policies for free trade zones and/or comprehensive innovation reform pilot zones;
(4) The employer is eligible for the preferential policies for the Chinese headquarters of multinationals;
(5) Personnel transfer between the group and its subsidiaries;
(6) Foreigners undertaking the intergovernmental agreements or cooperation projects;
(7) Representatives of foreign establishments in China who have entered China with valid work visas; or foreigners who have obtained FWP for less than 90 days in China and now are employed by domestic employers within the validity period of their stay;
(8) Other circumstances deemed eligible by the approving agencies.

>>> Procedures

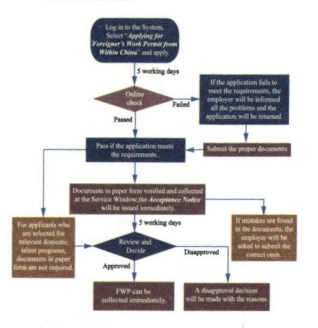

Log in to the System, Select *"Applying for Foreigner's Work Permit from Within China"* and apply

↓ 5 working days

Online check — Failed → If the application fails to meet the requirements, the employer will be informed all the problems and the application will be returned

Passed ↓

Pass (if the application meets the requirements) → Submit the proper documents

↓

Documents in paper form verified and collected at the Service Window, the *Acceptance Notice* will be issued immediately.

↓ 5 working days

For applicants who are selected for relevant domestic talent programs, documents in paper form are not required.

Review and Decide — Disapproved → If mistakes are found in the documents, the employer will be asked to submit the correct ones.

Approved ↓

FWP can be collected immediately. | A disapproval decision will be made with the reasons.

>>> Checklist

1. Application Form for FWP
2. Proof of work experiences
3. Certificate of the highest academic degree or related approval document and certificate of professional qualification
4. Certificate of no criminal record (issued in the last 6 months)
5. Physical examination certificate or Commitment Letter (issued in the last 6 months)
6. Employment contract or proof of employment (including the dispatch letter issued by a multinational employer)
7. The applicant's passport or international travel documents
8. A full-face photo of the applicant taken in the last 6 months
9. (Z or R) visa or valid residence permit held by the applicant
10. Relevant documents for the accompanying family members
11. Other documents

Notes:
Documents of No. 2, 3 and 4 are not required for a foreigner working in China and intending to work for a different company, with the job position (occupation) remaining the same, but Cancellation Certificate or the FWP of his/her last job are required.

>>> Tips

1. The applicant or the handler may collect the certificate with his/her valid identification document and *Acceptance Notice on FWP Application* at the accepting agency; or, the employer applies to deliver the certificate by EMS while working on the application online, and the accepting agency will mail the FWP to the employer upon approval (freight collect).
2. The applicant can apply for the residence permit at the exit-entry administration departments of local public security authorities with the FWP.

Guangzhou Municipal Science and Technology Bureau © 2021

070

Chapter III Living in Guangzhou

>>> Tips

1. The applicant or the handler (the Employer's Power of Attorney is required if the handler is not the authorized person in the system) may collect the certificates with his/her valid identification document and *Acceptance Notice on FWP Application* at the accepting agency; or, the employer applies to deliver the certificates by EMS while writing on the application, and the accepting agency will mail the FWP to the employer upon approval (freight collect).
2. The applicant can apply for the residence permit at the exit-entry administration departments of local public security authorities with the FWP.

Scan the QR Code for full version

Service Center

Guangzhou Service Center of Foreigner's Work Permit
(Huangpu District and Nansha District are not included)
Address: Counter 517-518, 5th Floor, No.61 Huali Rd, Zhujiang New Town, Tianhe District, Guangzhou

Foreign-related Comprehensive Service Platform, Guangzhou Nansha Government Affairs Service Center (only for Nansha District)
Address: Counter A-5, Comprehensive Service Platform for Foreign Affairs, Guangzhou Nansha Government Affairs Service Center, 1st Floor, No.1 Fenghuang Avenue, Nansha District, Guangzhou

Service Center of Science and Technology Bureau of Huangpu District (only for Huangpu District)
Address: Counter 401-402, Zone A, 4th Floor, Government Affairs Service Center, No.3 Xiangxue 3rd Rd, Huangpu District, Guangzhou

Office Hours: Monday to Friday
9:00-12:00, 13:00-17:00 (national statutory holidays excluded)

Hotline: 020-12345

Guide to Apply for Foreigner's Work Permit
From outside China
(over 90 days)

For Foreigner's Work Permit related issues, please log in the Service System for Foreigners Working in China a https://fuwu.most.gov.cn/lbgrwzb/

For Service Guide of Foreigner's Work Permit application, please visit the website of Guangzhou Municipal Science and Technology Bureau and refer to Service for Foreign Talents and Talents from Hong Kong, Macao and Taiwan at http://kjj.gz.gov.cn/attachment/6/6/777/6777216/7230754.pdf

---

>>> Application Criteria

1. Being at least 18 years old and healthy, with no criminal record, employed by a certain employer in Mainland China and obtaining the professional skills or certain level of knowledge necessary for the job.
2. Being a professional which is urgently needed in China and employed for a job which is in line with the social and economic development in China.
3. Complying with the provisions of other laws and regulations on employment of foreigners in China, if any.
(For details of categories, please see *Evaluation Criteria for Foreigners Employed in China (Trial)* at http://kjj.gz.gov.cn/attachment/6/6/777/6777216/7230754.pdf)

>>> Checklist

- Applying for *Notification Letter of FWP* before entering China
  ☐ Application Form for FWP
  ☐ Proof of work experiences
  ☐ Certificate of the highest academic degree or related approval document and certificate of professional qualification
  ☐ Certificate of no criminal record (issued in the last 6 months)
  ☐ Physical examination certificate or Commitment Letter (issued in the last 6 months)
  ☐ Employment contract or proof of employment (including the dispatch letter issued by a multinational employer)
  ☐ The applicant's passport or international travel documents
  ☐ A full-face photo of the applicant taken in the last 6 months
  ☐ Relevant documents for the accompanying family members
  ☐ Other documents

- Applying for *FWP* after entering China
  ☐ (Z or R) visa or valid residence permit held by the applicant
  ☐ Employment contract (no need to re-submit if provided before entering China)
  ☐ Physical examination certificate (no need to re-submit if provided before entering China)

Note:
All the scanned or photographed documents must be uploaded in original version of full color; the original documents of No. 1,4,5 and 10 should be submitted and will not be returned once collected; the original documents of No. 2,3,6,7,9,10,11 and 12 should be verified and submitted in photocopies (affixed with the employer's official seal).

>>> Procedures

Guide for Foreigners in Guangzhou (2021)

Scan the QR Code for full version

Service Center

Guangzhou Service Center of Foreigner's Work Permit (Huangpu District and Nansha District are not included)
Address: Counter 517-518, 5th Floor, No.61 Huali Rd, Zhujiang New Town, Tianhe District, Guangzhou

Foreign-related Comprehensive Service Platform, Guangzhou Nansha Government Affairs Service Center (only for Nansha District)
Address: Counter 4-5, Comprehensive Service Platform for Foreign Affairs, Guangzhou Nansha Government Affairs Service Center, 1st Floor, No.1 Fenghuang Avenue, Nansha District, Guangzhou

Service Center of Science and Technology Bureau of Huangpu District (only for Huangpu District)
Address: Counter 401-402, Zone A, 4th Floor, Government Affairs Service Center, No.3 Xiangxue 3rd Rd, Huangpu District, Guangzhou

Office Hours: Monday to Friday
9:00-12:00, 13:00-17:00 (national statutory holidays excluded)

Hotline: 020-12345

Guide for Online Registration by Employers to Apply for FWP

For Foreigner's Work Permit related issues, please log in the Service System for Foreigners Working in China at https://fuwu.most.gov.cn/lbgzweb/

For Service Guide of Foreigner's Work Permit application, please visit the website of Guangzhou Municipal Science and Technology Bureau and refer to Service for Foreign Talents and Talents from Hong Kong, Macao and Taiwan at http://kjj.gz.gov.cn/attachment/6/6777/6777216/7230754.pdf

>>> Application Criteria

1. Being an organization established according to the laws, with no record of serious violation of law or discredit; the jobs offered to foreigners should be special needs, short for Chinese candidates for the time being, and subject to relevant regulations in China; the payment and the salary of the job should be over the local minimum incomes.
2. Duly pre-approved by the competent departments as confined by the laws and regulations, if applicable.

>>> Checklist
(all the scanned or photographed documents must be uploaded in original version of full color)

1. Registration form
2. Legal registration certificate
3. Identification documents of the person in charge and the handler
4. Approval documents of competent departments, if applicable
5. Other documents

>>> Procedures

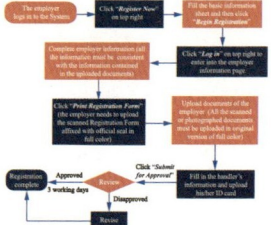

The employer logs in to the System → Click "*Register Now*" on top right → Fill the basic information sheet and then click "*Begin Registration*"

Complete employer information (all the information must be consistent with the information contained in the uploaded documents) → Click "*Log in*" on top right to enter into the employer information page

Click "*Print Registration Form*" (the employer needs to upload the scanned Registration Form affixed with official seal in full color) → Upload documents of the employer (All the scanned or photographed documents must be uploaded in original version of full color)

Registration complete ← Approved — 3 working days — Review — Click "*Submit for Approval*" ← Fill in the handler's information and upload his/her ID card

Disapproved → Revise

>>> Tips

1. For employers handling with FWP in the System for the first time, the first step is to register an account. After completing the registration, the employer can submit applications and check the status; registered users can log in with their registered account directly.
2. If the application for the account has not been checked after submitting, the application can be revoked by clicking "*Revoke*". The application can be revised.
3. To update the basic information (such as business license, legal representative, the handler, etc.), please click "*Change Employer Information*" on top right. Click "*Submit for Approval*" at the bottom after updating, and the registered information will be updated upon approval.

Guangzhou Municipal Science and Technology Bureau © 2021

the criteria for innovative and entrepreneurial talents, professional and skilled talents, excellent foreign graduates, meet the criteria for foreign professional talents set in the point-based system, or are introduced due to implementation of inter-government agreements or protocols, the restrictions on age, education or working experience can be relaxed. For details, see the *Categorization Criteria of Foreigners Working in China (Trial)*. If there are national regulations on professionals and government project personnel, the said regulations shall apply.

3. Other foreigners (Category C)

Other Foreigners (Category C) refers to foreigners employed to meet the demand of the domestic labor market in line with the state policies and regulations. For details, see the *Categorization Criteria of Foreigners Working in China (Trial)*.

V. Foreigner's Work Permit

(I) Applicable scope

Foreigners working in China shall obtain work permits and work-type residence permits in accordance with relevant regulations. Organizations or individuals shall not employ a foreigner without obtaining a work permit and a residence permit.

(II) Service contents

The relevant services include: Foreigner's Work Permit (FWP) applications from outside China or within China, application for short-term FWP, as well as FWP extension, update, cancellation of FWP and Notification of FWP.

(III) Where to apply

Service System for Foreigners Working in China (https://fuwu.most.gov.cn/lhgzweb/) accepts on-line applications on a year-round basis at no cost.

(IV) Categorization criteria of foreigners working in China

1. High-end foreign talents (Category A)

High-end Foreign Talents (Category A) include scientists, leading S&T talents, international entrepreneurs, special talents and other foreign high-end talents urgently needed in the economic and social development of China who fall in line with the national priority list for foreign talents or fulfill the market demand for government-encouraged posts as well as those who meet the criteria for high-end foreign talents set in the points-based system (grade 85 points or more). Foreign high-end talents are free from restriction on quota not subject to age, education and work experience restrictions. For details, see the Categorization Criteria of Foreigners Working in China (Trial).

2. Foreign professional talents (Category B)

Foreign Professional Talents (Category B) include foreign professionals who meet the requirements of the *Guiding Catalog and Positions for Foreigners Working in China*, fulfill the urgent demands of the economic and social development of China, hold bachelor's degree or above, have relevant working experience for two years or more, and are aged below 60 or obtaining 60 points or more in the points- based system; for those who are in urgent need and meet

Canadian International School of Guangzhou
Address: 122 Dongyi Lu, Panyu District, Guangzhou
Postcode: 511400
Tel: 020-39939920
Website: www.cisgz.com

BASIS International School Guangzhou
Address: 8 Jiantashan Lu, Guangzhou Guangzhou Science City, Huangpu District, Guangzhou
Postcode: 510663
Tel: 020-82222888
Fax: 020-89856222
Website: www.bigz.basischina.com

Britannia International School Guangzhou
Address: 4 Chuangjia Lu, Jinshazhou, Baiyun District, Guangzhou
Postcode: 510168
Tel: 020-66606886
Website: www.bisgz.com

ISA Science City International School
Address: 66 Yushu Nanlu, Huangpu District, Guangzhou
Postcode: 510700
Tel: 020-37362580
Website: www.isagzsc.com

Utahloy International School Guangzhou
Address: 800 Shatai Beilu, Baiyun District, Guangzhou
Postcode: 510515
Tel: 020-87202019
Website: www.utahloy.com/gz/

Utahloy International School Zengcheng
Address: Dapuwei Village, Zengjiang Sub-district, Zengcheng District, Guangzhou
Postcode: 511325
Tel: 020-82913201
Website: www.utahloy.com/zc/

광저우한국학교/Guangzhou Korean School
Address: 6 Xinghai lu, Shilou Town, Panyu District, Guangzhou
Postcode: 511447
Tel: 020-39298661
Fax: 020-39298663
Website: www.gks.or.kr

ISA International School of Guangzhou
Address: Block C2-2, Redtory, 128 Yuancun Siheng Lu, Tianhe District, Guangzhou
Postcode: 510655
Tel: 020-88900909
Website: www.isagzth.com

American International School of Guangzhou
Address: 3 Yanyu Nanjie, Ersha Island, Yuexiu District, Guangzhou (Grade K-5)
19 Kexiang Lu, Huangpu District, Guangzhou, Guangdong Province (Grade 6-12)
Postcode:
510105 (Grade K-5)
510663(Grade 6-12)
Tel: 020-3213555
Website: www.aisgz.org

广州日本人学校 / Japanese School of Guangzhou
Address: 10 Fengxin Lu, Guangzhou Science City, Guangzhou
Postcode: 510663
Tel: 020-61397023
Website: jsgcn.com

オイスカ広州日本語幼稚園/OISCA Guangzhou Japanese Kindergarten
Address: 10 Fengxin Lu, Guangzhou Science City, Guangzhou
Postcode: 510663
Tel: 020-61397023

Guangzhou Grace Academy
Address: Complex A and B, Wanxingwei, Jushu Village, Dashi Town, Panyu District, Guangzhou
Postcode: 511431
Tel: 020-84500180
Fax: 020-34506248

Affiliated School of JNU for Hong Kong and Macao Students
Address: 18 Huilong Lu, Longdong Sub-district, Tianhe District, Guangzhou
Postcode: 510520
Tel: 020-87085090
Fax: 020-87085090

international students.

To study in higher education institutions in Guangzhou, international students may follow the Administrative Measures for Schools Recruiting and Training International Students issued by the Ministry of Education, the Ministry of Foreign Affairs, and the Ministry of Public Security. Before entering China, international students should apply for X1 or X2 visas to the Chinese embassies or consulates in their countries of origin or residence, or other agencies entrusted by the Ministry of Foreign Affairs, and submit relevant materials such as the certificates filed with their education authorities and the admission letters issued by the higher education institutions as regulated. If an international student holds a study visa indicating that he/she needs to apply for a residence permit after entering China, the student shall apply to the exit-entry administration department of Guangzhou Public Security Bureau for a residence permit for foreigners studying in Guangzhou within 30 days from the date of entry. (For details, please visit the official website of Guangzhou Public Security Bureau: www.gzjd.gov.cn)

(III) Schools for children of foreigners in Guangzhou

The British School of Guangzhou
Address: 983-3 Tonghe Lu, Baiyun District, Guangzhou
Postcode: 510515
Tel: 020-87094788
Website: www.bsg.org.cn

IV. Education

As China's current academic system stipulates, the compulsory education lasts 9 years, high school education 3 years, junior college education 2 to 3 years, undergraduate education 4 to 5 years, graduate education for master's degree 2 to 3 years, and graduate education for doctoral degree 3 to 4 years.

(I) Compulsory education and high school education

Guangzhou has released policies that include the "children of overseas Chinese", "children of foreigners holding the Permanent Residence Permit for Foreigner (including minor holders themselves)", "school-age children of diplomatic personnel in consulates in Guangzhou" in the scope of compulsory education. These children are enrolled in schools near them as if they were locals as arranged by the district education bureaus without examinations. Other foreign school-age children may also apply for eligible private schools offering compulsory education according to the guidelines of the district they are in.

Guangzhou has released policies that include the "school-age children of diplomatic personnel in consulates in Guangzhou" in the scope of high school education. They may take high school entrance examinations and apply for public high schools, private high schools and secondary vocational schools as if they were locals. Children of foreigners attending junior high school in Guangzhou, or overseas students approved to attend high schools in the city may apply for private high schools and secondary vocational schools.

Foreign students who need to transfer to primary and secondary schools in Guangzhou may contact the school by themselves in accordance with the *Implementation Rules of Guangdong Department of Education on the Management of Primary and Secondary School Students (Trial)*. After the school verifies and approves the application, it will handle the transfer and admission as required.

In addition, school-age children of foreigners may apply for admission to the school for children of foreigners in Guangzhou by themselves.

(II) Higher education

Healthy foreign citizens who have education equivalent to Chinese high school graduate or above and hold an ordinary passport may apply for study or further education in higher education institutions qualified to recruit

(II) Banking services

Outlets of major banks in Guangzhou provide foreign currency exchange and reexchange services, and three-star hotels or above provide foreign currency exchange services. Star hotels, some restaurants, large department stores and supermarkets accept overseas credit cards. Most outlets of the Bank of China provide traveler's check cashing or collection services.

(III) Postal and courier services

The Post and Telecommunications Bureau has a city-wide service network. The Bureau is open seven days a week, and operates the collection and delivery of international/domestic letters, parcels, express mails and international business letters, telegraphs, telephones and telexes. In addition, some postal savings bank outlets provide services such as postal savings, remittances, and telegraphic remittances. There are green post boxes on the sides of the main road for people to post domestic and international letters.

III. Communications, Banking, Post and Telecommunications Services >

(I) Telecommunications and mobile communications

Generally, you may use the telephone in the guest room to make International Direct Dialing (IDD) calls. In addition to the telecommunications fees, the hotels will charge an additional service fee of about 10% - 15%. You may directly make international and domestic long-distance calls using an IP phone card or a prepaid card bought in stores on a public telephone. To apply for telephone and broadband Internet services, please call telecom operators at 10000 (China Telecom) or 10050 (China Railway Signal & Communication), or visit the operators' business outlets. Internet services are also available in hotels' guest rooms and business centers, and Internet cafes. Guangzhou has two mobile communication networks, GSM and CDMA, which provide wireless Internet services.

For details, please visit the operators' business outlets or call 10086 (China Mobile) or 10010 (China Unicom)

of the coach rides from or to passenger stations in Guangzhou, or the public transportation, please call 12345 to consult customer service, provide feedback or file real-name complaints. If you accidentally leave your luggage or items in buses or taxis, please contact the operators of the public transport vehicles according to the *Notice of the General Office of Guangzhou Municipal People's Government on Printing and Distributing the Regulations on the Management of Lost and Found Items in Guangzhou* (Sui Fu Ban Gui [2021] No. 1).

The QR code and ticket query interface of Xing Xun Tong App

trips on APM and tramcar lines is RMB 2 per person. To ride the metro lines, passengers may use the Passenger Code, Yang Cheng Tong, Ling Nan Tong, National All-in-One Card, Metro Day Pass, UnionPay credit card or a single trip ticket. At present, the Passenger Codes for Guangzhou Metro are available on the Guangzhou Metro App, WeChat applet, Alipay applet and Yang Cheng Tong App. What's more, the Passenger Code on the Guangzhou Metro App can also be used in three cities, Beijing, Shanghai and Chongqing, making it convenient for citizens to take urban rail transit in different cities.

As the preferred mode of public transportation for citizens and passengers, Guangzhou Metro has always been fulfilling its social responsibilities and living up to the brand philosophy of "all the way for you". To boost passenger satisfaction, Guangzhou Metro has offered services such as courtesy waiting areas, courtesy seats and courtesy direct trains, and launched passenger-friendly programs such as convenience umbrella, convenience medical kit, mother-to-be badge and green channel to meet the passengers' needs.

Guangzhou Metro Hotline: 96891
Guangzhou Metro Website: www.gzmtr.com
Guangzhou Metro App:

(IV) Public transport

Taxi fare in Guangzhou is as follows: starting price: RMB 12/3km; renewal price: RMB 2.6/km for the trip exceeding 3 kilometers; no-occupancy surcharge: 20% of the renewal price (15-25 kilometers), 50% of the renewal price (over 25 kilometers), or 30% of the renewal price (23:00-5:00). Passengers will pay any separately charged road/bridge fees. Drivers and passengers must wear seat belts. After paying the fare, passenger may ask for a receipt and get off the taxi with all their luggage and items.

If you need information about the coach schedule, bus and water bus routes, etc., Xing Xun Tong App is available for you to check the schedule and availability of tickets, purchase tickets, generate ticket codes, and check the bus position in real time. When taking public transportation or entering the passenger stations, please take relevant pandemic prevention and control measures as required. If you are dissatisfied with the operation or services

(III) Metro lines

Established in 1992, Guangzhou Metro Group is a large state-owned enterprise wholly-owned by the Guangzhou Municipal Government. At present, Guangzhou Metro has 14 lines in operation, namely Line 1, Line 2, Line 3 (including the northern extension of Line 3), Line 4, Line 5, Line 6, Line 7, Line 8, Line 9, Line 13, Line 14 (including the Knowledge City Line), Line 18, Line 21, APM Line (Zhujiang New Town Automated People Mover) and Guangzhou-Foshan Metro Line. With a total of 290 stations (including 40 interchange stations), these lines are 589.4 kilometers long. They span two cities, Guangzhou and Foshan, run through 11 administrative districts in Guangzhou, and connect major transportation hubs such as Baiyun Airport, high-speed rail stations, railway stations and other major passenger stations, realizing the "integration of Guangzhou and Foshan" and "access to metro lines in all districts". There are two tramcar lines in Guangzhou, namely, Guangzhou Tramcar Haizhu Circle Line (THZ1) and Huangpu Tramcar Line 1 (THP1), which are about 22.1 kilometers long and have a total of 30 stations.

The fares for trips on Guangzhou metro line network are calculated by travel distance: for the first 4 kilometers: RMB 2; for the next 4-12 kilometers: RMB 1 for every 4 kilometers; for the next 12-24 kilometers: RMB 1 for every 6 kilometers; RMB 1 for every 8 kilometers beyond 24 kilometers. The fare for

Jinan, Xi'an, Nanning, Guiyang, Chengdu, Chongqing, Lanzhou, Yinchuan, Kunming and Hong Kong within one day. Except Taiwan and Macao, there are regular-speed passenger trains to other provincial capital cities.

There are four railway stations in Guangzhou: Guangzhou Railway Station in Yuexiu District, Guangzhou East Railway Station in Tianhe District, Guangzhou South Railway Station in Panyu District, and Guangzhou North Railway Station in Huadu District.

Passenger trains from Guangzhou Station mainly go to cities such as Beijing, Shanghai, Wuhan, Chengdu, Chongqing, Guiyang, Lhasa, Urumqi, Nanning, Haikou, Xi'an, Yinchuan and Ningbo. Those from Guangzhou East Station mainly go to cities such as Hong Kong (Hung Hum), Shenzhen, Shantou, Meizhou, Xiamen, Harbin and Changchun, and some go to cities in East China (Beijing-Kowloon Railway), Beijing, Shanghai and other major cities; trains from Guangzhou South Railway Station are mainly high-speed EMU trains and Zhuhai Intercity EMU trains that reach the destinations within one day.

Passengers may log in to the China Railway Customer Service Center website at www.12306.cn or use "Railway 12306" App to buy or endorse a ticket or get a refund. These services are also available offline at the ticket offices in the railway stations. Additionally, passengers may buy an e-ticket using the self-service vending machines in the stations, or order a ticket by calling 95105105. E-tickets are available for sales at all sales agencies in Guangzhou.

From Qingcheng Station to Huadu Station, it takes as short as about 16 minutes if the train only stops at large stations, and about 33 minutes if it stops at every station. From Huadu Station to Baiyun Airport North Station, the travel time is about 14 minutes and 21 minutes respectively.

Baiyun Airport Customer Service Hotline
Tel: (020) 96158
Website: http://www.gbiac.net

(II) Railway

China Railway Guangzhou Group Co., Ltd. operates EMU trains and regular-speed passenger trains. High-speed EMU trains offer tickets to business seats (only a few trains), special seats, second-classseats and no seats. Regular-speed passenger trains offers tickets to premium soft sleepers and soft sleepers (only a few trains for both), hard sleepers, soft seats, hard seats and no seats, with or without air conditioners. EMU trains and long-distance trains are equipped with dining cars for passengers to order meals.

In recent years, the fast-developing railways have become a fast, convenient, safe, comfortable and affordable option for traveling. At present, Guangzhou has high-speed railways to Beijing, Shijiazhuang, Zhengzhou, Wuhan, Changsha, Shanghai, Nanjing, Hangzhou, Fuzhou, Hefei, Nanchang,

II. Transportation

(I) Guangzhou Baiyun International Airport

Located in Huadu District, north of downtown Guangzhou, Baiyun International Airport is one of the three major hub airports in China. It boasts convenient transportation. In addition to the airport expresses, this large comprehensive transportation hub can be conveniently accessed in various ways, including driving, taxi, Metro Line 3, Airport Express bus, and intercity rail transit.

At present, Baiyun Airport has 8 parking lots open to the public, namely P1, P2, P3, P4, P5, P6, P7 and P8. Specifically, P1 - P5 are around Terminal 1 (T1) and P6 - P8 around Terminal 2 (T2), providing a total of more than 8,400 parking spaces. Parking fees: Free for the first 15 minutes (inclusive); RMB 10 per hour for the first 2 hours (less than 1 hour is counted as 1 hour); RMB 5 per hour starting from the third hour; and RMB 60 for 24 hours a day.

Passengers may take the Airport Express buses from Baiyun Airport to Guangzhou Baima Building, Huashi Hotel in Tianhe District, Rosedale Hotel & Suites in Haizhu District, Vanke Shangcheng Yufu in Guangzhou Development District in downtown Guangzhou; from Baiyun Airport to Conghua, Zengcheng, Zhuhai (stops: Guantang, Tangjia, Xiangzhou), Shenzhen (stop: Bao'an), Zhongshan, Zhongshan Guzhen (stop: Henglan), Zhongshan Xiaolan (stop: Dongsheng), Huizhou (stop: Boluo), Foshan, Foshan Shunde (stop: Chencun), Shunde Longshan, Foshan Guicheng (stop: Dali), Foshan Gaoming (stop: Sanshui), Foshan Xiqiao (stop: Shishan), Zhaoqing (stop: Sihui), downtown Dongguan (stop: Nancheng), Dongguan Songshan Lake (stop: Dongcheng), Dongguan Wanjiang, Jiangmen, Jiangmen Taishan, Qingyuan (stop: Holyton Hotel), Yangjiang (stops: Zhishan, Enping), Heyuan, Yunfu and Shaoguan in the Pearl River Delta. Likewise, passengers may take the buses from these places to Baiyun Airport. Tickets are available at local bus stops, city terminals or self-service ticket vending machines and ticket offices at Baiyun Airport.

Guangzhou-Qingyuan Intercity Railway (Huadu Station to Qingcheng Station) and Guangzhou East Ring Intercity Railway (Huadu Station to Baiyun Airport North Station) offer great convenience to passengers traveling between Qingyuan, Huadu and Baiyun Airport. These two intercity railways are connected through stops at Qingcheng, Huadu and Baiyun Airport North.

(IV) Cultural and recreational activities

Guangzhou is a place to enjoy a variety of recreational activities and experience cultural feasts. Guangzhou Opera House, Xinghai Concert Hall, Friendship Theater and Sun Yat-sen Memorial Hall often put on classic Chinese and foreign shows. Guangzhou Art Museum, Guangzhou Museum of Art, Guangzhou Library and Guangdong Museum of Art present various kinds of exhibitions. Chimelong Paradise, Teemall and Grandview Mall offer motorized rides for relaxation. Xiangjiang Safari Park, Crocodile Park, Guangzhou Zoo and Baiyun Mountain Scenic Area are ideal destinations for relaxation, sightseeing and getting close to nature. Conghua Hot Springs, Bishuiwan Hot Spring Resort, Golden Leaf Hot Spring Resort and Jinxiu Xiangjiang Hot Spring Villa are places to not only enjoy the hot springs but also host large conferences. The Pearl River Night Cruise, Warner Jinyi Cinema, KTV, bars, etc. are your best choices to enjoy romantic nights in Guangzhou. The city has many bar areas, and the popular ones are: Fangcun Bar Streets on the north and south banks of the Pearl River, Binjiang Lu Bar Street, downtown Huanshi Lu Bar Street where foreigners gather, and Zhujiang Party Pier Bar Street.

There are also many large-scale sports venues in Guangzhou, such as Luhu golf course, tennis and badminton courts on Shamian and Ersha Island, yoga studios and Total Fitness for one to keep fit and relax.

(II) Lingnan fruits

Located in the south subtropical zone, Guangzhou has fresh fruits on the market all year round, and earns the reputation of the "Hometown of Fruits". It is blessed with over 200 kinds of fruits, among which lychee, banana, papaya and pineapple are known as the "Four Famous Fruits in Lingnan". In addition, other fruits such as mango, star fruit, pomegranate, longan, white olive, black olive, wampee, bayberry, jackfruit, Sanhua plum and watermelon are also well-received.

(III) Shopping

Guangzhou enjoys a well-deserved reputation of being a "Shopping Paradise", offering commodities from well-known brands and luxury goods worldwide to daily necessities, food, clothing from different countries in the supermarket. There are also specialized wholesale markets that export products globally and well meet the different needs of foreigners who visit Guangzhou for business, living or traveling.

Foreign tourists who wish to buy special local products as gifts for their families and friends may go to the Xindaxin Department Store on Beijing Lu, Lian Xiang Lou offering pastries and cakes, Guangzhou Restaurant Likoufu Franchise offering cured food, and Teemall, Grandview Mall and tourist attractions offering souvenirs.

I. Food and Recreation

(I) Capital of gourmet food

Guangzhou has been known as the Capital of Gourmet Food for 2,000 years. As one of the eight major cuisines in China, Cantonese cuisine features vastly diverse ingredients and exquisite production, emphasizing the color, fragrance, taste, shape and freshness of food. Cantonese dishes are of light taste, and change seasonally to highlight freshness and nutrition. In areas around Beijing Lu, Shangxiajiu Pedestrian Street and Xiguan Food Street, well-known snacks, dim sum and flavored food are everywhere. Soup, tea and late-night snacks are also part of Guangzhou's food culture.

The city is home to a large number of time-honored Cantonese restaurants, Chaozhou cuisine restaurants, bustling tea houses and restaurants serving other Chinese cuisines, such as Hunan restaurants, Sichuan restaurants, hot pot restaurants, Shandong restaurants and Huaiyang restaurants. There are also many good places to go for western cuisines, such as western restaurants, coffee shops, McDonald's and Pizza Hut. Additionally, a lot of affordable small restaurants, food stalls, traditional snack bars which serve special dishes, hot pots, barbecues and snacks also thrive in the city.

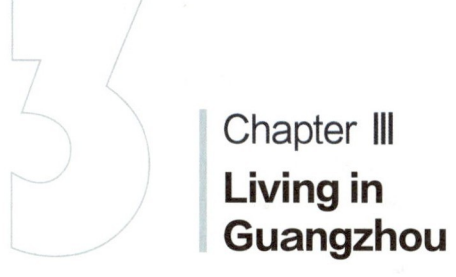

Chapter III
Living in Guangzhou

Guide for Foreigners in Guangzhou (2021)

District	Sub-district/Town	Office Set-up	Address	Telephone	Contact Person
Conghua District (1)	Wenquan	Independent (facing the street)	167 Chongkou Lu, Wenquan Town	87990806	Liang Jiawen 18826262295
Zengcheng District (1)	Yongning	Phoenix Town Community Office of Yongxin Police Station	8 Country Garden Phoenix Town Fengyan Yuan 5 Jie, Yongning Jie	32169393	Lie Zhaoqiang 13580510980 Zhan Jialin 13430365849

Chapter II Entry-Exit, Stay and Residence

District	Sub-district/Town	Office Set-up	Address	Telephone	Contact Person
Huangpu District (3)	Lianhe	Public Order, Complaints and Proposals Center	Lianhe Jiedao Management and Service Station for Foreigners	62208797	Sun Yuting 13660064405
Huadu District (1)	Huadong	Independent	A1 Dong, East Zone of RF Jingang City, Huadong Town	36977400	Jiang Jingyi 13710364240
Panyu District (8)	Luopu	Independent	40 Yansha Donglu, Panyu District	84581515	Chen Shuhui 13570480270. Huang Zixian
	Zhongcun	Binfenhui Community Party and Residents Affairs Center	20 Xueyuan Lu, Clifford Estates	84788095	Wen Chengfeng 13824409885
	Dashi	Government Affairs Center	149 Gangdong Lu	84785011	Han Junqing 18688204768 Li Jing 15920515616
	Nancun	Government Affairs Cente	1042 Xingye Dadao	84763275	Liang Minshan 15814536732 Guo Zhaohua 13922739433
	Xiaoguwei	Government Affairs Center	Zhongxinnan Dajie	34729905	Huang Siya 13535477741 Chen Zijun 13711254950
	Shilou	Property Service Center for the Media Village of the Asian Games City	1 Xingya 2 Lu, Asian Games City, Guangzhou	84658890	Chen Jiewen 13560430003 Liang Bingpei 13560320403
	Xinzao	Migrants Service Center	9 Xinghua Lu	None	Li Jiekai 15914398101 Chen Yaofeng 18820000796
	Shibi	Public Order, Complaints and Proposals Center of Guangzhou South Railway Station	Public Order, Complaints and Proposals Center of Guangzhou South Railway Station, Huijun Lu	39267235	Huang Yaodong 15322062854 Li Taoyu 13678973738
Nansha District (1)	Nansha	Independent	Second shop on the left side, 2 Country Garden Tianxi Bay, Nansha District (not numbered yet)	34684563	Luo Feifei 13535438848

047

District	Sub-district/Town	Office Set-up	Address	Telephone	Contact Person
Baiyun District (21)	Jingtai	Government Affairs Center	31 Yunyuan 3 Jie	None	Zhou Jiaying (auxiliary police officer of Jingtai Police Station 15920131617)
	Junhe	RF Town Community Police Office	1F, 26 Huayu Jie, RF Town, Junhe Jie	None	Zhang Yan 13826463520 Du Yanyi 17322080816 Zhang Hao 18316985517
	Shimen	Government Affairs Center	Window 10, Government Affairs Center, 12 Shijing Industrial Zone 1 Henglu, Shisha Lu	86166640	Qiu Yujie 13119590278
	Tongde	Government Affairs Center	78 Tongya Jie, Tongde Garden, Xicha Lu	None	Liang Yingxin 15017561882
	Xinshi	Government Affairs Center	89 Xinda Lu	None	Zhou Yingxin 18926211023
	Yongping	Government Affairs Center	1 Huixian Lu	None	Liu Zheng 18122717680
	Yuncheng	Migrants and House Leasing Managemente Center	1 Lvtai Xijie	None	Peng Qian 15218862190
	Shijing	Jinbi Xincheng Community Committee	40 Jinxin 3 Jie	None	Lin Haizheng 13922425228. Huang Yongzhao 15521065069.
	Renhe	Government Affairs Center	6 Helong 6 Lu	36031153	Zhou Xueying 15915812338
	Zhongluotan	Community Police Office	2 Changzhong Lu	36774468	He Mao 15602238851
	Jianggao	Migrants and House Leasing Management Service Center	1 Jinsha Nanlu	None	Li Yan 18826466876
Huangpu District (3)	Luogang	Xiangxue Community Committee	7 Shanxiang Lu, Huangpu District	89851230	Nie Min 15251516566
	Yunpu	Public Order, Complaints and Proposals Center	2 Rongyue 1 Jie	82207380	Jin Yinghu 13073070066

Chapter II Entry-Exit, Stay and Residence

District	Sub-district/Town	Office Set-up	Address	Telephone	Contact Person
Tianhe District (18)	Yuangang	Government Affairs Center	1F, 600 Yuangang Lu	None	Xiong Lei 18198971532
	Changxing	Government Affairs Center	1F, 289 Changxing Lu	None	Li Jianzhong 13302211462
	Zhuji	Migrants and House Leasing Management Center	2F, 2 Zhucundong Heng 5 Lu	32351603	Liao Yuechen 13828467376
	Xiancun	Government Affairs Center	167 Pingyun Lu	38392756	Lin Wanli 13760715404
Baiyun District (21)	Songzhou	RF Peninsula (Independent)	39 Hepan Dongjie	None	Tan Pianpian 13539479069
	Songzhou	RF Taoyuan (Independent)	36 Fulin Jie	None	Shen Jiaying 18814106457
	Tangjing	Government Affairs Center	907 Sanyuan Li Dadao	None	None
	Jingxi	Government Affairs Center	18 Jingxi Zhonglu	None	Chen Ying, 18825049495 Wu Zhiyong 13828413825
	Jinsha	Independent	22 Huicai 2 Jie	37614323	Shen Chunquan 13640692933 Feng Xinwen 18928872886
	Tonghe	Government Affairs Center	2077 Guangzhou Dadao Bei	None	Gong Jun 13560451633
	Huangshi	Guangdong University of Foreign Studies Community Police Office	19 Congyun Lu	None	Li Bin 13609012072
	Baiyunhu	Government Affairs Center	201, 288 Shixia Lu, Baiyun District, Guangzhou	None	Liu Sijia 13631570625 Luo Yongxian 13760726629 Li Huijuan 15914269467
	Helong	Migrants and House Leasing Management Center	629 Helong 1 Lu, Baiyun District, Guangzhou	None	Li Xianzhao 18826101044
	Jiahe	Public Order, Complaints and Proposals Center	1179 Helong 2 Lu	81310021	Liu Qiyan 13609027965

District	Sub-district/Town	Office Set-up	Address	Telephone	Contact Person
Tianhe District (18)	Shipai	Independent	Room 612, 6F, Regal Court Business Center, 570 Tianhe Beilu	87558146	Guan Guixian 13922110662 Wang Hong 13760758316
	Linhe	Government Affairs Center	101 Linhe Xilu	83629417 38848305	Zheng Yudong 13826087771 Wu Liling 13760777330
	Wushan	Migrants and House Leasing Management Center	201 Huijing Nanlu (left of Villandry Club)	38298306 85287435	Liu Yan 13570550988 Feng Guanxing 13751834628
	Liede	Independent	20 Haiming Lu	38211191	Lin Lin 13650713017
	Tianhe Nan	Government Affairs Center	193 Tiyuxi Hengjie	37343867	Li Bohao 18565090409 Shen Sihui
	Tangxia	Tangxia Jie Government Affairs Centre	1F, Tangdedong Henglu, Tangxia	None	Pan Jinxia 1351276620 Manhua Yun 13609007890
	Tianyuan	Government Affairs Center	2 Dongfang 3 Lu, Tianhe District	88527736	Hong Junmei 13924001202
	Longdong	Government Affairs Center	Hall, 1F, 1 Longdong Beilu	32108252	Xie Zhenxing 13480265474
	Chebei	Migrants and House Leasing Management Center	6 Beidong Lu, Dongpu	32205635	Yang Huimei 13824431416 Lin Xianjie 18198971207
	Qianjin	Government Affairs Center	3 Taoyuan Lu	None	Pan Tingting 13570350731 Zhang Xiaowen 18126713681
	Fenghuang	Public Order, Complaints and Proposals Center	88 Huamei Lu	None	Liu Lifeng 13560242029 Wu Junan 13828407222
	Huangcun	Government Affairs Center	1F, 5 Liyuan Lu	82307272	Yuan Jiaqi 18602072823
	Shahe	Government Affairs Center	1F, 89 Shahe Dajie	None	Zhang Zhicong 15914390030
	Xintang	Government Affairs Center	141-147 Hejing Lu	82357233 ext812	Wu Yilin 13143114510

Chapter II Entry-Exit, Stay and Residence

District	Sub-district/Town	Office Set-up	Address	Telephone	Contact Person
Liwan District (22)	Chongkou	Government Affairs Center	3F, 88 Fangcun Dadao Dong, Liwan District, Guangzhou	81803162	Chen Siqiong 13450472346
	Duobao	Migrants and House Leasing Management Center	1F, 121 Duobao Lu	None	Cai Xiaoting 13826401131
	Hailong	Government Affairs Center	1F, 107 Longxi Zhonglu	81415269	Chen Xuefeng 19966230753 13570376393
	Huadi	Party and Residents Affairs Center	187 Fangcun Dadao Zhong	None	Liang Xinyi 15017568391
	Qiaozhong	Government Affairs Center	169 Qiaozhong Nanlu	None	Zhang Hengfeng 15622341831
	Changhua	Government Affairs Center	1F, 33 Zhier, Enning Lu, Fengqing Shouyue	None	Cheng Jiamin 18126844491
	Dongjiao	Sub-district Office	4 Huannan Jie, Huanhua Lu	81502025	Huang Guihong 13928840306
	Dongsha	Sub-district Office	3 Yulan Lu, Dongsha Dadao	None	Wei Zhibin 15625093106
	Jinhua	Government Affairs Center	79 Jinhua Zhijie, Xihua Lu	81089535	Li Xiaocong 13535209329
	Shamian	Government Affairs Center	Basement, 1 Shamian 1 Jie	81218880	Luo Yi 13611429608
	Hualin	Migrants and House Leasing Management Center	1F, 34 Xingxian Fang	None	Cai Leshi 13725324074 Zhang Hongmei 15014242905
	Lingnan	Government Affairs Center	1F, 99 Shanmulan Lu	81859261	Wang Liting 13610222016
	Longjin	Government Affairs Center	52-54 Oujia Yuan, Liwan District	None	Chen Yinling 13570202420
	Caihong	Migrants and House Leasing Management Center	17 Xianjiazhuang	81021610	Chen Manyu 13411160010 Mai Sheng 13826076482
	Zhongnan	Migrants Service and Rental Management Service Center	3F, 52 Zengnan Lu	None	

Guide for Foreigners in Guangzhou (2021)

District	Sub-district/Town	Office Set-up	Address	Telephone	Contact Person
Yuexiu District (18)	Nonglin	Government Affairs Center	64 Zhixin Nanlu	87660519	Fu Xuelin 13710907401
	Zhuguang	Government Affairs Center	54 Zhuguang Lu	None	Yang Yingying 13543432917
	Baiyun	Government Affairs Center	54 Zhuguang Lu	83884653	
	Guangta	Public Order, Complaints and Proposals Center	26 Yuntai Li, Jiefang Zhonglu	83335087	Liang Jian, 13724840290
Haizhu District (22)	Chigang	Government Affairs Center	2F, Choi Chi Building, 448 Guangzhou Dadao Nan	None	Lao Dacheng 18922187577
	Xingang	Government Affairs Center	38 Zhier Xingang Xilu	None	Lin Qianting 13570480532
	Binjiang	Binjiang Police Station	Basement, 15 Yiminli, Binjiang Zhong, Haizhu District	None	Li Jinle 18664877452
	Pazhou	Dongbei Community Committee	9 Chenyue Lu	89260554	Su Minying 15818157347
Liwan District (22)	Nanyuan	Independent	Back Building, 14 Huiwen Fourth Street, Nanan Lu (next to Police Office)	81022953	Chen Xueping 13430258771 Xie Peiyi 13642779684
	Fengyuan	Independent	1F, S Dong, Viva Plaza, Liwan District	81708945	Li Sui 13326492523
	Xicun	Independent	151 Xiwan Lu	81670229 81670251	Chen Shi 18030592925
	Zhanqian	Independent	51 Chengang Lu (opposite Yuexiu Vehicle Administration Office)	None	Li Yingmei 13450203808
	Baihedong	Independent	East of 1F, 42 Zhier Hedong Lu, Liwan District	81557390	Zhang Minli 15914370900
	Shiweitang	Independent	7 Zhiyi Xingdong Lu	None	Chen Qian 13828485969
	Chajiao	Migrants and House Leasing Management Center	96 Chajiao Lu	81579169	Guan Shanming 13560089961

Chapter II Entry-Exit, Stay and Residence

(VII) Foreigners Service Centers in Guangzhou (98 in total as of May 12, 2021)

District	Sub-district/Town	Office Set-up	Address	Telephone	Contact Person
Yuexiu District (18)	Dengfeng	Independent	2F (on the right side), 5 Tongxin Lu (next to Guangdong Trust Real Estate Development Corp)	83492672	Liang Ye 19966290490 Chi Yulong 13640728742
	Huale	Foreigners Service Center	1F, 68 Taojinkeng	83498020	Yang Zhiyuan 13533201059
	Meihuacun	Government Affairs Center	Window 14, 1F, 21 Meihua Lu	31651312	Huang Yingya 37592527
	Huanghuagang	Migrants and Houses Leasing Service Center	84 Xianlie Zhonglu	37619431	Liu Zhongqin 18802032316
	Jianshe	Independent	2 Jianshe Zhong Malu	83523382	Dang Conghui 83523382
	Kuangquan	Independent	85 Yaotai Xijie	86326382	Wu Xueting 15099979894
	Liurong	Liurong Sub-district Service Center	109 Zhiyi Liurong Lu	83185971	Xu Suizhuo 13632244019
	Beijing	Migrants and House Leasing Management Center	482 Huifu Donglu	31058899 31058897	Lu Wenzhao 13632292991
	Dadong	Party and Residents Affairs Service Center	1F, 8 Dongren Xinjie	None	Chen Jiaheng 13710078144
	Datang	Government Affairs Center	17 Bingzheng Jie	83350595	Zeng Qihui 15914421516
	Dongshan	Government Affairs Center	2F, 26 Zhiyi Siyou Bei 2 Jie	87383516	Qiu Honglian 13719037175
	Hongqiao	Beiyuan Community Committee	1F, 220 Xiaobei Lu	None	You Chengzhu 13925001352
	Liuhua	Independent	209 Zhier Huanshi Zhonglu	86661620	Sun Shujing 83127280 18818854205
	Renmin	House Leasing Management Center	257 Daxin Lu	81092131	Song Lin 13826026221

041

3. Entry and Exit Office Hall of Tianhe District Public Security Bureau
Address: 13 Ruanjian Lu, Tianhe District
Tel: 12345
Office hours: 9:00-12:00 / 13:00-17:00 from Monday to Friday

4. Entry and Exit Office Hall of Baiyun District Public Security Bureau
Address: 11 Guangyun Lu, Baiyun District
Tel: 12345
Office hours: 9:00-12:00 / 13:00-17:00 from Monday to Friday

5. Entry and Exit Office Hall of Huangpu District Public Security Bureau
Address: 2F, 13 Xiangxue 3 Lu, Huangpu District
Tel: 12345
Office hours: 9:00-12:00 / 13:00-17:00 from Monday to Friday

6. Entry and Exit Office Hall of Huadu District Public Security Bureau
Address: 101 Tiangui Lu, Huadu District
Tel: 12345
Office hours: 9:00-12:00 / 13:00-17:00 from Monday to Friday

7. Entry and Exit Office Hall of Panyu District Public Security Bureau
Address: 550 Yayun Dadao, Panyu District
Tel: 12345
Office hours: 9:00-12:00 / 13:00-17:00 from Monday to Friday

8. Entry and Exit Office Hall of Nansha District Public Security Bureau
Address: 2F, Building 5 China Tiejian Global Center, 6 Huameng Jie, Huangge Town, Nansha District, Guangzhou
Tel: 12345
Office hours: 9:00-12:00 / 13:00-17:00 from Monday to Friday

9. Entry and Exit Office Hall of Yuexiu District Public Security Bureau
Address: 72 Yuexiu Zhonglu, Yuexiu District
Tel: 12345
Office hours: 9:00-12:00 / 13:00-17:00 from Monday to Friday

10. Entry and Exit Office Hall of Liwan District Public Security Bureau
Address: 328 Zhongshan 7 Lu, Liwan District
Tel: 12345
Office hours: 9:00-12:00 / 13:00-17:00 from Monday to Friday

11. Entry and Exit Office Hall of Zengcheng District Public Security Bureau
Address: 7 Jingguan Dadao, Lihu Jie, Zengcheng District
Tel: 12345
Office hours: 9:00-12:00 / 13:00-17:00 from Monday to Friday

12. Entry and Exit Office Hall of Conghua District Public Security Bureau
Address: 128 Hebin Beilu, Chengjiao Jie, Conghua District
Tel: 12345
Office hours: 9:00-12:00 / 13:00-17:00 from Monday to Friday

(3) Foreigners who stay in host families: the host's identity papers.

(4) Foreigners who reside in relevant institutions: a certificate issued by the host institution or the host unit, and the identity papers of the legal representatives of the institution.

(V) Self declaration by foreigners for temporary accommodation registration

1. Platform URL link:

http://crjyw.gzjd.gov.cn/ELSCommunityinfoPutup

Log in through the link of "www.gzid.gov.cn – Entry and Exit Business - Self Declaration for Accommodation Registration for Foreigners". Google Chrome is recommended, as Internet Explorer may not fully display the information.

2. Applicable scope

(1) The self-help declaration platform for temporary accommodation registration for foreigners is applicable to foreign nationals residing in Guangzhou only.

(2) Foreigners whose current passports have no entry and exit records, foreign infants born in China, foreigners and residents of Hong Kong, Macao and Taiwan who enter and leave China with People's Republic of China Entry and Exit Permit shall go to the police station for on-site application.

3. Notes

(1) Please provide a valid Chinese mobile phone number to receive the latest important notices.

(2) After filling in the form as required, please pay attention to the SMS alerts sent by the entry-exit department. If the application fails, the applicant shall apply with the local police station on-site.

(VI) Offices for visa and permit application in Guangzhou

1. Entry and Exit Administration of the Guangzhou Public Security Bureau

Address: 155 Jiefang Nanlu, Guangzhou

Tel: 12345

Office hours: 9:00-12:00 / 13:00-17:00 from Monday to Friday

2. Entry and Exit Office Hall of Haizhu District Public Security Bureau

Address: 18 Zilong Dajie, Jiangnan Xilu, Haizhu District

Tel: 12345

Office hours: 9:00-12:00 / 13:00-17:00 from Monday to Friday

(1) They are near relatives of Chinese nationals;

(2) They have settled in China; or

(3) They have other legitimate reasons.

3. Renounce Chinese nationality

Eligible applicants: Chinese nationals who meet one of the following conditions may renounce their Chinese nationality upon approval of their applications:

(1) They are near relatives of foreign nationals;

(2) They have settled abroad; or

(3) They have other legitimate reasons.

(IV) Accommodation registration for foreigners

After arriving in Guangzhou, foreigners shall register for temporary accommodation according to Article 39 of the *Exit and Entry Administration Law of the People's Republic of China*.

Where foreigners stay in hotels in China, the hotels shall register their accommodation.

For foreigners who reside or stay in domiciles other than hotels, they or the persons who accommodate them shall, within 24 hours after the foreigners' arrival, go through the registration formalities with the public security organs in the places of residence.

If the validity of the accommodation registration expires or the visa has changed, the temporary accommodation registration shall be updated promptly.

Houses leased to foreigners shall meet the safety requirements and be registered and filed for the purpose of leasing as is required.

The following documents shall be submitted for accommodation registration:

1. The identity information page (with photo) and valid visa page of the passport or valid identity papers (including but not limited to passport, international travel documents, temporary documents, refugee certificate, asylum-seekers certificate, etc.) of the lodger (one photocopy shall be provided and the original be presented for verification);

2. Residence certificate (one photocopy shall be provided and the original be presented for verification)

(1) Foreigners who purchase their own houses: immovable property ownership certificate or real estate ownership certificate.

(2) Foreigners who live in rental houses: the identity papers of the leaser and the House Leasing Contract signed with the leaser. Where the leaser entrusts a housing agency with full authority for leasing and management, the agency shall be regarded as the lodger and provide the legal person's identity certificate of the agency.

(3) A valid passport;

(4) Permanent residence permit of the applicant;

(5) Supporting materials before and after the change of relevant information (applicable for change of information);

(6) A Proof of Loss issued by the local public security authority or the loss statement written and signed by the applicant (applicable for permit loss);

(7) Other certificates as required by the public security authority.

3. Notes

(1) A foreigner who holds a valid permanent residence permit may apply for replacement of the permit within one month before the validity expires.

(2) If the information in permanent residence permit changes, he or she may apply for replacement of the permit within one month after the changes.

(3) Where the permanent residence permit is damaged or lost, he or she shall apply for replacement or reissue of the permit promptly.

(III) Nationality-related service

1. Restore Chinese nationality

Eligible applicants: Foreigners who once held Chinese nationality and abide by China's Constitution and other laws.

2. Acquire Chinese nationality

Eligible applicants: Foreign nationals or stateless persons who are willing to abide by China's Constitution and laws and who meet one of the following conditions may apply for Chinese nationality:

personnel recognized by market (whose annual wage income is not less than 6 times the average wage of in-service employees in the cities or towns where they are located in the previous year) can apply for permanent residence in China together with the applicant.

(2) Children: children of personnel recognized by the government, with outstanding contribution, with required positions, or making general investment, Chinese holding a doctoral degree, employed personnel, or personnel recognized by market (whose annual wage income is not less than 6 times the average wage of in-service employees in the cities or towns where they are located in the previous year), who are of foreign nationality, unmarried and aged below 18, can apply for permanent residence in China together with the applicant.

5. Family reunion

(1) Spouses: foreigners married to a Chinese citizen with permanent household registration in Guangzhou or a foreigner who has obtained permanent residence status in China; the marriage relationship has lasted for five years; have stayed in China for five consecutive years and not less than nine months each year.

(2) Children: unmarried foreigners aged under 18, one or both of whose parents are Chinese citizens with permanent household registration in Guangzhou or foreigners who have obtained permanent residence status in China.

(3) Dependent relatives: foreigners aged over 60 who have no immediate family abroad; have resided in China for five consecutive years before the date of application and for not less than nine months every year; and live as a dependent on immediate family within China.

(II) Renewal and reissue of permanent residence permit

1. Application conditions

A foreigner who holds a valid permanent residence permit and has not lost his or her permanent residence status in China, may apply for replacement or reissue of the permit if he or she meets one of the following conditions:

(1) The validity of the permanent residence permit expires;

(2) The information in permanent residence permit changes;

(3) The permanent residence permit is damaged or lost.

2. Application documents

(1) Application Form for Foreigners to Renew or Reissue Permanent Residence Permit (in triplicate);

(2) Four recent photos of the applicant, bareheaded, full face and colored with blue background (specification: 48 × 33mm);

(2) Personnel marked as "talents": foreign high-level talents whose work-type residence permit are marked with a note of "talent" and have worked for three years in China.

(3) Personnel recognized by the market: foreigners who have worked in Guangdong for four consecutive years and lived in China for no less than six months each year within these four years, have earned an annual wage income (before tax) of over RMB 400,000 for four consecutive years and have paid personal income tax of more than RMB 70,000 each year for four consecutive years; or those whose annual wage income is no less than 6 times of the average wage of urban working employees in the city or town where they are located in the previous year, and the annual individual income tax paid is no less than 10% of the annual wage income.

(4) Personnel with required positions: foreigners holding a position of vice general manager, vice chairman, or above in qualifying organizations, or those holding titles of associate professor, associate researcher, or above, or those receiving the equivalent treatment for at least four years, and having lived in China for no less than three years cumulatively in these four years with good taxation records.

(5) Overseas Chinese holding a doctoral degree: Chinese with a foreign nationality who have a doctoral degree and work in Guangzhou with a work-type residence permit.

(6) Overseas Chinese employees: Chinese with a foreign nationality who have worked in an enterprise in Guangzhou with a work-type residence permit for 4 consecutive years and have actually lived in China for at least 6 months each year.

3. Foreign investors

(1) General investment: foreigners who have invested a total of USD 2 million in China as a natural person or more than USD 500,000 in industries encouraged by the *Catalogue for Guidance of Foreign Investment Industries* promulgated by the state, have made stable investment for three consecutive years and have a good taxation record.

(2) Investment in the Greater Bay Area: foreigners who make direct investment in nine cities of the Greater Bay Area as natural persons or through companies that they themselves are controlling shareholders as natural persons, with stable investment for three consecutive years and a total investment of USD one million (a total investment of more than USD 500,000 in industries encouraged by the *Catalogue for Guidance of Foreign Investment Industries* promulgated by the state) and a good taxation record.

4. Accompanying family members

(1) Spouses: foreign spouses of personnel recognized by the government, with outstanding contribution, with required positions, or making general investment, Chinese holding a doctoral degree, employed personnel, or

V. Application for Permanent Residence

(I) Types of personnel eligible for permanent residence in China

1. Special personnel

(1) Personnel recommended by government: high-level foreign talents who meet the criteria and recommended by Guangzhou Municipal People's Government or the Guangdong Free Trade Office.

(2) Personnel with outstanding contribution: foreigners who make major and outstanding contributions or are badly needed by China.

2. Employed personnel

(1) Personnel meeting evaluation standard: foreign members in an innovation and entrepreneurship team or foreign technical personnel recruited by enterprises whose credit points are over 70 in accordance with the foreign talents' credit points rating standards implemented in Guangdong Free Trade Zone or nine cities in Guangdong, Hong Kong and Macao Greater Bay Area.

receipt and decide whether to issue the visa within the prescribed time of the receipt. The time limit for processing the visa is 7 working days (investigation time excluded if the public security authority needs to investigate and verify relevant matters). When the passport or other international travel documents are kept for the purpose of visa application, the applicant can legally stay in China with the acceptance receipt. If he or she needs to travel to other cities in China by plane or train, the applicant can apply to affix the special entry-exit seal on the acceptance receipt. The applicant shall collect the passport from the entry-exit administration department of the public security authority on the date indicated in the acceptance receipt.

C. A statement from the embassy or consulates of his or her home country in China if there is;

D. Foreign employees and students shall submit a confirmation letter from their organizations;

E. The original and photocopy of the visa held at the time of entry if the residence permit is damaged abroad;

F. A new physical examination if the residence permit is damaged abroad and the applicant stays abroad for more than 30 days.

(VII) Notes for visa and permit application

1. To apply for a visa, stay and residence permit, foreigners need to log into the service application page of www.gzjd.gov.cn (the official website of Guangzhou Public Security Bureau) and select "foreigner's certificate processing" for online appointment, or visit the online application desk of Guangzhou Entry-Exit Administration Building for on-site appointment. Organizations issuing confirmation letter for foreigners' application for visa, stay and residence permit need to log into the service application page of www.gzjd.gov.cn and select "foreign-related organizations filing" for online filing. Those passing the filing review are waived of registration certificate when applying for foreigners' visa, stay and residence permit.

2. Foreigners working in China shall hold both work permit and work-type residence permit.

3. When the registered information in a foreigner's residence permit has changed, the holder shall, within 10 days from the date of change, report to the issuing organ for the change of the information.

4. Applicants aged between 18 and 70 shall submit Health Certificate issued by Guangdong Entry-Exit Inspection and Quarantine Bureau when applying for residence permit for the first time.

5. Marriage certificate, birth certificate, kinship certificate, adoption certificate, certificate of information change such as name change, issued by organizations of a foreign country shall be authenticated by the Chinese embassy or consulates in that country.

Certificates in a foreign language shall be translated into Chinese by a notary office in China.

6. Foreigners residing in China who apply for an extension of their residence period shall submit an application to the entry-exit administration department of the public security authority at or above the county level in the place of residence 30 days before the expiration of the validity period of their residence permit.

7. If a foreigner's visa application meets the acceptance requirement, the entry-exit department of the public security authority shall issue an acceptance

(VI) Documents required for visa and permit reissue

After entering China, where a foreigner applies for visa and permit reissue due to the loss, theft or damage of a valid general visa, stay permit or residence permit held, a general visa, stay permit or residence permit which is the same with the original can be issued. The applicant is required to submit the following documents:

1. Basic documents

(1) His or her valid passport or other international travel documents and the original and photocopy of his or her passport and visa;

(2) The Overseas Personnel Temporary Accommodation Form valid in Guangzhou;

(3) A digital photo for the purpose of Guangdong entry/exit documents and its Inspection Note;

(4) Other certificates as required by the public security authority.

2. Relevant supporting documents

(1) Where a visa or stay permit is lost or stolen:

Proof of Passport Loss or the statement from the embassy or consulate of his or her home country in China or Police Reporting Receipt;

(2) Where a visa or stay permit is damaged:

A. The damaged passport;

B. Completed Case/Incidence Report Form;

C. A statement from the embassy or consulates of the applicant's home country in China if there is.

(3) Where a group visa is lost, stolen or damaged:

A. A receipt of case reporting issued by the police station;

B. A letter of certification from the local travel agency;

C. Photocopy of the group visa.

(4) Where a residence permit is lost or stolen:

A. A Proof of Passport Loss or a statement from the embassy or consulate of applicant's home country in China or Police Reporting Receipt;

B. Foreign employees and students are required to submit a confirmation letter from their organizations;

C. Where the residence permit is lost or stolen abroad, the original and photocopy of the visa held at the time of entry shall also be submitted;

D. Where the residence permit is lost or stolen abroad and the applicant stays abroad for more than 30 days, he or she shall take a new physical examination.

(5) Where a residence permit is damaged:

A. The damaged passport;

B. Completed Case/Incident Report Form;

(5) Family member relationship certificate, photocopy of passport, visa or stay/residence permit of the person visited (the original document need to be verified), and a letter issued by the person visited;

(6) Other certificates as required by the public security authority.

4. Documents required for private business residence permit for family members of employees

Spouses, parents, children under the 18 years of age and parents-in-law of foreigners residing in Guangzhou due to work and study shall enter China with S1visa if they intend to reside in China and apply for private business residence permit within 30 days from the date of entry.

The applicant shall respond to questions and provide the following documents during application:

(1) The original and photocopy of his or her valid passport and visa;

(2) Completed Foreign National Visa and Residence Application Form;

(3) A digital photo for the purpose of Guangdong entry/exit documents and its Inspection Note;

(4) The Overseas Personnel Temporary Accommodation Form valid in Guangzhou;

(5) Health Certificate issued by Guangdong Entry-Exit Inspection and Quarantine Bureau (required when applying for residence permit for the first time);

(6) To visit a permanent resident foreigner in China, the applicant shall also provide photocopies of the valid passport and residence permit of the former (the original document needs to be verified), as well as the certification letter, and kinship certificate issued by the organization where he works or studies;

(7) Other certificates as required by the public security authority.

5. Documents required for stay permit application

If an employee needs to stay for humanitarian reasons after the end of his or her employment, he or she may apply to the entry-exit administration department of the local public security authority for a stay permit. The applicant shall respond to questions and provide the following materials during application:

(1) Valid passport or other international travel documents and the original and photocopy of his or her valid passport and visa;

(2) Completed Foreign National Visa and Residence Application Form;

(3) A digital photo for the purpose of Guangdong entry/exit documents and its Inspection Note;

(4) The Overseas Personnel Temporary Accommodation Form valid in Guangzhou;

(5) Letter of Employment Termination from his/her previous employer;

(6) Other certificates as required by the public security authority.

China, Permit for Foreign Nationals to Engage in Offshore Oil Operations in the People's Republic of China, or photocopy of approval document for performances issued by agencies authorized by the cultural authority (the original document need to be verified);

(6) A confirmation letter from the employer;

(7) Other certificates as required by the public security authority.

3. Documents required for S2 visa extension for family members of employees

Family members of foreigners who stay or reside in China for work and study ("family members" refer to spouses, parents, parents-in-law, sons, daughters, brothers, sisters, grandparents, grandsons, granddaughters, sons-in-law and daughters in law) shall hold a S2 visa when they come to China for family visit over a short period of time. If they intend to stay longer than the visa stay period, they shall apply for a visa extension 7 days before the visa validity expires.

The applicant shall respond to questions and provide the following documents during application:

(1) Valid passport or other international travel documents and the original and photocopy of his or her valid passport and visa;

(2) Completed Foreign National Visa and Residence Application Form;

(3) A digital photo for the purpose of Guangdong entry/exit documents and its Inspection Note;

(4) The Overseas Personnel Temporary Accommodation Form valid in Guangzhou;

China with S1 visa and apply for private business residence permit within 30 days from the date of their entry.

(V) Documents required for Visa and Permit application

1. Documents required for application of work-type residence permit for the first time

Foreigners coming to work in Guangzhou shall enter with Z Visa and apply for work-type residence permit within 30 days from the date of their entry.

The applicant shall respond to questions and provide the following documents during application:

(1) The original and photocopy of his or her valid passport and visa;

(2) Completed Foreign National Visa and Residence Application Form;

(3) A digital photo for the purpose of Guangdong entry/exit documents and its Inspection Note;

(4) The Overseas Personnel Temporary Accommodation Form valid in Guangzhou;

(5) Health Certificate issued by Guangdong Entry-Exit Inspection and Quarantine Bureau (required when applying residence permit for the first time);

(6) Notification Letter of Foreigners Work Permit, Foreign Expert Certificate or Foreigners Employment Permit of the People's Republic of China, Permit for Foreign Nationals to Engage in Offshore Oil Operations in the People's Republic of China, or photocopy of approval document for performances issued by agencies authorized by the cultural authority (the original document need to be verified);

(7) A confirmation letter from the employer;

(8) Applicants who enter China with other types of visa may apply for work-type residence permit valid for one year or less with work permit certificate issued by human resources and social security department or foreign experts department;

(9) Other certificates as required by the public security authority.

2. Documents required for work-type residence permit extension

(1) The original and photocopy of applicant's valid passport and visa;

(2) Foreign National Visa and Residence Application Form;

(3) A digital photo for the purpose of Guangdong entry/exit documents and its Inspection Note;

(4) The Overseas Personnel Temporary Accommodation Form valid in Guangzhou;

(5) Notification Letter of Foreigners Work Permit, Foreign Expert Certificate or Foreigners Employment Permit of the People's Republic of

(III) Visa replacement

If a foreigner applies for a replacement due to loss, theft or damage of a general visa after entry, a general visa with the same type, validity of entry, number of entries and validity of stay as the original can be issued. The applicant shall apply in accordance with the following requirements:

1. A foreigner whose passport is lost or stolen shall provide a Proof of Loss or a statement from the embassy or consulate of his or her home country in China as well as a new passport or other international travel document.

2. A foreigner whose passport is damaged shall provide the damaged passport or a statement from the embassy or consulate of his or her home country in China as well as a new passport or other international travel document.

3. A foreigner whose group visa is lost, stolen or damaged, shall provide a letter of certification from the local travel agency and a photocopy of the group visa.

4. In addition to the above information, the applicant shall also provide his or her Foreigners' Accommodation Registration Form valid in Guangzhou, a visa photo for foreigners in Guangdong Province and its Inspection Note.

5. Other certificates as required by the public security authority.

(IV) Types of residence permit

1. Work-Type Residence Permit is issued to foreign nationals who work in Guangzhou. They shall enter China with Z visa and apply for work-type residence permit within 30 days from the date of their entry.

2. Study-Type Residence Permit is issued to foreign students who study in Guangzhou for a long time. They shall enter China with X1 visa and apply for study-type residence permit within 30 days from the date of their entry.

3. Foreign Journalist Residence Permit is issued to resident foreign journalists in China. They shall enter China with J1 visa and apply for foreign journalist residence permit within 30 days from the date of their entry.

4. Family Reunion Residence Permit is issued to Chinese citizens or foreign family members of foreigners with permanent residence status in China who apply for residence in Guangzhou due to family reunion, as well as foreign children under 18 years of age of Chinese with a foreign nationality or overseas Chinese in Guangzhou due to foster care. They shall enter China with Q1 visa and apply for family reunion residence permit within 30 days from the date of their entry.

5. Private Business Residence Permit is issued to the spouse, parents, children under 18 years of age, parents-in-law of foreigners residing in Guangzhou for work and study as well as foreigners who need to reside in China for medical assistance, service or other private affairs. They shall enter

7. M visa is issued to those who come to China for commercial and trade activities.

8. Q1 visa is issued to those who are family members of Chinese citizens or of foreigners with Chinese permanent residence and apply to go to China for family reunion, or to those who intend to go to China for the purpose of foster care. Q2 visa is issued to those who apply to visit their relatives who are Chinese citizens residing in China or foreigners with permanent residence in China for a short period of time.

9. R visa is issued to those who are high-level talents needed by China or with specialized skills urgently needed in China.

10. S1 visa is issued to those who intend to stay in China for a long time to visit the foreigners working or studying in China to whom they are spouses, parents, sons or daughters under the age of 18 or parents-in-law, or to those who intend to go to China for other private affairs.

S2 visa is issued to those who intend to stay in China for a short period of time to visit their family members who are foreigners working or studying in China, or to those who intend to go to China for other private matters.

11. X1 visa is issued to those who intend to study in China for a long time.

X2 visa is issued to those who intend to study in China for a short period of time.

12. Z visa is issued to those who intend to take up employment in China.

(II) Documents required for visa extension and renewal

Application for visa extension and renewal shall be made 7 days before the expiration of the visa validity. The applicants shall respond to questions and provide the following documents during the application:

1. Valid passport or other international travel documents and the original and photocopy of his or her valid passport and visa;

2. Completed Foreign National Visa Application Form;

3. A digital photo for the purpose of Guangdong entry/exit documents and its Inspection Note;

4. The Overseas Personnel Temporary Accommodation Form valid in Guangzhou;

5. Other relevant supporting documents;

6. Other certificates as required by the public security authority.

The extension of the visa stay may not exceed, in aggregate, the period of stay originally indicated in the visa. The period of stay for renewed visa may not exceed one year in total from the date of the current entry.

IV. Visa and Permit Application

(I) Types of visa

Chinese visas are classified as Diplomatic visa, Courtesy visa, Business visa, and General visa. General visas are further classified into following types, which are marked by a corresponding Chinese phonetic alphabet:

1. C visa is issued to crew members of trains, aircraft and ships on international travels, flights or voyages, their accompanying family members and motor vehicle drivers engaged in cross-border transport activities.

2. D visa is issued to foreign nationals who come to reside permanently in China.

3. F visa is issued to foreign nationals who come to China for visits, inspection tours, lectures, and exchanges.

4. G visa is issued to foreign nationals who transit through China.

5. J-1 visa is issued to resident foreign journalists of foreign news organizations stationed in China, and J-2 Visa is issued to foreign journalists who come to China for short-term news coverage.

6. L visa is issued to foreign nationals who come to China for tourism. Those who come as a tourist group may be granted a group visa.

Railway Station Office of Guangzhou Customs is mainly responsible for the supervision and clearance of luggage and goods carried by inbound and outbound passengers at Tianhe Railway Station.

Address: 1 Dongzhan Lu, Tianhe District, Guangzhou, China.

Public transportation: Exit G – Guangzhou East Railway Station - Metro Line 1 and Line 3

Panyu Office of Guangzhou Customs is mainly responsible for the supervision and clearance of luggage and goods carried by inbound and outbound passengers at Panyu Lotus Mountain Passenger Port.

Address: Lotus Mountain Passenger Port, 1 Gangqian Lu, Shilou Town, Panyu District, Guangzhou, China.

Public transportation: Pan 160 (Bus); Exit A - Shiji Station - Metro Line 4 to Pan 92, 93 (Metro to Bus).

Nansha Office of Guangzhou Customs is mainly responsible for the supervision and clearance of luggage and goods carried by inbound and outbound passengers at Nansha Passenger Port and Nansha International Cruise Homeport.

Address: Inside Nansha Passenger Port, Dong 1 Lu, Shangmao Dadao, Haibin New Town, Nansha District, Guangzhou; Inside Guangzhou Nansha International Cruise Home Port, Xingsha Lu, Nansha District, Guangzhou

Public transportation: Exit G - Nansha Passenger Port Station - Metro Line 4

Guangzhou Post Office of Guangzhou Customs is mainly responsible for the supervision and clearance of inbound and outbound postal articles, print and audio-visual products in Guangdong Province (except Shenzhen, Zhuhai, Shantou, Jiangmen and Dongguan), Hebei Province, Gansu Province, Qinghai Province and NingxiaHui Autonomous Region, the supervision of transit international mail bags entering and leaving China through Guangzhou Post Office to/from other cities and provinces, as well as the supervision and clearance of inbound and outbound goods, express goods and cross-border e-commerce handled by postal enterprises.

Address: Guangzhou Liuhua Postal Compound, 4 Zhannan Lu, Yuexiu District, Guangzhou

Public transportation: Exit D2 - Guangzhou Railway Station - Metro Line 2 and Line 5

Tianhe Office of Guangzhou Customs is mainly responsible for the inspection of imported and exported articles for public and personal use in the administrative area of Guangzhou Customs.

Address: 4 F, Guangzhou Government Affairs Center, 61 Huali Lu, Tianhe District, Guangzhou.

Public transportation: Exit B1- Zhujiang New Town Station -Metro Line 3

> **For rules and procedures, please contact:**
> Tel: 020-12360
> **Guangzhou Customs**
> Address: 83 Huacheng Dadao, Zhujiang New Town, Guangzhou
> Website: http://guangzhou.customs.gov.cn
> **Huangpu Customs**
> Address: No.333 Dashadi Dong, Huangpu District, Guangzhou
> Website: http://huangpu.customs.gov.cn

(III) Main Responsibilities of Guangzhou Customs Offices at border crossings and public transportation information

Baiyun Airport Office of Guangzhou Customs is mainly responsible for the supervision and clearance of luggage and goods carried by inbound and outbound passengers at Baiyun International Airport.

Address: Heng 1 Lu, Konggangsi Lu, Guangzhou Baiyun International Airport, Renhe Town, Baiyun District, Guangzhou.

Public transportation: Airport South Station - Metro Line 3 (North Extension).

III. Import and Export of Articles for Public and Personal Use

(I) Equipment and vehicles of resident offices

Resident offices may apply for the importation and exportation of office equipment and motor vehicles and permanent personnel may apply for the importation of duty-free motor vehicles in accordance with relevant regulations.

A motor vehicle which has been imported duty-free as described above may be transferred to another resident office or to another staff member of the resident office or sold to an authorized operating entity after it has been released by the Customs for four years or the term of office of the staff member has expired. When the six-year period of customs supervision expires, the vehicle may be transferred, sold or used for other purposes.

(II) Motor vehicles for personal use

Permanent members of staff may, after obtaining long-term residence permit, import a motor vehicle, limited to one each person. Written applications shall be submitted by the permanent personnel or their appointed customs declaration agency to the competent Customs. Upon the approval of the competent Customs, the motor vehicle can be released by presenting the approval notice and/or other required documents. The vehicle is subject to duties according to the relevant regulations. To apply for the importation of such a vehicle, the following documents shall be submitted to the competent Customs:

1. Identity papers;

2. Long-term residence permit;

3. Application Form of the Customs of the People's Republic of China for Importation and Exportation of Articles for Personal Use;

4. Bill of lading (waybill), packing list and other required documents;

5. Other documents as required by the Customs.

After being approved by the competent Customs and obtaining a *Notice of the Customs of the People's Republic of China on the Issuance/Revocation of Licenses for Supervised Imported/Exported Vehicles*, permanent personnel shall complete the vehicle transfer formalities with the public security and traffic administration authority.

travel history and contact history truthfully, and cooperate with the Customs for quarantine investigation.

6. Passengers shall pay close attention to their physical conditions after entering China. In case of symptoms of infectious diseases, they shall seek medical treatment immediately, disclose their travel history and contact history in detail, and inform the Customs of their medical treatment.

According to *Frontier Health and Quarantine Law of the People's Republic of China* and detailed rules for its implementation, "passengers carrying microorganisms, human tissues, biological products, blood, blood products and other special articles into or out of the country shall apply in advance to the Customs directly administering their destinations for examination and approval of special articles, and declare to the Customs when entering or leaving the country. Those who bring blood products or biological products for their own use and for the purpose of prevention or treatment of diseases only into and out of the country are not subject to the examination and approval procedures of health and quarantine, and the relevant certificates of the hospital shall be presented to the Customs at the time of entry and exit; the amount allowed is limited to one course of treatment specified by the prescription or instruction".

In order to protect the health and safety of Chinese citizens, in accordance with *Frontier Health and Quarantine Law of the People's Republic of China* and its implementation rules, inbound and outbound passengers shall pay attention to health issues in their international travel.

1. Before leaving, passengers can log in to the official websites of General Administration of Customs and Guangzhou Customs to check the global situation of infectious diseases, or consult the offices of Guangzhou Customs and its international travel health care center for health information.

2. In case of fever, headache, cough, dyspnea, nausea, vomiting, abdominal pain, diarrhea, muscle pain, joint pain, rash, jaundice and other infectious disease symptoms (hereinafter referred to as "infectious disease symptoms") when leaving the country, passengers shall report to the customs, and may consider canceling or delaying the trip and seeking medical treatment promptly.

3. Passengers shall enhance disease prevention awareness during international travel and try to avoid contact with people showing infectious disease symptoms; avoid being bitten by rats, ants, ticks and other vector organisms, and maintain good hygiene habits. In case of symptoms of infectious diseases, passengers shall seek medical treatment in a timely manner and seek help from the Chinese embassy or consulate where they stay if necessary.

4. In case of infectious disease symptoms on the way back to China, passengers shall inform the crew on the means of transport promptly and truthfully, and cooperate with the crew for self-isolation and personal protection.

5. In case of infectious disease symptoms at the time of entry, passengers shall report to the health quarantine personnel of the Customs, disclose their

Non-resident long-term visitors (foreign nationals, residents from Hong Kong, Macao and Taiwan or overseas Chinese who are approved to enter by the public security authority and stay in China continually for one year or longer and return to their original place of residence outside China when their residence period expires) may import and export items for personal use according to the procedures set forth in the *Provisions of the Customs of the People's Republic of China on the Importation and Exportation of Articles for Personal Use by Non-Resident Long-Term Visitors*. To bring items for personal use into China, an applicant shall file a written application with the competent Customs or the Customs at the border crossings in person or through his or her appointed customs declaration agency, and produce the following documents:

1. Identity papers;
2. Long-term residence permit;
3. Application Form of the Customs of the People's Republic of China for Importation and Exportation of Articles for Personal Use;
4. Bill of lading (waybill), packing list and other required documents.

Dutiable items imported by non-resident, long-term visitors for personal use are subject to the customs duty in accordance with the *Regulations of the People's Republic of China on Import and Export Duties*. The Customs does not levy duties on items which are imported by long-term, non-resident visitors for personal use and which are exempted from duty under intergovernmental protocols. Domestic articles, in a reasonable amount, which are imported into China by staff members of foreign consulates, the United Nations and its affiliations, and representative offices of international organizations in China, as well as by their family, are exempted from duty and inspection.

Under the principle of personal use and reasonable amount, books and teaching and scientific research materials/objects, which are imported by high-level international students or international science and technology experts recognized by the Ministry of Human Resources and Social Security, Ministry of Education, or institutions authorized by them, are exempted from import duty.

For rules and procedures, please contact:
Tel: (8620) 12360
Guangzhou Customs
Address: 83 Huacheng Dadao, Zhujiang New Town, Guangzhou
Website: http://guangzhou.customs.gov.cn
Huangpu Customs
Address: No.333 Dashadi Dong, Huangpu District, Guangzhou
Website: http://huangpu.customs.gov.cn

Passengers coming from or leaving for Hong Kong and Macao may carry 200 cigarettes or 50 cigars or 250 grams of tobacco duty-free each time; and a bottle of alcoholic beverage (0.75 litres or less) with alcohol content of 12% or above duty-free. Other passengers may bring in 400 cigarettes or 100 cigars or 500 grams of tobacco each time duty-free; and two bottles of alcoholic beverages (1.5 litres or less) with alcohol content of 12% or above duty-free. Passengers who make a round trip to Hong Kong and Macao on the same day or multiple round trips in a short period of time may carry 40 cigarettes or 5 cigars or 50 grams of tobacco duty-free. Wine cannot be brought in duty-free.

Inbound passengers shall declare truthfully to the Customs personal items other than a camera, a portable cassette player, a minicam, a portable video cam and a word processor needed for the trip and shall go through the relevant formalities.

Inbound and outbound passengers carrying more than RMB 20,000 or more than USD 5,000 or an equivalent amount in other foreign currencies in cash, shall make a declaration to the Customs in writing (Passengers who make multiple trips on the same day or within a short period of time are subject to separate provisions for the currencies they carry). For foreign passengers who make multiple round trips within 15 days or make frequent inbound and outbound trips, the Customs will only release items needed for their journey duty-free.

Inbound and outbound passengers holding a diplomatic or courtesy visa granted by the competent authority of the People's Republic of China, or those who are given the inspection-exemption courtesy, are not required to fill out the declaration form; however, they shall present their valid identity papers to the Customs to enjoy the courtesy of inspection-exemption.

A passenger can carry no more than RMB 150 worth of Chinese medicinal materials and Chinese patent medicines if bound for Hong Kong or Macao and no more than RMB 300 if bound for a foreign country.

Chinese laws and regulations expressly provide that precious cultural relics and other cultural relics prohibited from leaving the country cannot leave. Passengers carrying, consigning or mailing cultural relics out of the country shall declare to the Customs. The identification mark affixed with the seal of the cultural department and cultural relics export invoice or the export license issued by the cultural administrative department designated by the Ministry of Culture are required for the Customs inspection before they are released.

Guangdong Office of National Cultural Relics Entry and Exit Administration
Address: 32 Shuiyin 4 Henglu, Guangzhou, China
Zip Code: 510075
Tel: (8620) 87047165

II. Passenger Customs Clearance and Declaration

Luggage and goods carried by inbound and outbound passengers, under the principle of personal use and reasonable amount, shall be declared truthfully to the Customs and subject to its inspection.

Personal items brought in by a non-resident passenger, which will remain in China, if valued at RMB 2,000 or less, are exempt from duty. Duty-exempt items in a single category shall be for personal use only and in a reasonable amount. Tobacco products and alcoholic beverages, however, are subject to separate rules and regulations.

Personal items beyond the exemption of RMB 2,000 are subject to the customs duty. A single indivisible item shall be taxed for its full value.

The dutiable value of inbound and outbound goods is determined by the Customs pursuant to the law.

(3) Animal carcasses;

(4) Soil;

(5) Articles listed in the Catalogue of Animals and Plants, and Animal and Plant Products Prohibited from Being Carried or Posted into the People's Republic of China;

(6) Waste and used articles, radioactive substance and other objects prohibited from entering the country in accordance with the State provisions. (Excerpt from *No.146 Administrative Measures on Quarantine of Articles Carried by Entry and Exit Passengers*, issued by the General Administration of Quality Supervision, Inspection and Quarantine of the People's Republic of China.)

Guangzhou Customs
Address: 83 Huacheng Dadao, Zhujiang New Town, Guangzhou
Postcode: 510623
Tel: (8620) 81102000
Website: http://guangzhou.customs.gov.cn

(5) Inbound and outbound corpses and human bones;

(6) Inbound and outbound luggage and objects originating from epidemic areas or contaminated by a contagious disease or deemed likely to transmit a contagious disease;

(7) Other articles that shall be declared to and quarantined by inspection and quarantine authorities, specified by the General Administration of Quality Supervision, Inspection and Quarantine of the People's Republic of China. (Excerpt from *No.146 Administrative Measures on Quarantine of Articles Carried by Entry and Exit Passengers*, issued by the General Administration of Quality Supervision, Inspection and Quarantine of the People's Republic of China.)

2. Inbound and outbound personnel are prohibited from carrying the following articles into the country:

(1) Pathogenic micro-organisms (including seed cultures of bacteria and viruses, etc.) of animals and plants, insect pests and other harmful organisms;

(2) Relevant animals and plants, their products and other quarantine objects from countries or regions with prevalent epidemic animal or plant diseases;

designated by the government of the country of their current residence or one issued by any other medical institution and certified by a notary public. The health certificate shall be valid for 6 months from the date of issue. (Excerpt from *Detailed Rules for the Implementation of the Law of the People's Republic of China Governing the Administration of Entry and Exit of Foreigners*)

2. People coming from a Yellow Fever prevalent area are required to present valid certificate of inoculation against Yellow Fever to the health and quarantine organ upon entry. (Excerpt from *Rules for the Implementation of Frontier Health and Quarantine Law of the People's Republic of China*)

3. Foreigners suffering from serious psychosis, infectious tuberculosis or other infectious diseases which may seriously endanger the public health shall not be permitted to enter China. (Excerpt from *Detailed Rules for the Implementation of the Law of the People's Republic of China Governing the Administration of Entry and Exit of Foreigners and Rules for the Implementation of Frontier Health and Quarantine Law of the People's Republic of China*)

(III) Inspection and quarantine instructions for outbound personnel

1. A passenger bound for a foreign country infected with Yellow Fever shall present a vaccination certificate on exit. (Excerpt from *The Health and Quarantine Inspection Rules for Inbound and Outbound Personnel*, SN/T 1344-2003)

2. An outbound passenger shall provide a relevant vaccination certificate according to the requirements of his or her destination country. (Excerpt from *The Health and Quarantine Inspection Rules for Inbound and Outbound Personnel*, SN/T 1344-2003)

(IV) Luggage instructions for inbound and outbound personnel

1. Inbound or outbound personnel carrying the following objects shall declare to the quarantine and inspection authority and subject the objects to quarantine:

(1) Inbound animals, plants or their products and other objects subject to quarantine;

(2) Inbound and outbound biological species resources, endangered wild animals, plants or their products;

(3) Outbound national key protected wild animals and plants or their products;

(4) Inbound and outbound microorganisms, human tissues, biological products, blood, blood products, and other special objects;

2. When there is a major epidemic reported in China or abroad, temporary compulsory inspection and quarantine measures announced by the General Administration of Quality Supervision, Inspection and Quarantine of the People's Republic of China with regard to inbound and outbound means of transport, personnel and their luggage shall apply, and means of transport from epidemic areas shall be parked at designated places. Inbound and outbound personnel shall truthfully fill out the "Entry-Exit Quarantine and Health Declaration Card", enter or exit through the dedicated lane for inspection and quarantine, and have their luggage scanned by an X-ray machine. (Excerpt from *2008 No. 62 Notice on Streamlining Health Declaration Procedures for Inbound and Outbound Passengers at Border Crossings Nationwide,* issued by the General Administration of Quality Supervision, Inspection and Quarantine of the People's Republic of China.)

(II) Inspection and quarantine instructions for inbound personnel

1. Foreigners who are to come to China for permanent residence or for residence of one year or more shall in addition, in applying for entry visas, produce for examination a health certificate issued by a medical institution

I. Entry-Exit Inspection and Quarantine

(I) Health declaration at border crossings

1. When there is no major epidemic reported in China or abroad, inbound and outbound personnel do not need to fill out an "Entry-Exit Quarantine and Health Declaration Card". However, inbound and outbound personnel exhibiting symptoms of fever, vomiting, cough, breathing difficulty, diarrhea, contagious disease or psychiatric disorders or who may be judged to be carrying microorganisms, human tissues, biological products, blood or its products, and animals, plants or their products shall verbally declare their status to quarantine officers and subject themselves to inspection and quarantine. (Excerpt from *2008 No. 62 Notice on Streamlining Health Declaration Procedures for Inbound and Outbound Passengers at Border Crossings Nationwide*, issued by the General Administration of Quality Supervision, Inspection and Quarantine of the People's Republic of China.)

Chapter II
Entry-Exit, Stay and Residence

V. Government Services

Most foreign-related functional departments in Guangzhou are able to handle enquiry, complaints and formalities in English. All government departments have websites in Chinese and English bilingually to provide information on policies, regulations and guidelines. Online services are available for businesses relating to industry, commerce and taxation. The office hours of government departments are from 9:00 am to 12:00 pm, and 2:00 pm to 6:00 pm, Monday to Friday (except statutory holidays). Those who need service on public holidays may contact relevant government departments in advance to make an appointment. Please visit the portal of Guangzhou municipal government (website: www.gz.gov.cn) to learn more about the latest government policies and everyday information.

Guangzhou Multilingual Public Service hotline 960169 established by the Foreign Affairs Office of Guangzhou Municipal People's Government provides free interpretation service for inquiries concerning public services and policy consultancy in English, Japanese and Korean. This hotline may be connected with other government and public service hotlines such as 12345, 110, 119, 120, 96158 (Baiyun Airport), and 96900 (Guangzhou Traffic) to provide real-time interpretation through three-way call. The hotline in English operates 24 hours a day, and that in Japanese and Korean between 9:00 am and 9:00 pm.

> **Foreign Affairs Office of Guangzhou Municipal People's Government**
> Address: 311 Yuexiu Beilu, Guangzhou
> Website: http://www.gzfao.gov.cn

IV. Foreign Exchanges

Guangzhou is a renowned international metropolis with a long history. In as early as B.C. years, it has maintained close and friendly exchanges with foreign countries. As one of the starting points of the famous Maritime Silk Road, the city has been engaging in foreign trade for more than 2,000 years.

As of December 2021, Guangzhou has established sister city ties with 38 cities of 35 countries on six continents, including 12 cities of 10 countries in Europe, 2 cities of 2 countries in North America, and 6 cities of 6 countries in Latin America, 12 cities of 11 countries in Asia, 4 cities of 4 countries in Africa, and 2 cities of 2 countries in Oceania.

As of December 2021, the city has forged friendship city relationships with 62 cities of 44 countries on six continents, including 23 cities of 13 countries in Europe, 5 cities of 2 countries in North America, and 7 cities of 6 countries in Latin America, 15 cities of 13 countries in Asia, 7 cities of 7 countries in Africa, and 3 cities of 2 countries in Oceania. (See the official website of the Foreign Affairs Office of Guangzhou Municipal People's Government for details.)

opium campaign, Hong Xiuquan who led peasant uprisings, Zhang Zhidong a representative of the Westernization Movement, thinkers and political reformers Kang Youwei and Liang Qichao, and Sun Yat-sen who led the Chinese democratic revolution and overthrew the feudal system of monarchy which had ruled China for several thousands of years. They all made great contribution to the formation and development of this reputed historic city.

Guangzhou features a wealth of cultural relics and historic sites. The outstanding examples include: the Mausoleum of Nanyue King of more than 2,000 years of history, Guangxiao Buddhist Temple, Liurong Temple and Huaisheng Mosque of more than 1,000 years of history, Nanhai God Temple built in the Sui Dynasty, Wuxian Taoist Temple, Zhenhai Tower and Lotus Pagoda in the Ming Dynasty, and Chen Clan Ancestral Hall and Yuyin Garden in the Qing Dynasty. Memorial sites of modern revolution include the site of Peasant Movement Institute where Comrade Mao Zedong once hosted the workshop, Guangzhou Martyrs' Memorial Garden, Cemetery of the 72 Martyrs in Huanghuagang, the site of Whampoa Military Academy, Sun Yat-sen Memorial Hall and the former residence of Hong Xiuquan. There are also many scenic spots in the city. Back in the Song, Yuan, Ming and Qing dynasties, it was a tradition to select the Eight Views of the city. After the founding of the People's Republic of China in 1949, the city has seen rapid progresses in urban construction and development. On May 18, 2011, the results of the New Eight Views of Guangzhou were announced, namely the Tower in the Zhujiang New Town (Canton Tower), the Flowing River (the Pearl River), the Verdant Mountain (Baiyun Mountain), the Glamor of Yuexiu (Yuexiu Mountain), the Renowned Ancient Academy (Chen Clan Ancestral Hall), the Wonderland in Liwan (Lychee Bay River), the Splendid Science City (Guangzhou Science City), and the Sunset at the Wetland (Nansha Wetland).

III. History

Guangzhou is among the first national historic cities recognized by the State Council. In as early as the Neolithic Age six to seven thousand years ago, the ancestors lived and multiplied on this land, creating a splendid prehistoric civilization and opening the first chapter of humanities in the city. Guangzhou is also known as Ram City and Rice Ear City. Legend has it that in ancient times, five immortals arrived in Guangzhou riding five-color rams that carried ears of rice to the people, blessing the city to be free from famine. Today, the Five Ram Statue in Yuexiu Park has become a symbol of Guangzhou.

For more than 2,000 years from the Qin and Han dynasties to the Ming and Qing dynasties, Guangzhou had been a prominent port city for foreign trade in China. During Emperor Wu's reign in the Han Dynasty, China's fleets set off from the city and sailed to the Southeast Asian and South Asian countries for trade, and during the Eastern Han Dynasty they sailed even farther to the Persian Gulf. In the Tang Dynasty, Guangzhou was known as a world-famous oriental port city, as well as the starting point of the then world's longest sea route, Guangzhou Maritime Route. The Maritime Trade Commissioner appointed by the central government came to Guangzhou to administer the foreign trade. Later in the Song Dynasty, Maritime Trade Superintendency, the country's first agency to manage foreign trade, was established in the city. During the Ming and Qing dynasties, Guangzhou became a special open port, and for a long time it was the only port city for foreign trade in the country.

Guangzhou is a heroic city rooted in a glorious revolutionary tradition. In modern times, the city bore witness to the battle against the British invaders in Sanyuanli, the Huanghuagang Uprising against the feudal regime led by Sun Yat-sen, and Guangzhou Uprising led by the Communist Party of China. It is not only the cradle of bourgeois revolution in China, but also a heroic city where the people were engaged in revolutionary struggle led by the proletarian party leaders.

Guangzhou is home to generations of great achievers, such as Ren Xiao in the Qin Dynasty, Zhao Tuo in the Han Dynasty, Ge Hong in the Jin Dynasty, Huineng in the Tang Dynasty, Zhan Ruoshui in the Ming Dynasty, scholars Qu Dajun and Ruan Yuan in the Qing Dynasty, Lin Zexu who led the anti-minority village (She Ethnic Minority Village, Zhengguo Town, Zengcheng District, with 385 villagers form 88 households); 10 schools enrolling 1,366 Xinjiang and Tibetan students (including 6 schools, namely Guangya High School, Guangzhou No. 6 Middle School, Guangzhou No. 75 Middle School, Yuyan Middle School, Xiehe High School and Yushan High School offering high school classes for Xinjiang students, two schools, namely Guangzhou Vocational School of Finance and Business and Guangzhou Vocational School of Municipal Administration offering vocational classes for Xinjiang students, and two schools, namely Guangzhou Vocational School of Medicine and Guangzhou Health Science College offering vocational classes for Tibetan students); nearly 2,000 halal ramen stores and restaurants; four ethnic organizations at municipal level, namely Guangzhou National Unity and Progress Association, Guangzhou Manchu History and Culture Research Association, Guangzhou Hui History and Culture Research Association, and Guangzhou Society of Ethnic Minority Sports.

II. Administrative Districts and Population

Guangzhou covers a total area of 7,434.40 km^2, accounting for 4.21% of the total land area of Guangdong Province. It has 11 districts under its administration, namely Yuexiu, Haizhu, Liwan, Tianhe, Baiyun, Huangpu, Huadu, Panyu, Nansha, Conghua and Zengcheng.

In 2020, the permanent residents in Guangzhou stood at 18,676,605, with 13.87% aged between 0 and 14, 74.72% between 15 and 59, 11.41% aged 60 and above, and 7.8% aged 65 and above.

There are 55 ethnic minorities with a total population of 827,000 in Guangzhou. Among them, those with a register certificate (Hukou) is about 118,000, mainly coming from ethnic groups such as Zhuang, Hui, Manchu, Tujia and Yao. Those without such certificate is about 709,000, mainly coming from ethnic groups such as Zhuang, Hui, Tujia, Miao, Yao and Dong. Guangzhou has recorded one of the fastest and largest increase in the population of ethnic minorities among Chinese cities. There are three ethnic primary schools including Hui Primary School, Manchu Primary School, and She Primary School, enrolling 327 ethnic minority students; one ethnic peasant uprising led by Hong Xiuquan during the Qing Dynasty, the Hundred Days' Reform advocated by the reformist thinkers Kang Youwei and Liang Qichao, and the 1911 Revolution against the feudal regime and the famous Huanghuagang Uprising led by Sun Yat-sen.

Today, as a pioneer in China's reform and opening up and a window for foreign trade, the city witnesses tremendous economic growth and all-round development. It is one of the most economically active cities in China and ranks among the country's top three major cities in terms of comprehensive economic strength.

The economic growth has propelled the continuous improvements in the city's appearance and living environment. As the intersection of Beijing-Guangzhou Railway, Guangzhou-Shenzhen Railway, Guangzhou-Maoming Railway and Guangzhou-Meizhou-Shantou Railway as well as the civil aviation hub in South China, the city is easily accessible from different parts of the country. The successful completion of major projects, such as Guangzhou Metro consisting of 15 lines, the Ring Expressway, the Yajisha Bridge, Guangzhou International Convention and Exhibition Center, Guangzhou Baiyun International Airport, and Guangzhou Higher Education Mega Center, testifies that Guangzhou, a thousand-year-old city, still thrives as a modern international metropolis in the 21st century.

Guangzhou is a preeminent historical and culture city. As documented in ancient literature, the city walls were built in as early as 214 B.C. With a historical legacy of more thar 2200 years, it boasts many cultural relics that vividly reflect its development at various historical stages.

Guangzhou is one of the starting point of the ancient Maritime Silk Road. For more than 2,000 years since the Qin and Han dynasties, it has been an important port for foreign trade, as evidenced by the large wooden ships with rudders and anchors excavated from the remains of shipyards of the Qin and Han dynasties, the African ivory and Persian silver boxes unearthed from the mausoleum of the second King of Nanyue Kingdom, and the foreign trade agency established during the Tang and Song dynasties.

Guangzhou is also the cradle of Chinese modern democratic revolution. It has witnessed many significant revolutionary events in the country's history, such as the Sanyuanli Uprising against the British invaders in 1840 when the British Empire invaded China from its "Southern Gateway", the

I. Basic Information

Guangzhou is the capital city of Guangdong Province, serving as its political, economic, science and technology and education center. Located in the south of the Chinese Mainland and southeast of the Province, the city lies at the northern edge of the Pearl River Delta, bordering on the South China Sea, and neighboring Hong Kong and Macau. As a regional central city and transportation and communication hub in South China, it is known as the "Southern Gateway" to China.

Guangzhou has a sub-tropical monsoon climate, which is characterized by plentiful rain, mild temperature, absence from extreme weather conditions and flowers in full bloom all year round. The annual mean temperature ranges between 21 and 23°C, with the annual mean relative humidity at 75% and the annual rainfall in the urban area over 2,100 mm.

Chapter I
City Overview

Chapter IV **Safety Rules and Regulations** 113

I. Safety	114
II. Tax Payment and Exemption	116
III. Individual Income Tax	117
IV. Vehicles and Vessels Tax	124
V. Traffic Laws and Regulations	127
VI. Legal Disputes	141

Chapter V **Business and Investment Guide** 145

I. Investment Environment and Business Development	146
II. Industrial Support Policies	148
III. Introduction to Key Economic Development Zones	155
IV. Protection of Intellectual Property Right	160

Contents

Chapter I City Overview — 001

I. Basic Information — 002
II. Administrative Districts and Population — 005
III. History — 007
IV. Foreign Exchanges — 009
V. Government Services — 010

Chapter II Entry-Exit, Stay and Residence — 011

I. Entry-Exit Inspection and Quarantine — 012
II. Passenger Customs Clearance and Declaration — 017
III. Import and Export of Articles for Public and Personal Use — 022
IV. Visa and Permit Application — 025
V. Application for Permanent Residence — 034

Chapter III Living in Guangzhou — 049

I. Food and Recreation — 050
II. Transportation — 053
III. Communications, Banking, Post and Telecommunications Services — 059
IV. Education — 061
V. Foreigner's Work Permit — 066
VI. Marriage and Adoption — 076
VII. Religions and Venues of Religious Activity — 085
VIII. Medical Service — 090
IX. Funeral Service — 108
X. Learning Chinese — 110